MW00667044

Spatial Analysis for the Social Sciences

Many theories in the social sciences predict spatial dependence or the similarity of behaviors at neighboring locations. *Spatial Analysis for the Social Sciences* demonstrates how researchers can diagnose and model this spatial dependence and draw more valid inferences as a result. The book is structured around the well-known Galton's problem and presents a step-by-step guide to the application of spatial analysis. The book examines a variety of spatial diagnostics and models through a series of applied examples drawn from the social sciences. These include spatial lag models that capture behavioral diffusion between actors, spatial error models that account for spatial dependence in errors, and models that incorporate spatial heterogeneity in the effects of covariates. *Spatial Analysis for the Social Sciences* also examines advanced spatial models for time-series cross-sectional data, categorical and limited dependent variables, count data, and survival data.

David Darmofal is an associate professor of political science at the University of South Carolina. His research focuses on spatial analysis and political geography and has appeared in a variety of journals including the *American Journal of Political Science*, *Journal of Politics*, and *Political Geography*. He has received best article awards from the *Journal of Politics* and *Political Research Quarterly*. He teaches regularly in the Inter-University Consortium for Political and Social Research (ICPSR) Summer Program in Quantitative Methods of Social Research.

Analytical Methods for Social Research

Analytical Methods for Social Research presents texts on empirical and formal methods for the social sciences. Volumes in the series address both the theoretical underpinnings of analytical techniques as well as their application in social research. Some series volumes are broad in scope, cutting across a number of disciplines. Others focus mainly on methodological applications within specific fields such as political science, sociology, demography, and public health. The series serves a mix of students and researchers in the social sciences and statistics.

Series Editors:

R. Michael Alvarez *California Institute of Technology*
Nathaniel L. Beck *New York University*
Stephen L. Morgan *Johns Hopkins University*
Lawrence L. Wu *New York University*

Other Titles in the Series:

Time Series Analysis for the Social Sciences, by Janet M. Box-Steffensmeier, John R. Freeman, Matthew P. Hitt, and Jon C. W. Pevehouse
Counterfactuals and Causal Inference, Second Edition, by Stephen L. Morgan and Christopher Winship
Statistical Modeling and Inference for Social Science, by Sean Gailmard
Formal Models of Domestic Politics, by Scott Gehlbach
Counterfactuals and Causal Inference: Methods and Principles for Social Research, by Stephen L. Morgan and Christopher Winship
Data Analysis Using Regression and Multilevel/Hierarchical Models, by Andrew Gelman and Jennifer Hill
Political Game Theory: An Introduction, by Nolan McCarty and Adam Meirowitz
Essential Mathematics for Political and Social Research, by Jeff Gill
Spatial Models of Parliamentary Voting, by Keith T. Poole
Ecological Inference: New Methodological Strategies, edited by Gary King, Ori Rosen, and Martin A. Tanner
Event History Modeling: A Guide for Social Scientists, by Janet M. Box-Steffensmeier and Bradford S. Jones

Spatial Analysis for the Social Sciences

DAVID DARMOFAL
University of South Carolina

CAMBRIDGE
UNIVERSITY PRESS

CAMBRIDGE
UNIVERSITY PRESS

32 Avenue of the Americas, New York, NY 10013-2473, USA

Cambridge University Press is part of the University of Cambridge.

It furthers the University's mission by disseminating knowledge in the pursuit of education, learning, and research at the highest international levels of excellence.

www.cambridge.org
Information on this title: www.cambridge.org/9780521716383

First published 2015

Printed in the United Kingdom by Clays, St Ives plc

A catalog record for this publication is available from the British Library.

Library of Congress Cataloging in Publication data
Darmofal, David, 1968–
Spatial analysis for the social sciences / David Darmofal.
pages cm. – (Analytical methods for social research)
Includes bibliographical references and index.
ISBN 978-0-521-88826-4 (hardback) – ISBN 978-0-521-71638-3 (paperback)
1. Spatial analysis (Statistics) 2. Social sciences–Research–Methodology. I. Title.
HA30.6.D37 2015
001.4'22–dc23 2015016112

ISBN 978-0-521-88826-4 Hardback
ISBN 978-0-521-71638-3 Paperback

Contents

List of Figures

List of Tables

Preface

This book is designed for social scientists who seek to model the spatial dimension of behavior that is inherent in substantive social science theories. The social sciences are united by their focus on subjects that are inherently social and interdependent. Unlike more individuated concerns, the units studied by social scientists often interact with each other and affect each other's behavior as a consequence. This interaction is promoted by spatial proximity – units that are more geographically proximate are more likely to interact with each other and influence each other as a consequence. Shared concerns combine with spatial proximity to promote familiarity. Just as familiarity has long been observed to breed contempt, so also does it promote cooperation. Even when spatially proximate units do not interact with each other, they often exhibit similar behaviors as a result of shared environmental influences. In short, there is a strong spatial component to many of the behaviors studied by social scientists and this is reflected in many of our theories in the social sciences.

It might surprise social scientists who have not seriously considered the spatial dimension of behavior to learn that all social science data are, in fact, spatial data. The behaviors, processes, and events of interest to social scientists occur at specific geographic locations. The past two decades have seen an explosion in social science data that are geocoded – coded to include the geographic locations of the observations. This increase in the availability of geocoded data has been matched by advances in geographic information system (GIS) software, such as ESRI's (Environmental Systems Research Institute) popular ArcGIS package. At the same time, significant advancements have been made in the development of spatial diagnostics and estimators, many of which are now included in dedicated spatial software such as GeoDa as well as standard statistical packages such as R, Stata, and WinBUGS. The time has never been better for scholars wishing to model spatial relationships in their data.

This book is organized around Galton's problem, a common reference point across many of the social sciences. In the late nineteenth century, well before

modern spatial diagnostics and estimators had even been imagined, Galton raised an important concern that would shape subsequent research in the social sciences. Galton noted that behaviors should not be assumed to be independent across units of observation. Instead, units may share similar behaviors as a result of behavioral diffusion. Alternatively, units may exhibit similarity in their behaviors as a result of shared exposure to common factors that influence behavior. Galton's problem and the two alternative sources of spatial similarity (and dissimilarity) in behaviors serve as organizing principles for the book's discussion of how social scientists can diagnose and model spatial dependence in their data.

The book is designed to guide researchers through the sequential steps of diagnosing and modeling spatial dependence in their data. The book begins by introducing social scientists to the principal forms of spatial data. Next, the critical question of how "neighboring" observations are defined is discussed. The book then examines the principal differences between spatial dependence and the more familiar temporal dependence in time series analysis. The book next presents diagnostics that researchers can employ to diagnose spatial dependence in their data. The book discusses alternative approaches to modeling this dependence. The latter chapters are devoted to specialized, advanced models for spatial dependence. The book concludes by examining software and web resources for diagnosing and modeling spatial dependence.

The methods discussed in this book are demonstrated through a variety of examples. Among these are applications to demographic change, poverty rates, immigrant demographics, civil wars, partisan voting, legislative roll-call voting behavior, voter turnout, state spending on higher education, the New Deal realignment, government ideology and representation, and the timing of position announcements on the North American Free Trade Agreement (NAFTA). These applications employ many different types of areal units, including census tracts, counties, congressional districts, states, and countries. A variety of spatial methods are demonstrated through these applications. These spatial topics include the diagnosis of spatial dependence at the global and local levels in the absence of covariates, spatial lag and spatial error models, models for spatial time-series cross-sectional (TSCS) data, geographically weighted regressions (GWR), spatial binary dependent variable models, and spatial survival models. The data and code for the applications in this book are available at http://thedata.harvard.edu/dvn/dv/David.

As with any project, this book has benefited from countless conversations. My work in spatial analysis began in graduate school. I was fortunate to be a graduate student in the Political Science Department at the University of Illinois at Urbana-Champaign, an engaging and supportive environment for graduate students. At the time I was working on a dissertation employing county-level data that presented some unique challenges – and opportunities – for analysis. One of my advisors, Wendy Tam Cho, was herself beginning to explore the effects of spatial dependence on political behavior and suggested that I also

explore the leverage that spatial analysis could provide for my research. As it turned out, Illinois was a fortuitous place to be, as one of the leading scholars in spatial econometrics, Luc Anselin, had recently joined the faculty. Like Wendy, Luc also became a valuable guide for my burgeoning interest in spatial analysis. I thank Wendy and Luc for their encouragement and support for me as a young scholar.

I also thank the series editors, R. Michael Alvarez, Neal Beck, Stephen Morgan, and Lawrence Wu, and my editor at Cambridge University Press, Robert Dreesen, for their guidance and support on this project. I thank the University of South Carolina for its support during the writing of this book and for providing an active and engaging academic environment in which to write it. Thanks also to Janet Box-Steffensmeier and the Political Science Department at Ohio State University, who provided me the opportunity to explore my thinking on spatial analysis further and to plan and teach my own graduate course on spatial analysis during a year as a postdoctoral fellow in the Program in Statistics and Methodology (PRISM) at Ohio State.

I also want to thank the many other scholars whose conversations, advice, and discussions over the years have shaped my understanding of spatial analysis. In addition to those already mentioned, these scholars include Brady Baybeck, Kyle Beardsley, Fred Boehmke, Jake Bowers, Sarah Brooks, Greg Caldeira, Mike Crespin, Chuck Finocchiaro, Rich Fording, Rob Franzese, Brian Gaines, Andrew Gelman, Elisabeth Gerber, Jeff Gill, Jim Gimpel, Kristian Gleditsch, Michael Greig, Jude Hays, Zaryab Iqbal, Jennifer Jerit, Aya Kachi, Luke Keele, Holger Kern, James Kuklinski, Marcus Kurtz, Andrew Lawson, Suzanna Linn, Arthur Lupia, Stephen A. Matthews, Scott McClurg, Daniel McMillen, James Monogan, Jacob Montgomery, Clayton Nall, Peter Nardulli, Brendan Nyhan, John Patty, Mark Peffley, Maggie Penn, Thomas Plümper, Kirk Randazzo, Jon Rogowski, Norman Schofield, Betsy Sinclair, Anand Sokhey, Sarah Wilson Sokhey, Lyndsey Young Stanfill, Harvey Starr, Tracy Sulkin, Rocio Titiunik, Craig Volden, Lee Walker, Mike Ward, Justin Wedeking, Alan Wiseman, Chris Witko, Jack Wright, and Chris Zorn. I apologize to any scholars who were inadvertently left off this list, as I have benefited from numerous conversations with scholars on spatial analysis over the years. I also thank seminar participants at the University of Illinois at Urbana–Champaign, the Quantitative Institute for Social Science at the University of Kentucky, the Center for Political Studies at the University of Michigan, the Methods Speaker Series at Ohio State University, the Biostatistics Forum in the Department of Epidemiology and Biostatistics, Arnold School of Public Health, University of South Carolina, the Political Science Research Workshop at the University of South Carolina, the Center for New Institutional Social Sciences at Washington University in St. Louis, and faculty and students in the Interactive Television (ITV) Program in Advanced Political Methodology at Ohio State University, the University of Illinois, the University of Minnesota, and the University of Wisconsin for feedback on spatial presentations. I thank Lynn Shirley at the

University of South Carolina for help in identifying and accessing spatial data and Michael Fix and Adam Pernsteiner for helpful research assistance on this project. I also thank SAGE Publications for the permission to reprint portions of my *American Politics Research* article, "The Political Geography of the New Deal Realignment" in Chapter 7 and Blackwell Publishing for the permission to reprint portions of my *American Journal of Political Science* article, "Bayesian Spatial Survival Models for Political Event Processes" in Chapter 9.

Finally, I want to thank my mother. The past few years have been a rewarding time, as roles have reversed and I've been able to repay her for the support and encouragement she has provided throughout my life. These years have also reinforced the importance of spatial proximity for all of our relationships. This book is dedicated to her.

PART I

GENERAL TOPICS

1

The Social Sciences and Spatial Analysis

> "[F]ull information should be given as to the degree in which the customs of the tribes and races which are compared together are independent. It might be, that some of the tribes had derived them from a common source, so that they were duplicate copies of the same original. ...It would give a useful idea of the distribution of the several customs and of their relative prevalence in the world, if a map were so marked by shadings and colour as to present a picture of their geographical ranges."
>
> Sir Francis Galton at The Royal Anthropological Institute, 1888
> *The Journal of the Anthropological Institute of Great Britain and Ireland* 18: 270.

1.1 INTRODUCTION

Concepts of space and geography play prominent roles in many social science theories. In fields as diverse as anthropology, criminology, demography, political science, sociology, and public health, our theories predict that spatially proximate units are more likely to behave similarly than spatially distant units. These theories, in short, predict positive spatial autocorrelation or spatial dependence, the spatial clustering of similar behaviors, processes, and events among neighboring observations. This common interest in geography across the social sciences is not surprising. The social sciences are defined by their focus on phenomena that are inherently social and interdependent. Shared concerns combine with spatial proximity to promote familiarity. This familiarity in turn breeds both contempt and conflict and interaction and interdependence.

Until recently our ability to incorporate the spatial dimension of our theories in our models was quite limited, relying primarily on dummy variables to capture differences in behavior across geographically disparate units. Such an approach is suboptimal, as it is unable to address some of the central issues posed by spatially dependent data. Consider, for example, Sir Francis Galton's comment in the epigraph to this chapter. Sir Galton's comment

in response to Edward Tylor's presentation at the Royal Anthropological Institute in November 1888 clearly ranks among the most influential comments expressed at an academic presentation, remembered as it is more than a century later. Sir Galton's critique, which has since come to be known as Galton's problem, focuses on the critical substantive distinction between two alternative explanations for spatially dependent behavior.

On the one hand, spatial dependence may be produced by the diffusion of behavior between neighboring units. If so, the behavior is likely to be highly social in nature, and understanding the interactions between interdependent units is critical to understanding the behavior in question. For example, citizens may discuss politics across adjoining neighborhoods such that an increase in support for a candidate in one neighborhood directly leads to an increase in support for the candidate in adjoining neighborhoods.

Alternatively, neighboring units may independently adopt similar behaviors simply because the units share characteristics that promote the behavior in question. If so, the spatial dependence observed in our data does not reflect a truly spatial process, but merely the geographic clustering of the sources of the behavior of interest. For example, citizens in adjoining neighborhoods may favor the same candidate not because they talk to their neighbors, but because citizens with similar incomes tend to cluster geographically, and income also predicts vote choice. Such spatial dependence can be termed attributional dependence, as neighboring units have shared attributes that produce the clustering of behaviors. Clearly, determining which process is producing spatial dependence is critical to our understanding the behavior of interest. As a consequence, we need a way to determine which of the two forms of spatial dependence is at work in our data and model the particular form of spatial dependence.

Often our model specifications in the social sciences do not take space seriously. We may include regional, country, or state nominal variables that capture the uniqueness of particular geographic units. But rarely do we think of these dummy variables as spatial variables. Moreover, this standard dummy variable approach is unable to distinguish between the two quite different explanations for spatial dependence. As proxies for our ignorance of the sources of spatial autocorrelation, statistically significant parameters on dummy variables for geographic areas merely tell us that behaviors differ for units in these particular areas in contrast to the reference category. Such an approach cannot tell us whether the spatial dependence is consistent with diffusion or with the spatial clustering of the behaviors' sources.

Recent advances in spatial analysis, however, now allow us to address Galton's problem econometrically and model the alternative sources of spatial dependence. Although spatial econometric models come in a variety of forms, at their most basic level they share a common feature that distinguishes them from standard econometric models: they explicitly model spatial autocorrelation.

Spatial econometric models allow us to address Galton's problem because each of the two alternative sources of spatial dependence posed by Galton presents its own distinct spatial econometric specification.

1.2 SPATIAL LAG AND SPATIAL ERROR MODELS

Spatial diffusion occurs because units' behavior is directly influenced by the behavior of "neighboring units." (The definition of neighbors is generalizable and need not imply a geographic relationship. Spatial models, as a consequence, are quite flexible for a variety of modeling situations involving dependent data). This diffusion effect corresponds to a positive and significant parameter on a spatially lagged dependent variable capturing the direct influence between neighbors.

Conversely, the geographic clustering of the sources of the behavior implies an alternative specification. Assuming that we are unable to model fully the sources of spatial dependence in the data generating process (DGP), these sources will produce spatial dependence in the error terms between neighboring locations. This spatial error dependence can be modeled via a spatially lagged error term. Spatial error dependence is also consistent with spatial clustering in measurement errors.

The substantive implications of properly modeling spatial dependence are intimately linked with methodological implications. Ignoring either form of spatial dependence in our models poses its own distinct implications for inference. For example, estimating an ordinary least squares (OLS) model that ignores a diffusion effect in the DGP can produce biased and inconsistent parameter estimates. Estimating an OLS model that ignores spatial clustering in the sources of the behavior can produce inefficient parameter estimates, standard error estimates that are biased downward, and type I errors.

Many social scientists are familiar with problems that dependent data pose for inference in time series analysis. And the two alternative sources of spatial dependence bear a surface similarity with lagged dependent variables and lagged error terms in time series analysis. However, time series methods for modeling temporal dependence cannot simply be applied to the case of spatial dependence because spatial dependence is not simply the cross-sectional analogue of serial dependence. In the time series context, influence flows in one direction, from the past to the present. In contrast, spatial dependence is simultaneous: in the diffusion case, neighbors influence the behavior of their neighbors and vice versa. In the case of attributional dependence, errors for neighboring observations exhibit simultaneous dependence. As a consequence of this multidimensional, simultaneous spatial autocorrelation, OLS cannot be used to estimate a model with spatially lagged dependent variables, and simple iterative estimators for unidimensional dependence such as the Cochrane–Orcutt estimator cannot be used to estimate a model with

* biased estimates * std error

spatially lagged errors. Instead, either maximum likelihood or instrumental variables approaches must be employed to estimate spatial models.

Happily, the diagnosis and modeling of spatial dependence is a straightforward process that can be adapted easily by applied researchers in the social sciences. First, global and local measures of spatial autocorrelation are estimated to determine whether the data exhibit spatial autocorrelation. If the data do exhibit spatial autocorrelation, the researcher simply applies diagnostics to an OLS specification to determine whether the variables in the model sufficiently capture this spatial dependence. If the variables do not fully model the dependence, the diagnostics indicate whether the researcher should estimate a model with a spatially lagged dependent variable or a spatially lagged error term.

This book examines how social scientists can diagnose and model the spatial dependence that is predicted by our theories. It is designed to provide a comprehensive, up-to-date introduction to spatial analysis for applied researchers in the social sciences. As such, examples are employed throughout the book to demonstrate how spatial analysis can be applied to research questions in the social sciences. The book assumes little in the way of prerequisites, although training in linear regression and maximum likelihood estimation will prove helpful.

1.3 OUTLINE OF THE BOOK

The book is structured as follows. Chapter 2 examines a critical but often underexplored question in spatial analysis: Which units are to be considered "neighbors of each other"? Neighbors are defined via a spatial weights matrix. This is a critical step in any spatial analysis, as it limits the spatial dependence that can be diagnosed and modeled in one's data. As a consequence, the definition of neighbors in the spatial weights matrix should in most cases be guided by substantive theory.

With the importance of a theoretically based weights matrix in hand, Chapter 3 returns to Galton's problem introduced in this chapter. The discussion in Chapter 3 focuses on the two alternative explanations for spatial dependence and the corresponding spatial lag and spatial error models. The distinction between multidimensional spatial dependence and unidimensional temporal dependence is expanded on and the performance of OLS for multidimensional spatial models is contrasted against the performance of OLS for unidimensional time series models. Chapter 3 also examines the performance of OLS when a spatially lagged dependent variable or spatially lagged errors are inappropriately omitted from the model specification. The analytical and empirical results of these analyses argue for the use of explicitly spatial methods for modeling spatial data.

Chapter 4 begins the discussion of the sequential process of diagnosing and modeling spatial autocorrelation. The chapter focuses on the initial step: the

diagnosis of univariate spatial autocorrelation in the absence of covariates. The discussion builds on the previous chapters, examining how theoretically based weights matrices and measures of spatial autocorrelation are employed to diagnose univariate spatial autocorrelation in the absence of covariates. A variety of global and local measures of spatial autocorrelation are examined. The chapter also examines how spatial autocorrelation measures can be used as an initial diagnostic for possible spatial heterogeneity in the effects of substantive covariates in one's model.

Chapter 5 examines how the spatial dependence diagnosed via the methods presented in Chapter 4 can be modeled. OLS models with which social scientists are most familiar will perform well if attributional dependence, and not diffusion, is responsible for the spatial autocorrelation that has been diagnosed, and if these common causal factors can be modeled fully with covariates. As a consequence, the next step in treating spatial dependence in models for continuous dependent variables is to estimate an OLS model and apply diagnostics to determine whether the covariates fully model the spatial autocorrelation. The chapter considers several spatial autocorrelation diagnostics for OLS models and demonstrates how they can be employed in social science applications.

Chapter 6 turns to maximum likelihood, instrumental variables, and generalized method of moments (GMM) approaches for modeling spatial lag dependence and maximum likelihood and GMM estimation of models for spatial error dependence. The chapter presents applied examples of the estimation of both spatial lag and spatial error models. The chapter also discusses estimation approaches for large sample sizes, the interpretation of substantive effects, and goodness of fit statistics for spatial models.

Chapter 7 returns to the topic of spatial heterogeneity first introduced in Chapter 4. Because spatial dependence can be produced by differing effects of substantive covariates across geographic areas, it is important to examine whether such spatial heterogeneity exists in one's data. This chapter examines models for spatial heterogeneity such as spatial random coefficients models, spatial switching regressions, spatial expansion models, and geographically weighted regressions.

Having focused on cross-sectional analyses in the preceding chapters, Chapter 8 examines the modeling of spatial dependence in time-series cross-sectional (TSCS) and panel data. The space–time model with a spatially lagged dependent variable is examined, as is the space–time model with spatially lagged errors. Both fixed effects and random effects models are considered, as is the TSCS spatial lag model with a temporal lag. A spatial Hausman testing framework is discussed next, followed by nonparametric covariance matrix estimation for space–time models. The chapter also discusses recently developed Lagrange multiplier tests for space–time models.

Chapter 9 examines the modeling of spatial dependence in specialized models. Three broad classes of models are examined. Spatial models for

limited and categorical dependent variables are discussed by examining recent innovations in spatial logit and probit models as well as spatial multinomial models. Next, spatial event count models are examined. Finally, spatial survival models are discussed in which spatial dependence in risk propensity is incorporated in the survival model specifications.

Chapter 10 summarizes and reviews how social scientists can employ spatial models in their research. The chapter also examines emerging research frontiers in spatial analysis. The book concludes with three appendices and a glossary. The first appendix presents a brief introduction to getting one's data ready for a spatial analysis, an important issue in that social science datasets do not come with geometry included for the areal units such as countries, states, cities, and census tracts whose behavior social scientists seek to explain. The second appendix examines routines for spatial analysis in both standard statistical packages and in dedicated spatial software. The third appendix examines Web resources for spatial analysis. The glossary provides definitions of many of the central concepts in spatial analysis that are discussed in the book.

1.4 FOR FURTHER READING

Researchers interested in exploring the roles of space and geography in social science theories will find examples in a variety of disciplines. These include fields as diverse as anthropology, criminology, demography, political science, sociology, and public health. The following list of publications is by no means exhaustive, but instead provides some examples of research in these and other disciplines. In anthropology, examples include White, Burton, and Dow's (1981) network autocorrelation analysis of the sexual division of labor in agriculture in Africa. In sociology, Baller and Richardson (2002) examine geographic patterns in suicide and Farley and Frey (1994) examine residential segregation (see also Gieryn's [2000] review essay on the role of place in sociology). In demography there is Loftin and Ward's (1983) work on the effects of population density on fertility; Logan, Zhang, and Alba's (2002) study of immigrant enclaves and ethnic communities; and Yang, Shoff, and Matthews' (2013) study of the relationship between the second demographic transition and infant mortality. In migration studies, Johnson et al. (2005) examined age-specific migration in the United States and Hunter (2000) explored immigrant residential concentration and environmental hazards.

In criminology, Land, McCall, and Cohen (1990) studied the structural covariates of homicide rates, and Sampson and Raudenbusch (1999) studied public disorder and crime in urban neighborhoods. In the field of communication, Øyen and De Fleur (1953) studied the effects of dropping leaflets on the spatial diffusion of information. In political science, there is Most and Starr's (1980) work on spatial proximity and international conflict and Gleditsch and Ward's (2006) work on democratization. In public health, there is Snow's (1855) pioneering work on the London cholera epidemic. These are, of course,

only a small subset of the examples of work on spatial theory in the social sciences. Many additional examples can be found in these and other social science disciplines.

The renewed interest in spatial concerns in the social sciences is also reflected in a variety of special issues on spatial topics in social science journals. Readers interested in this spatial turn in the social sciences may be interested in reading further in the following special issues: *Social Science History* 24(3), 2000; *Agricultural Economics* 27(3), 2002; *Political Analysis* 10(3), 2002; *Political Geography* 21(2), 2002; *Journal of Economic Geography* 5(1), 2005; *American Journal of Preventive Medicine* 30(2), 2006; *Proceedings of the National Academy of Sciences* 102(43), 2005; *Population Research and Policy Review* 26(5-6), 2007 and 27(1), 2008; *Environmetrics* 19(7), 2008; *Children and Youth Services Review* 31(3), 2009; and *Historical Social Research* 39(2), 2014.

2

Defining Neighbors via a Spatial Weights Matrix

2.1 THE IMPORTANCE OF SPACE IN THE SOCIAL SCIENCES

All social science data are spatial data. The behaviors, processes, and events we seek to explain occur at specific geographic locations. As discussed in Chapter 1, these geographic locations are often central to our understanding of these phenomena. Consider, for example, research on behavioral interactions between units in shared networks (see, e.g., Huckfeldt and Sprague 1987, 1988). Research has shown that spatial proximity affects the nature of interactions between actors in these networks (Baybeck and Huckfeldt 2002). This mirrors a long line of research in international relations that has found that spatial proximity between countries promotes interactions between countries (Most and Starr 1980; Starr 2002). This spatial proximity in turn affects a variety of behaviors and processes of interest to scholars and observers alike, including democratization (Gleditsch and Ward 2006), civil wars (Salehyan and Gleditsch 2006; Gleditsch 2007), and war (Gleditsch and Ward 2000).

Similarly, consider the interest of both observers and scholars in the causes and consequences of poverty (see, e.g., Wilson 1987). Here, both researchers and pundits have recognized that geographic locations marked by deep poverty are increasingly segregated from economic opportunity and the opportunity for the residents in these locations to participate fully in American society. Inherent here again is the recognition that geography matters and that understanding the factors that produce poverty at the local level is a critical first step in producing policy options that can alleviate this poverty and produce positive outcomes for both the residents of these locations and for society as a whole.

These are but two of many prominent examples that reflect a growing interest in spatial concerns within the social sciences. It's easy to think of a myriad of additional examples that highlight how we are increasingly becoming attuned to the importance of geography in our lives. From capital tax competition (Franzese and Hays 2008) to crime (Getis 2010) to legislative

behavior (Rogowski and Sinclair 2012), from policy dependence (Neumayer and Plümper 2012) to policy diffusion (Berry and Baybeck 2005) to migration (Koser and Salt 1997), geography has become a key conceptual and empirical concern in the social sciences. The techniques examined in this book allow researchers to model more effectively this spatial component in our analyses.

2.2 TYPES OF SPATIAL DATA

There are three principal types of spatial data that social scientists may work with: areal data, geostatistical data, and point pattern data. In the case of areal data, a spatial plane is partitioned into a finite number of areal units, or polygons. In the case of regular areal data, the polygons take the form of a regular grid of square or rectangular objects, such as on a chessboard. Such regular areal data, however, are rare in the social sciences, where aggregate units of analysis typically are irregular and differ in shape from unit to unit. Irregular areal data in the social sciences include block groups, census tracts, zip codes, legislative districts, counties, states, regions, and countries. Areal data are the most common spatial data in the social sciences. As a consequence, most of the diagnostics and models discussed in this book employ an areal data perspective.

Figure 2.1 provides an example of irregular areal data in a map of Illinois block groups in the 2000 census. Block groups have been employed as areal units in a variety of disciplines, including criminology, sociology, political science, and public health. As can be seen from Figure 2.1, the Illinois block groups are irregular polygons, varying in both size and shape, that cover the full spatial plane within the Illinois state boundaries. These Illinois block groups are used throughout the remainder of this chapter to demonstrate various neighbor definitions in areal data.

In contrast to areal data, geostatistical data occur when the observed data are sample data from a continuous underlying surface. Examples of geostatistical data include fertility rates (Guilmoto and Rajan 2001), political campaign contributions (Cho and Gimpel 2007), and housing prices (Chica-Olmo 2007) that are observed at particular sampled locations and unobserved at other, unsampled locations. The researcher's principal interest in geostatistical data is to infer information about values on the variable of interest at unobserved locations on the spatial plane from the sample data.

Point pattern data occur when the observed spatial locations are the locations of discrete events. Where the central concern with geostatistical data is interpolating values at unobserved locations, the central concern with point pattern data is the locations of the events themselves. Often, the null hypothesis in a point pattern analysis is complete spatial randomness (CSR), in which events are distributed independently with regard to space (Gatrell 1996, 258). If the null of CSR is rejected, the researcher can then examine whether departures from the null reflect spatial clustering (in which events are more concentrated spatially than predicted under CSR) or spatial regularity

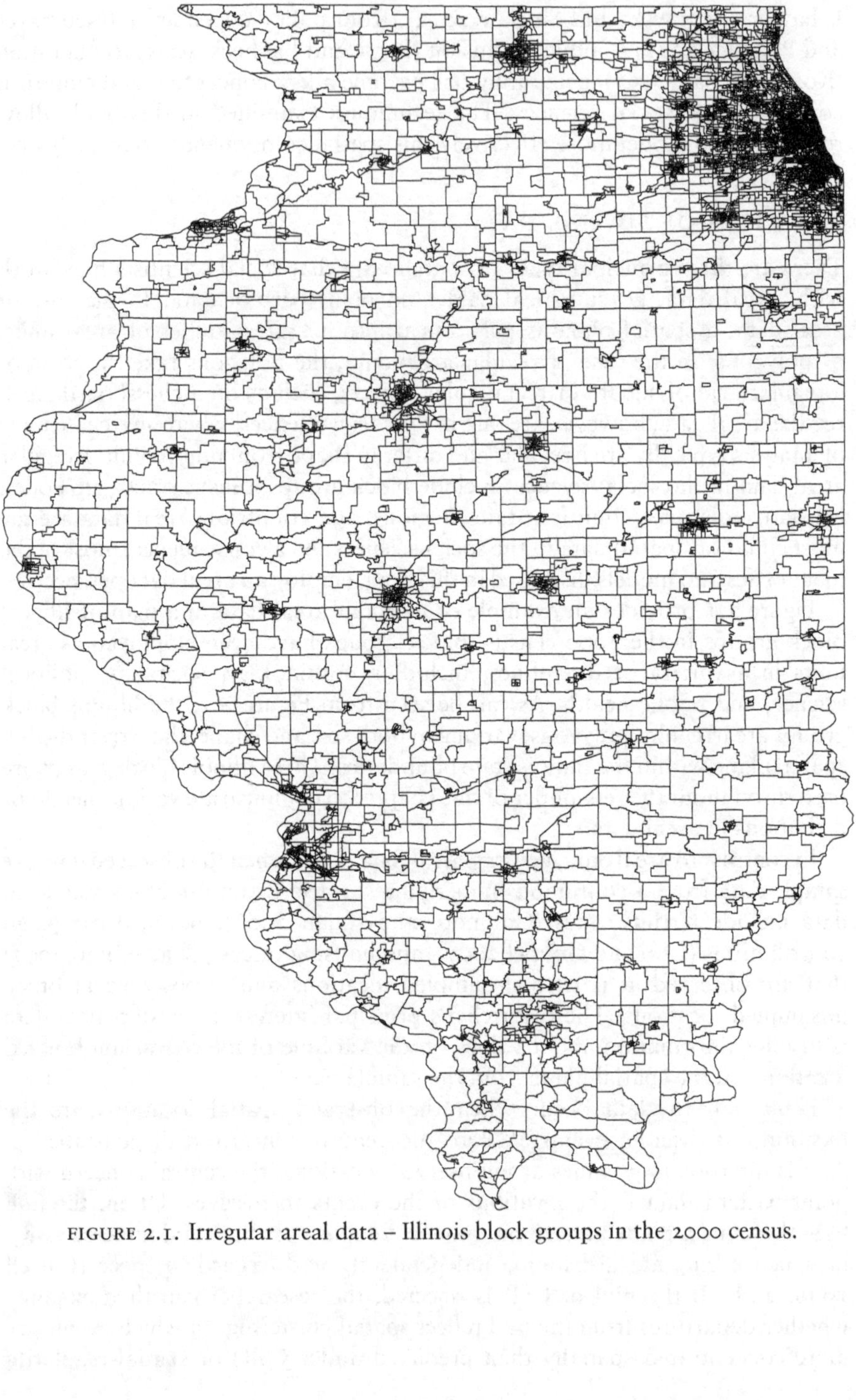

FIGURE 2.1. Irregular areal data – Illinois block groups in the 2000 census.

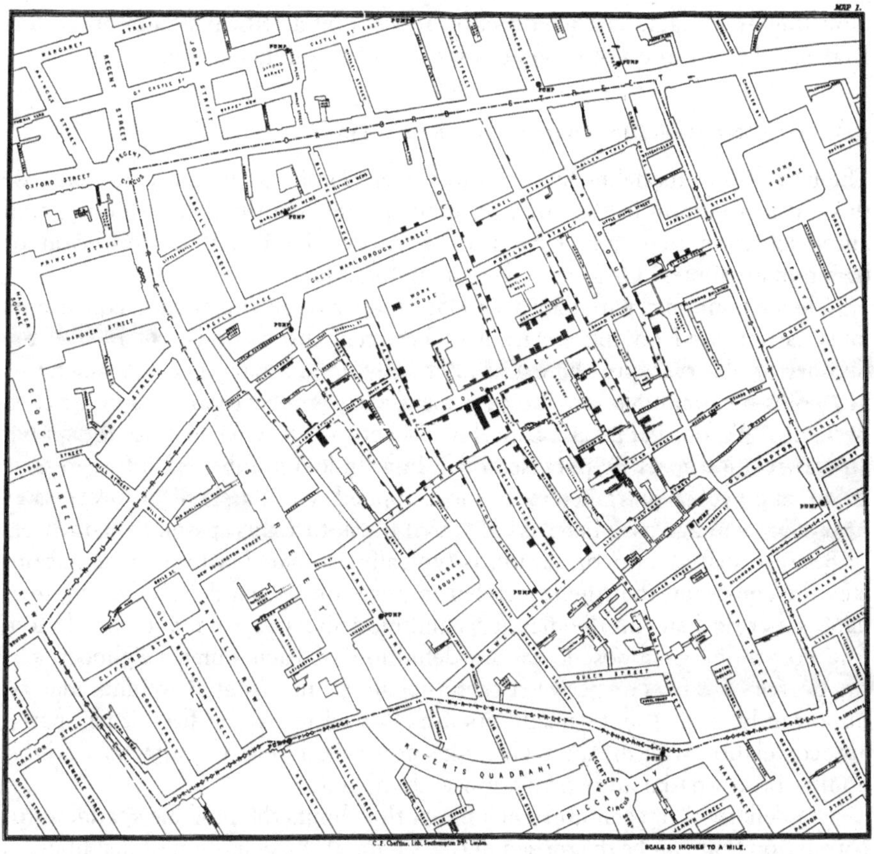

FIGURE 2.2. John Snow's map of the 1854 London cholera epidemic.

(in which events are more spatially dispersed than predicted under CSR). Here, alternative parametric models may be fit to determine the data generating point process producing the observed point pattern.

The modern discipline of epidemiology can be traced to Dr. John Snow's (1855) highly influential use of a primitive form of point pattern analysis in his study of the London cholera epidemic of 1854 (see Gatrell et al. 1996, 257). Snow mapped the geographic locations of cholera cases during this epidemic to identify spatial "clustering" of these cases. Snow's map of these cholera cases, originally published in 1855, is presented in Figure 2.2. Snow's mapping of these disease cases led him to trace the epidemic to the Broad Street water pump in Soho.

Although geostatistical or point pattern data will be appropriate for particular applications, the principal spatial data in the social sciences, as stated earlier, are areal data. As a consequence, this book focuses on strategies for

modeling areal data. The next section focuses on a critical step in areal data analysis: the definition of neighbors via a spatial weights matrix.

2.3 DEFINING NEIGHBORS IN AREAL DATA

The first step in modeling spatial autocorrelation in areal data is to diagnose this autocorrelation in the absence of covariates. Do the data exhibit spatial autocorrelation that may have been produced by behavioral diffusion or common attributes? Or are the data spatially independent?

When examining spatial autocorrelation in cross-sectional data, constraints must be imposed on the covariances between observations. With n as the number of observations, there are potentially $n \times n$ separate covariance terms in a cross-sectional dataset, and thus insufficient information to estimate each of the correlations in the data (Anselin and Bera 1998, 242). Instead, the spatial autocorrelation must be parameterized in a limited number of autoregressive or moving average parameters. In most applied work, a single autoregressive or moving average parameter is estimated to capture this spatial dependence.

Because spatial autocorrelation is typically estimated with a single parameter, the constraint that the researcher imposes on spatial dependence in areal data is a critical step in the diagnosis and modeling of spatial autocorrelation. The constraint is imposed via the definition of each unit's neighbors and the degree of influence between these neighbors in a spatial weights matrix. Importantly, only a unit's neighbors are allowed to exhibit first-order spatial autocorrelation with the unit. The unit's non-neighbors are assumed to exhibit no first-order spatial autocorrelation with the unit.[1]

The definition of each unit's neighbors thus limits the possible spatial autocorrelation that can be diagnosed in one's data. If the definition of neighbors is not consistent with the range of social interaction at which diffusion occurs, the resulting spatial autocorrelation estimate will not accurately capture diffusion processes at work in the data generating process (DGP). Similarly, if the neighbor definition is not consistent with the spatial clustering of non-diffusion sources of the behavior of interest, estimates of spatial autocorrelation will not accurately capture attributional dependence.

Closely related is the form and extent of spatial dependence between neighbors. Do all of the neighbors of i exert the same influence on i? Or is this influence greater for neighbors closer to i? Given the importance of accurately capturing the nature of spatial interaction and spatial dependence, substantive theory should, as much as possible, guide the construction of the

1 First-order spatial autocorrelation exists when neighbors exhibit significant spatial dependence with each other. Higher order spatial autocorrelation exists when spatial autocorrelation between units exists through dependencies between shared neighbors. Thus, for example, second-order spatial autocorrelation exists if neighbors of neighbors exhibit spatial dependence. The popular Six Degrees of Kevin Bacon game provides an intuitive introduction to first- and higher order dependencies between units.

spatial weights matrix and the constraints on potential spatial autocorrelation contained within it (see also Plümper and Neumayer 2010 on the importance of having theoretically motivated spatial weights matrices).

The standard spatial weights or connectivity matrix is an $n \times n$ matrix, W, in which $w_{ij} \neq 0$ if i and j are neighbors, or more generally, connected to each other; $w_{ij} = 0$ if i and j are not connected, and by convention, $w_{ii} = 0$ (i is not connected to itself). Typically the spatial weights matrix is then row standardized so that the sum of neighbors' weights for any particular observation equals 1. As Anselin and Bera (1998, 243) note, row standardization ensures that the values of all weights are between 0 and 1 and ensures comparability of spatial autocorrelation estimates across models. The latter occurs because the largest eigenvalue for a row-standardized weights matrix is always +1, thus facilitating the interpretation of the autoregressive parameter as a correlation.

Several alternative neighbor definitions and corresponding weights structures have been employed in practice. These range from simple contiguity definitions, to k-nearest neighbor definitions, to distance band neighbor definitions, to distance-decay neighbor definitions, and finally, given the generalizability of the approach, nonspatial neighbor definitions. Next, I consider each of these principal neighbor definitions in turn.

2.3.1 Contiguous Neighbors

The simplest definition of neighbors is the first-order contiguity case. Here, three principal alternatives exist for regular lattice data. Given the chessboard nature of regular lattice data, it is not surprising that these alternatives take the form of alternative chess pieces, with the contiguity definitions corresponding to the allowable moves of these chess pieces.

The first of these definitions is the rook definition, which defines as neighbors those areal units sharing a common edge, as shown in Figure 2.3. It can be seen that the rook neighbor definition corresponds to the horizontal and vertical moves of a rook in a chess game. Note the bidirectional arrows in Figure 2.3, which denote the simultaneous nature of spatial, as opposed to temporal dependence. In the typical spatial application, unit i would be allowed to influence its neighbor unit j's behavior *and* unit j would be allowed to influence its neighbor unit i's behavior.

Consider next a bishop neighbor definition, presented in Figure 2.4. As the name suggests, a bishop neighbor definition corresponds to the diagonal moves of a bishop in a chess game. In the bishop contiguity definition, objects sharing a common vertex with i are treated as neighbors of i.

The final contiguity neighbor definition is the queen contiguity definition. The queen contiguity neighbor definition incorporates both the rook and bishop definitions, as any object sharing either a common edge or vertex with i is defined as a neighbor of i. This queen contiguity neighbor definition is

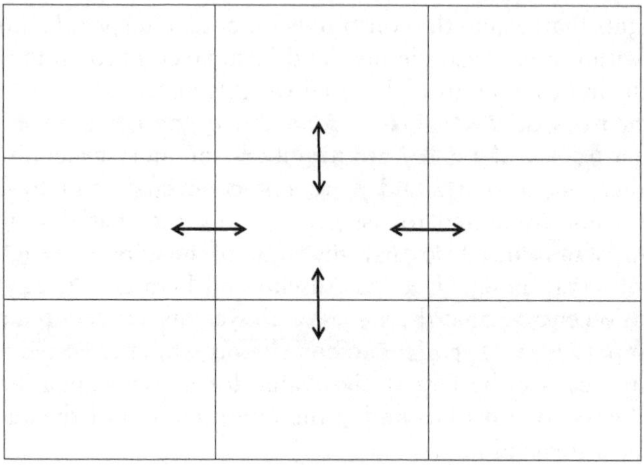

FIGURE 2.3. Rook neighbor definition.

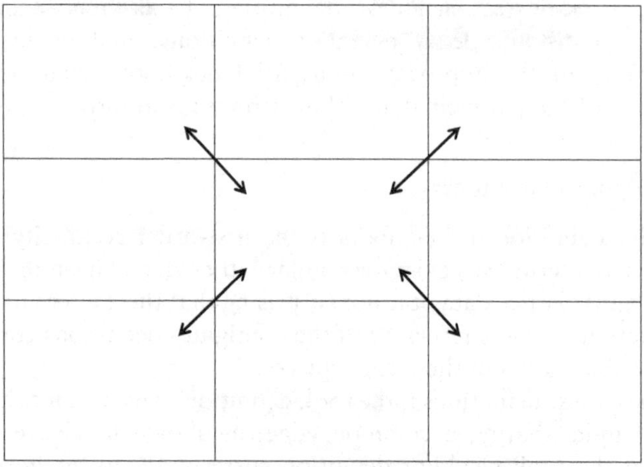

FIGURE 2.4. Bishop neighbor definition.

presented in Figure 2.5. The combination of the rook and bishop neighbor definitions reflects the queen's ability to move horizontally, vertically, or diagonally in a chess game. In short, in the queen contiguity definition, all polygons contiguous to *i* are neighbors of *i* (Anselin 1988c, 18).

Most applications in the social sciences employ irregular lattice data rather than the regular lattice data reflected in Figures 2.3–2.5. This limits the applicability of the rook and bishop neighbor definitions in practice. The queen contiguity definition typically has stronger theoretical justification than either the rook or bishop definitions. It is difficult to provide a theoretical rationale for why the types of polygons social scientists deal with would exhibit only spatial dependence with neighboring polygons with common edges or vertices, but not

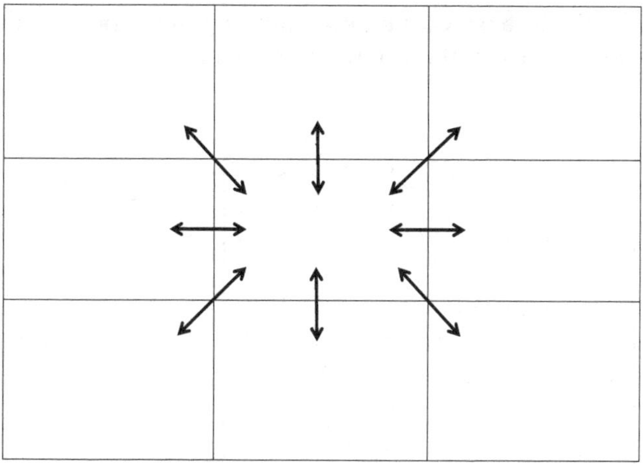

FIGURE 2.5. Queen neighbor definition.

all contiguous neighbors. As a consequence, researchers employing a contiguity neighbor definition will typically favor the queen contiguity definition over the two alternative contiguity definitions.

Consider the Illinois block groups in Figure 2.1. A criminologist may employ a queen contiguity neighbor definition for either of the two reasons corresponding to the alternative sources of spatial dependence in Galton's problem. On the one hand, she may employ this neighbor definition because she believes that crime diffuses across neighboring block groups. High crime rates in block groups neighboring block group *i* may directly increase the crime rate in block group *i* and vice versa. Alternatively, she may employ the queen contiguity neighbor definition because she believes that neighboring block groups share common attributes such as unemployment or poverty rates that influence crime rates.

A portion of the queen contiguity spatial weights matrix for the Illinois block groups is presented in (2.1). This matrix includes the neighbor definitions for the first five Illinois block groups in the 2000 census (block group numbers 1 through 5) and the last five Illinois block groups in the census (block group numbers 9846 through 9850). Block groups 1 through 5 are located in northwest Illinois while block groups 9846 through 9848 are located in Springfield (in central Illinois) and block groups 9849 and 9850 are located in southeast Illinois.

In this binary contiguity matrix, each unit's contiguous neighbors are given a value of 1 and its non-neighbors a value of 0 in the row corresponding to the unit. For example, Illinois block groups 1 and 3 are neighbors under the queen definition. This is reflected in the weights matrix. Row 1 lists the neighbors and non-neighbors for block group 1 among the first and last five Illinois block groups. As can be seen, of the first five Illinois block groups, only block group 3 is a queen contiguity neighbor of block group 1 and is coded accordingly with a

1 in the third cell. The binary contiguity matrix is symmetric, with this neighbor definition also reflected by the 1 in the first cell in row 3.

$$W = \begin{bmatrix} 0 & 0 & 1 & 0 & 0 & \cdots & 0 & 0 & 0 & 0 & 0 \\ 0 & 0 & 0 & 0 & 1 & \cdots & 0 & 0 & 0 & 0 & 0 \\ 1 & 0 & 0 & 1 & 0 & \cdots & 0 & 0 & 0 & 0 & 0 \\ 0 & 0 & 1 & 0 & 0 & \cdots & 0 & 0 & 0 & 0 & 0 \\ 0 & 1 & 0 & 0 & 0 & \cdots & 0 & 0 & 0 & 0 & 0 \\ \vdots & \vdots & \vdots & \vdots & \vdots & \ddots & \vdots & \vdots & \vdots & \vdots & \vdots \\ 0 & 0 & 0 & 0 & 0 & \cdots & 0 & 1 & 1 & 0 & 0 \\ 0 & 0 & 0 & 0 & 0 & \cdots & 1 & 0 & 1 & 0 & 0 \\ 0 & 0 & 0 & 0 & 0 & \cdots & 1 & 1 & 0 & 0 & 0 \\ 0 & 0 & 0 & 0 & 0 & \cdots & 0 & 0 & 0 & 0 & 1 \\ 0 & 0 & 0 & 0 & 0 & \cdots & 0 & 0 & 0 & 1 & 0 \end{bmatrix} \qquad (2.1)$$

Row standardization of the binary matrix in 2.1 produces the matrix in (2.2):

$$W = \begin{bmatrix} 0 & 0 & \frac{1}{3} & 0 & 0 & \cdots & 0 & 0 & 0 & 0 & 0 \\ 0 & 0 & 0 & 0 & \frac{1}{4} & \cdots & 0 & 0 & 0 & 0 & 0 \\ \frac{1}{4} & 0 & 0 & \frac{1}{4} & 0 & \cdots & 0 & 0 & 0 & 0 & 0 \\ 0 & 0 & \frac{1}{4} & 0 & 0 & \cdots & 0 & 0 & 0 & 0 & 0 \\ 0 & \frac{1}{4} & 0 & 0 & 0 & \cdots & 0 & 0 & 0 & 0 & 0 \\ \vdots & \vdots & \vdots & \vdots & \vdots & \ddots & \vdots & \vdots & \vdots & \vdots & \vdots \\ 0 & 0 & 0 & 0 & 0 & \cdots & 0 & \frac{1}{4} & \frac{1}{4} & 0 & 0 \\ 0 & 0 & 0 & 0 & 0 & \cdots & \frac{1}{6} & 0 & \frac{1}{6} & 0 & 0 \\ 0 & 0 & 0 & 0 & 0 & \cdots & \frac{1}{7} & \frac{1}{7} & 0 & 0 & 0 \\ 0 & 0 & 0 & 0 & 0 & \cdots & 0 & 0 & 0 & 0 & \frac{1}{4} \\ 0 & 0 & 0 & 0 & 0 & \cdots & 0 & 0 & 0 & \frac{1}{4} & 0 \end{bmatrix} \qquad (2.2)$$

As can be seen, the row standardization of a symmetric contiguity matrix typically produces a nonsymmetric matrix. This is because irregular areal objects typically have differing numbers of contiguous neighbors. As the row-standardized weights matrix in (2.2) shows, block group 1 has three neighbors, one of whom is block group 3 (the other neighbors are block groups 7 and 17, which are not shown in the matrix in [2.2]). In contrast,

block group 2 has four neighbors (one of whom is block group 5) and block group 3 also has four neighbors (two of whom are block groups 1 and 4). As is clear from the matrix, block groups 9849 and 9850 are each one of the other's four contiguous neighbors. As we would expect given the locations of these ten Illinois block groups, none of the first five block groups are contiguous to any of the final five block groups.

2.3.2 *k*-Nearest Neighbors

Alternatively, a researcher may wish to relax the strict contiguity neighbor definition, but still retain a proximity conception of spatial influence. A *k*-nearest neighbor definition retains the nearness conception while not assuming that there is any substantive importance to the Euclidean distance between units. In a *k*-nearest neighbor definition, all units among the *k* nearest neighbors of unit *i* are treated as neighbors of *i*, while the remaining units are treated as non-neighbors.

A *k*-nearest neighbor definition may be theoretically supported when one believes that units have a finite number of potential interactions and that these interactions are promoted by proximity. Thus it may be that the typical citizen is able to retain the political arguments of only five neighbors, at maximum, and that these neighbors with whom political discussion takes place are the individual's five most spatially proximate neighbors. If so, there may be an argument for employing a five-nearest neighbor definition. Clearly, the value *k* should be theoretically informed and the interaction potential should be promoted by spatial proximity if one is to employ a literal *k*-nearest neighbor definition.

A nonstandardized spatial weights matrix reflecting a five-nearest neighbor definition for the Illinois block groups is presented in (2.3). As can be seen, in contrast to the queen contiguity case, both block groups 3 and 4 are now neighbors of block group 1, as both are among the five nearest neighbors of the first block group. The row standardized form of this weights matrix is presented in (2.4). In this case, the portion of the matrix in (2.4) is symmetric. However, this is not always the case in practice, as a unit may be one of the *k*-nearest neighbors of unit *i*, even though unit *i* is not one of its *k*-nearest neighbors.

$$W = \begin{bmatrix} 0 & 0 & 1 & 1 & 0 & \cdots & 0 & 0 & 0 & 0 & 0 \\ 0 & 0 & 0 & 0 & 1 & \cdots & 0 & 0 & 0 & 0 & 0 \\ 1 & 0 & 0 & 1 & 0 & \cdots & 0 & 0 & 0 & 0 & 0 \\ 1 & 0 & 1 & 0 & 0 & \cdots & 0 & 0 & 0 & 0 & 0 \\ 0 & 1 & 0 & 0 & 0 & \cdots & 0 & 0 & 0 & 0 & 0 \\ \vdots & \vdots & \vdots & \vdots & \vdots & \ddots & \vdots & \vdots & \vdots & \vdots & \vdots \\ 0 & 0 & 0 & 0 & 0 & \cdots & 0 & 1 & 1 & 0 & 0 \\ 0 & 0 & 0 & 0 & 0 & \cdots & 1 & 0 & 1 & 0 & 0 \\ 0 & 0 & 0 & 0 & 0 & \cdots & 1 & 1 & 0 & 0 & 0 \\ 0 & 0 & 0 & 0 & 0 & \cdots & 0 & 0 & 0 & 0 & 1 \\ 0 & 0 & 0 & 0 & 0 & \cdots & 0 & 0 & 0 & 1 & 0 \end{bmatrix} \quad (2.3)$$

$$W = \begin{bmatrix} 0 & 0 & \frac{1}{5} & \frac{1}{5} & 0 & \cdots & 0 & 0 & 0 & 0 & 0 \\ 0 & 0 & 0 & 0 & \frac{1}{5} & \cdots & 0 & 0 & 0 & 0 & 0 \\ \frac{1}{5} & 0 & 0 & \frac{1}{5} & 0 & \cdots & 0 & 0 & 0 & 0 & 0 \\ \frac{1}{5} & 0 & \frac{1}{5} & 0 & 0 & \cdots & 0 & 0 & 0 & 0 & 0 \\ 0 & \frac{1}{5} & 0 & 0 & 0 & \cdots & 0 & 0 & 0 & 0 & 0 \\ \vdots & \vdots & \vdots & \vdots & \vdots & \ddots & \vdots & \vdots & \vdots & \vdots & \vdots \\ 0 & 0 & 0 & 0 & 0 & \cdots & 0 & \frac{1}{5} & \frac{1}{5} & 0 & 0 \\ 0 & 0 & 0 & 0 & 0 & \cdots & \frac{1}{5} & 0 & \frac{1}{5} & 0 & 0 \\ 0 & 0 & 0 & 0 & 0 & \cdots & \frac{1}{5} & \frac{1}{5} & 0 & 0 & 0 \\ 0 & 0 & 0 & 0 & 0 & \cdots & 0 & 0 & 0 & 0 & \frac{1}{5} \\ 0 & 0 & 0 & 0 & 0 & \cdots & 0 & 0 & 0 & \frac{1}{5} & 0 \end{bmatrix} \qquad (2.4)$$

2.3.3 Distance Band Neighbor Definition

Often, a researcher's conception of spatial dependence will incorporate the distances between observations. A distance band neighbor definition will be theoretically supported if the researcher believes that units within a particular distance of unit i exhibit spatial autocorrelation with unit i but that units beyond this critical distance are spatially independent from unit i. For example, returning to the crime rate example employed earlier, a researcher may employ a distance band neighbor definition if she has reason to expect that there is a geographic range of interaction within which crime diffuses. For example, it may be that crime diffuses not merely across contiguous block groups, but also across all block groups within twenty-five miles of each other. If so, the researcher will treat block groups within twenty-five miles of unit i as neighbors of i, and all block groups beyond this critical threshold distance as non-neighbors of i.

Critical questions must be addressed before creating a distance band weights matrix. First, from which points will the distance bands be measured? Is it more appropriate to estimate distance from the central points of the polygons (the average of the x,y coordinates of the vertices on the polygon's boundary); the centroid, or center of gravity of the polygon; the minimum distance between polygons; or the distance between the principal population centers or seats of government within the polygons? A second question is, What is the relevant critical distance for the distance band within which units will be treated as neighbors and beyond which units will be treated as non-neighbors? Clearly, the answers to these questions must reflect the scholar's substantive theory and understanding of the nature and range of spatial interdependence.

The matrix in (2.5) presents a distance band neighbor definition for the Illinois block groups. In this case, all block groups twenty-five miles or less from each other in great-circle distance are treated as neighbors while block groups beyond twenty-five miles are treated as non-neighbors. The distances

were measured from the central points of the block groups using GeoDa 0.9.5-i.[2] As can be seen, there are some differences between the distance band neighbors and the queen contiguity neighbors. For example, block group 1 is twenty-five miles or less from block groups 4 and 5 and thus is a neighbor of these block groups under the distance band definition. Similarly, block groups 3 and 5 are now neighbors of each other as well.

$$W = \begin{bmatrix} 0 & 0 & 1 & 1 & 1 & \cdots & 0 & 0 & 0 & 0 & 0 \\ 0 & 0 & 0 & 1 & 1 & \cdots & 0 & 0 & 0 & 0 & 0 \\ 1 & 0 & 0 & 1 & 1 & \cdots & 0 & 0 & 0 & 0 & 0 \\ 1 & 1 & 1 & 0 & 1 & \cdots & 0 & 0 & 0 & 0 & 0 \\ 1 & 1 & 1 & 1 & 0 & \cdots & 0 & 0 & 0 & 0 & 0 \\ \vdots & \vdots & \vdots & \vdots & \vdots & \ddots & \vdots & \vdots & \vdots & \vdots & \vdots \\ 0 & 0 & 0 & 0 & 0 & \cdots & 0 & 1 & 1 & 0 & 0 \\ 0 & 0 & 0 & 0 & 0 & \cdots & 1 & 0 & 1 & 0 & 0 \\ 0 & 0 & 0 & 0 & 0 & \cdots & 1 & 1 & 0 & 0 & 0 \\ 0 & 0 & 0 & 0 & 0 & \cdots & 0 & 0 & 0 & 0 & 1 \\ 0 & 0 & 0 & 0 & 0 & \cdots & 0 & 0 & 0 & 1 & 0 \end{bmatrix} \tag{2.5}$$

2.3.4 Distance-Decay Neighbor Definition

The distance band definition treated all neighbors within a certain distance of unit i as having the same weights, and thus exerting the same influence on measures of spatial autocorrelation as each other. This perspective would be justified if we believe that unit i is equally likely to interact or to share observed and unobserved characteristics with other units within particular distance bands. This may not, however, always be a realistic conception of spatial dependence. It may well be that spatial autocorrelation will be stronger among more spatially proximate units and decline as distance increases.

This latter perspective, in fact, is reflective of Tobler's (1970, 236) First Law of Geography in which "everything is related to everything else, but near things are more related than distant things." For Tobler, spatial autocorrelation extends across the full spatial plane, but is strongest at spatially proximate locations. This conception of spatial autocorrelation can be estimated via a distance-decay neighbor definition. If substantive theory suggests, we can also

2 GeoDa is a free downloadable software package for spatial analysis developed by Luc Anselin. The software can be downloaded from the GeoDa Center for Geospatial Analysis and Computation at Arizona State University at http://geodacenter.asu.edu/software/downloads. An active listserv, Openspace, exists for user queries for GeoDa and other software tools developed through the National Science Foundation–funded Center for Spatially Integrated Social Science (CSISS). Information on subscribing to Openspace can be found at http://geodacenter.asu.edu/support/community.

modify Tobler's law to specify a threshold distance beyond which units are spatially independent within the distance-decay neighbor definition.

Cliff and Ord (1973) proposed generalized distance weights that incorporate both a distance-decay effect and the extent of shared borders between units. Cliff and Ord propose that the elements of the spatial weights matrix take the form

$$w_{ij} = d_{ij}^{-a}[\beta_{i(j)}]^{b}, \tag{2.6}$$

where d_{ij} is the distance between contiguous units and $\beta_{i(j)}$ is the proportion of the border of unit i that is in contact with unit j. Positive values of the parameters a and b in (2.6) give greater weight, respectively, to units that are more spatially proximate and units with a higher proportion of a shared border (Cliff and Ord 1973, 13).

2.3.5 Nonspatial Weights

Beck, Gleditsch, and Beardsley (2006, 31) raise the important point that "Space is more than geography" and point toward shared language, social distance (Blau-space), and small world networks as examples in which the dependence between observations may be unrelated to geographic distance. Although spatial weights matrices were originally developed to estimate spatial autocorrelation, the areal data approach to estimating dependence between observations can be readily extended to these nonspatial neighbor definitions. As a consequence, the techniques of spatial analysis examined in this book are generalizable approaches to modeling dependent data. Beck et al., for example, employ a weights matrix in which the weights are defined by the proportion of country *i*'s total interstate trade that is accounted for by its trade with country *j* (33). This neighbor definition recognizes that the degree of interdependence between countries may be affected by economic interdependence.

Similarly, Leenders (2002) examined how influence in a social network can be modeled via a weights matrix. Here, nonzero elements in the weights matrix are given to unit *i*'s alters, where *i*'s alters are defined as the other units in the network that constitute *i*'s frame of reference (Leenders 2002, 33). Units given zero weights are those members of the social network who do not influence *i*'s opinions, attitudes, or behavior. The particular nonzero values that *i*'s alters receive reflect the potential for influence within the network rather than spatial proximity. Thus, alters who are expected to exert the strongest influences on *i* are given the largest weights. For example, in an individual-level analysis, particularly influential alters may be those with strong personalities or those whom *i* particularly respects. In such network autocorrelation models, it is particularly important to include asymmetries in social influence. While equals within the network may exert equivalent influences on each other, more asymmetric relationships should also typically be reflected in the cells of the

weights matrix. If unit j exerts greater influence on unit i than the reverse, then w_{ij} should take on a larger value than w_{ji}.

2.3.6 Higher Order Spatial Weights

All of the alternative neighbor definitions discussed thus far have been first-order neighbor definitions. The resulting weights matrices are thus all of the form where w_{ij} takes on a nonzero value when unit j has a direct neighbor relationship with unit i. Scholars may also be interested in higher order relationships in which neighbors of neighbors exhibit spatial autocorrelation. The researcher may, for example, wish to estimate spatial autocorrelation parameters for both first- and second-order spatial autocorrelation. Clearly, first- and second-order (and, more generally, higher order) relationships are not mutually exclusive, and in fact, frequently coexist. For example, Germany and France are first-order neighbors and are also second-order neighbors through Belgium, Luxembourg, and Switzerland. Clearly if the researcher wishes to estimate second-order spatial autocorrelation that does not account for first-order relationships, she will wish to exclude the first-order relationships from her second-order weights matrix.

2.4 MISSPECIFICATION OF THE WEIGHTS MATRIX

Clearly, a wide variety of spatial neighbor definitions are available to the researcher wishing to model spatial dependence. A variety of studies have demonstrated the importance of properly specifying the spatial weights matrix. Misspecifying how spatial dependence operates can affect the results of diagnostics for spatial dependence as well as coefficient estimates for both spatial and nonspatial effects (see Stetzer 1982; Anselin 1986; Anselin and Rey 1991; Florax and Rey 1995). As a consequence, spatial neighbor definitions should reflect guidance from substantive theory. Unfortunately, substantive theory regarding spatial effects remains an underdeveloped research area in most of the social sciences and an important agenda item for current research.

2.5 ESTIMATING A SPATIAL WEIGHTS MATRIX

Given how important the proper definition of neighbors is for the valid estimation of spatial dependence, researchers are increasingly exploring how neighbor definitions and resulting weights matrices can be estimated from data. In fact, this is a particularly active area of current research in spatial analysis. Aldstadt and Getis (2006) proposed "A Multidirectional Optimum Ecotope-Based Algorithm" (AMOEBA) for estimating a spatial weights matrix, which is optimum in employing the most local scale of spatial association in the data. Recently, Beenstock and Felsenstein (2012) developed a nonparametric method of moments approach for estimating a spatial weights matrix when

repeated observations are available on the units of interest. Much work remains to be done for developing estimation approaches for scholars employing cross-sectional spatial data.

2.6 APPLICATION: DEMOGRAPHIC CHANGE

The critical advantage of employing spatial methods for areal data is that they allow us to move beyond mere eyeball examinations of data to determine whether these data exhibit spatial dependence and if so, why they exhibit this dependence. This is of critical importance. The human mind is predisposed toward apophenia, the perception of structure where it does not exist, in data that are, in fact, random (see, e.g., Carroll 2003). Presented with a map, we are inclined to see a spatial structure to data, even when the data are randomly distributed in space. As a consequence, we do not want to rely on mere ocular, or eyeball, examinations of geography when we can test for the existence of a geographic structure to our data.

Consider, for example, demography, a key concern of scholars in a variety of social science disciplines. One of the most prominent and consequential developments in the demography of the United States in recent decades has been the dramatic growth in the size of its Hispanic population. Between 2000 and 2010, the United States' Hispanic population grew by 43 percent, more than four times the overall population growth rate in the country (Ennis, Ríos-Vargas, and Albert 2011, 2).

Changes in the Latino population in the continental United States are displayed in the map in Figure 2.6. This map presents the percentage change in the Hispanic population at the county level between 2000 and 2010. Percentage changes in the Hispanic population ranged from −100 percent (for Blaine County, Nebraska, which lost its sole Latino resident between 2000 and 2010) to more than +1740.5 percent (for Stewart County, GA). Figure 2.6 plots the percentage changes in the Hispanic population utilizing five categories.

Were these changes in the Latino population spatially structured so that neighboring counties exhibited similar percentage changes? Or were they randomly distributed with regard to space? It is not completely clear from Figure 2.6. Plausible arguments could be made either way, but given apophenia, we know that we may be biased toward seeing structure even where it doesn't exist. As a consequence, a mere eyeball test of the existence of a geographic structure will be neither reliable nor conclusive.

Happily, we don't have to rely on ocular judgments. We can employ diagnostics to determine whether there is a spatial structure to the data. In this case, there is. Employing the queen contiguity neighbor definition, the global Moran's I, one of the principal diagnostics for spatial dependence and one that will be presented in detail in Chapter 4, diagnoses positive spatial dependence. Percentage changes in the Latino population between 2000 and 2010 were not randomly distributed with regard to space. Instead, counties shared similar

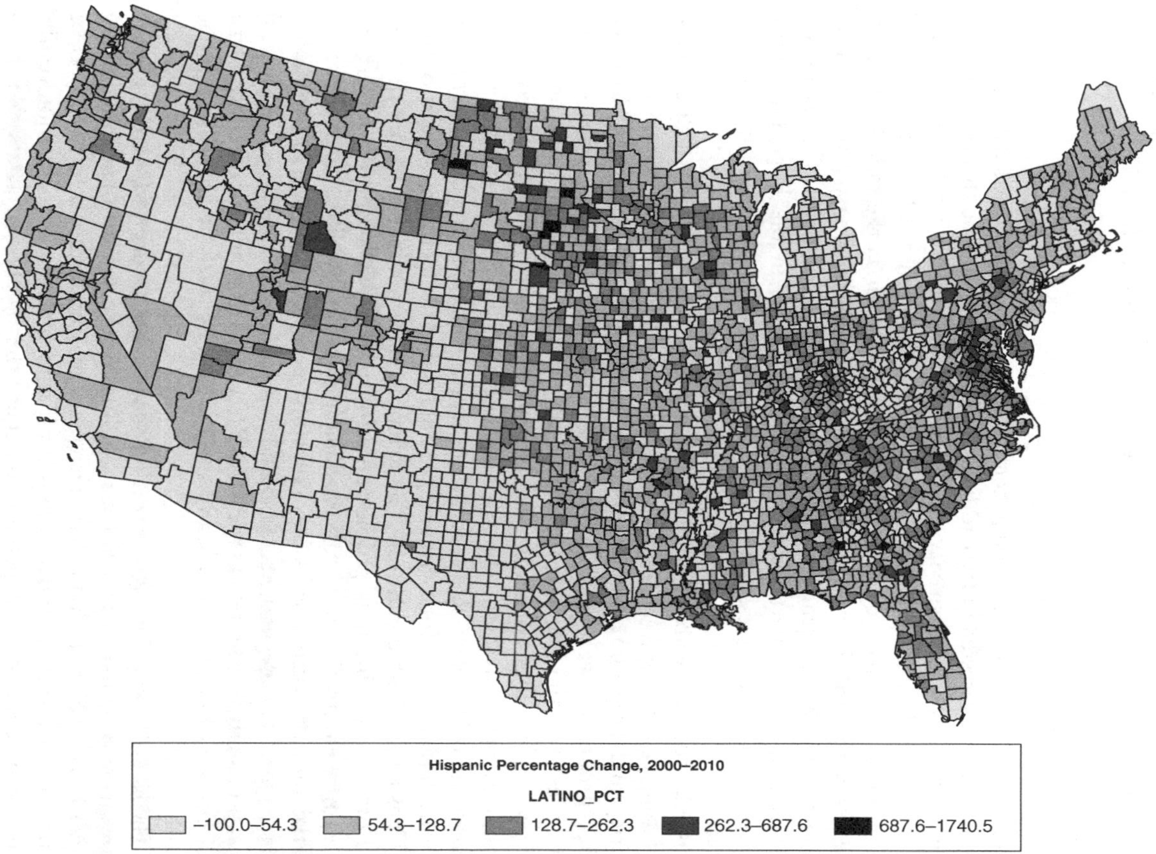

FIGURE 2.6. Percentage change in the Hispanic population, 2000–2010.

percentage changes in their Latino populations with their neighboring counties. Moreover, we can be quite confident of the existence of this spatial dependence. The pseudo p-value for the test of whether the observed Moran's I value of 0.176 is different from 0 is 0.001, the smallest possible value for the random permutation approach to significance employed in this test.[3]

2.7 ADDITIONAL TOPICS

Scholars interested in examining neighbor definitions for areal data in more detail will be interested in two additional concerns regarding this type of data. These issues are the sensitivity of spatial estimates to the areal units that are employed by the researcher and the effects of omitted areal units on spatial diagnosis and estimation. The first concern is known as the modifiable areal unit problem (MAUP) and the second is known as the boundary value problem. Important work is currently being done on both of these topics. The discussion here is intended to alert readers to these concerns in the hope that those interested in these topics will explore further some of the literature on these topics.

Block groups have been employed as areal units in a variety of disciplines, including criminology (McNulty 2001; Hannon and Knapp 2003), sociology (Farley and Frey 1994), and public health (Messer et al. 2006). However, block groups as well as many other areal objects, such as census tracts, zip codes, and the like are arbitrary units, defined principally for purposes of government administration, not because they carry particular theoretical rationales for analyses in the social sciences. (See Figure 2-3 [pp. 2–5] in *Census 2000 Summary File 1 Technical Documentation*, prepared by the U.S. Census Bureau, 2001, for a visual representation of the hierarchical relationship of Census geographic entities.) The arbitrary and modifiable nature of these and other areal objects is problematic, for as Openshaw and Taylor (1979) note, different areal objects can produce fundamentally different measures of spatial autocorrelation, or, as they colorfully note, "a million or so correlation coefficients." This dependence of spatial autocorrelation estimates on the areal objects of analysis is known as the MAUP (see also Glass and McAtee [2006] for a discussion of neighborhoods and specification of levels of analysis in public health).

The MAUP comprises two distinct problems. The *scale problem* refers to the dependence of spatial autocorrelation findings on the number of areal units into which a spatial plane is divided. A given plane may be divided into 5, 50, 500, or some other arbitrary number of polygons, with spatial autocorrelation results differing fundamentally depending on the n that is chosen. The *aggregation*

3 Note, I employed a permutation approach to inference on this test rather than assuming a normal distribution. This permutation approach and the rationale for it are presented in detail in Chapter 4.

problem refers to the dependence of spatial autocorrelation findings on the way that the spatial plane is divided into a particular set number of polygons. Thus, for example, there is a multitude of ways that a spatial plane can be divided into fifty polygons, and the spatial autocorrelation results will be dependent on the researcher's choice of how this division is accomplished. Unfortunately, there is ample empirical evidence that the scale and aggregation problems are common and can be quite severe (see, e.g., Openshaw 1983). As but one example, Openshaw and Taylor (1981) showed that correlation coefficients for the ninety-nine counties in Iowa varied from −0.97 to +0.99 depending on how these counties were aggregated. Moreover, equally problematic as Openshaw (1983, 5) notes, there is no general, systematic pattern to the effects on correlation coefficients that can aid with correction of these effects.

As Openshaw and Taylor (1981) show, although a variety of solutions have been proposed for the MAUP, many of these are problematic, as they impose additional, arbitrary criteria at the discretion of the researcher or ignore the fundamentally geographic nature of spatial data. For example, a spatial filtering approach due to Tobler (1969, 1975) may be employed to produce smoothed maps of underlying patterns that remove the noise resulting from aggregation effects. As Openshaw and Taylor note, however, this "solution" involves an infinite regress because any filtering analysis based on aggregate data will, by definition, be dependent on the aggregate areal units employed for the analysis. The best recourse for social scientists is to employ areal objects that are consistent with their substantive research questions. The plausibility of this approach, of course, will depend on the researcher's substantive question and the availability of appropriate areal objects.

Recent research on "bespoke neighborhoods" attempts to define areal units in a manner that can provide more verisimilitude to individuals' relevant neighborhood contexts than may be possible by utilizing predefined areal units such as block groups or census tracts. In this research, increasing neighborhood domains are built outward from each household unit by including the *n* nearest persons to that household, where *n* is an arbitrary threshold value such as 50, 500, or 1000 (see, e.g., MacAllister et al., 2001; Johnston et al., 2005). Although this bespoke neighborhood approach affords some increased verisimilitude by allowing neighborhood definitions to vary by household locations, the use of arbitrary thresholds is unlikely to distinguish precisely between actual neighborhoods.

The boundary value problem represents a second problem inherent in diagnosing and modeling spatial dependence. Assuming that observed units do not cover the full plane of possible spatial dependence, units at the boundaries of the observed data may be spatially autocorrelated with units outside of the observed data. Although this problem is generally referred to as the boundary value problem or the edge effect problem, both names are to some extent misnomers, as this problem can be more generalized and need not be restricted

to the boundaries of one's data. If data are missing in the interior of the plane, the same problem of biased autocorrelation estimates will also occur away from the boundary.

Assuming that units are autocorrelated with unobserved units outside the observed data, the boundary value or edge effect problem will produce biased estimates of spatial dependence in the subregion of the observed data that borders the units outside the observed data. The reason for this is clear: our estimates of spatial dependence are based only on the neighbors of unit *i* for which we have data, not those neighbors for which we do not have data but that also share spatial dependencies with our observed units. As Anselin (1988c, 173) notes, this may not be a concern in datasets with large numbers of observations, as maximum likelihood estimators of spatial dependence remain consistent even in the presence of edge effects. The bias induced in finite samples, however, may remain a concern for applied researchers working with smaller numbers of observations.

To date, solutions for the boundary value problem are suboptimal. Griffith (1983, 379) identifies five conventional approaches for dealing with the boundary value problem: mapping onto a torus, constructing an empirical buffer zone, constructing an artificial buffer zone, extrapolating into a buffer zone, and employing a correction factor. None of these "solutions," however, correct for the source of the boundary value problem: the fact that units affecting our observed units constitute missing data. At its base, the boundary value or edge effect problem is an insoluble problem when we do not know the values on the random variable for the polygons that are located outside the area of analysis but yet are spatially dependent with units located inside the area of analysis. We always risk biased spatial autocorrelation estimates by either ignoring this problem or by employing one of the standard approaches, as the solution to the problem may not accurately reflect the values located outside the observed data. As Anselin (1988c) notes, perhaps our best solution is to employ large samples to obtain consistent estimates in the presence of edge effects.

2.8 CONCLUSION

This chapter has focused on areal data, the principal spatial data social scientists are likely to employ in their spatial analyses. One of the first critical decisions that researchers must make when utilizing areal data is to determine the constraints that will be imposed on potential spatial autocorrelation. These constraints are imposed via a spatial weights matrix, which limits the potential spatial autocorrelation that can be diagnosed and modeled. Because the weights matrix plays such a critical role in the subsequent diagnosis and modeling of spatial dependence, researchers are advised either to employ a theoretically based weights matrix or to estimate the matrix from their data. Two additional important factors for the subsequent diagnosis and modeling

of spatial autocorrelation, the modifiable areal unit problem and the boundary value problem, were also discussed. To date, there are no perfect solutions for either of these problems that can apply to all cases. As a consequence, researchers must be sensitive to these concerns and examine the robustness of their findings both to the areal definitions of their units of analysis and to potential edge effects.

The definition of neighbors via the weights matrix is a necessary step before spatial dependence can be diagnosed via global and local measures of spatial autocorrelation and subsequently modeled via spatial econometric models (if these models are indicated by diagnostics for a nonspatial multivariate specification). Global and local measures of spatial autocorrelation are the subject of Chapter 4, while spatial diagnostics for nonspatial multivariate models and spatial econometric alternatives are the subjects, respectively, of Chapters 5 and 6. With the concepts of alternative neighbor definitions and weights matrices in hand, however, it is important to turn next to the question of how spatial dependence affects inferences in the social sciences. This is the subject of the next chapter, which examines the two alternative forms of spatial dependence implicit in Galton's problem, how multidimensional spatial dependence differs in its implications from unidimensional temporal dependence in time series analysis, the effects of omitted lag and error dependence on estimates, and the effects of spatial dependence on tests for other violations of ordinary least squares (OLS) assumptions.

3

Spatial Autocorrelation and Statistical Inference

Once the researcher has determined the appropriate weights structure based on theoretical expectations, or estimated this structure from the data, her next step is to diagnose and model the spatial dependence in the data. Before examining how spatial autocorrelation is diagnosed (the subject of Chapter 4) and modeled (the subject of Chapter 5), it is important to examine first the substantive implications of spatial autocorrelation and the effects of this dependence on inference in the social sciences. Here, it is useful to return to Galton's problem, which was first presented in the introductory chapter of this book.

As Galton's problem recognizes, there are two principal sources of spatial dependence. The first is an explicitly spatial source, focused on behavioral diffusion. Spatial proximity promotes behavioral interaction; generally, units of interest in the social sciences, be they individuals, states, nation-states, or other units, are more likely to interact with each other if they are spatially proximate to each other. Spatial diffusion occurs when spatially proximate units are influenced directly by the behaviors of their neighbors, and vice versa. From a modeling perspective, positive spatial diffusion corresponds to a positive and significant parameter on a spatially lagged dependent variable, where neighbors are defined via a weights matrix such as those presented in Chapter 2.

Alternatively, neighboring units may share similar behaviors even if there is no behavioral interaction between these units. In this case, the units' similarity in the behavior of interest is not affected directly by their neighbors' behavior. Instead, neighboring units in this case share similar behaviors as a result of the geographic clustering of the sources of these behaviors. Such spatial dependence may be called attributional dependence because it is traced not directly to the behavior of neighboring units, but instead to shared attributes at neighboring locations. If we are unable to model fully the attributional sources of spatial dependence in the data generating process (DGP), these sources will produce

spatial dependence in the error terms at neighboring locations. This spatial error dependence is modeled via a spatially lagged error term, where the error dependence is again modeled using a weights matrix such as presented in Chapter 2.

3.1 DEFINING SPATIAL AUTOCORRELATION

Formally, spatial autocorrelation implies a nonzero covariance between the values on a random variable for neighboring locations:

$$\text{Cov}(y_i, y_j) = E(y_i y_j) - E(y_i)E(y_j) \neq 0 \quad \text{for } i \neq j, \tag{3.1}$$

where the i, j locations have a spatial interpretation (Anselin and Bera 1998, 241–242).[1] The null hypothesis on a test of spatial autocorrelation is that the values on the random variable are distributed randomly in relation to space. That is, knowledge of units' spatial locations provides no leverage in predicting the units' values on the variable. Positive spatial autocorrelation exists when neighboring units share similar values on the variable, for example, when neighboring countries have similar economic policies or neighboring voters favor the same candidate. Negative spatial autocorrelation exists when neighboring units have dissimilar values on the variable. Negative spatial autocorrelation may reflect negative spatial externalities, such as when crime moves from one precinct to a neighboring precinct. Because spatial proximity is more likely to promote similarity than dissimilarity in behaviors, positive spatial autocorrelation is more likely than negative spatial autocorrelation in most social science applications.

What implications does spatial autocorrelation pose for inference? At first glance, spatial autocorrelation exhibits a surface similarity with the more familiar temporal dependence in time series analysis. Both are instances of dependent data. And in both the cross-sectional spatial case and the longitudinal time series case, the dependence can be modeled either via a lagged dependent variable or via the error term.

Spatial dependence, however, is not the cross-sectional analogue of serial dependence. The critical distinction between the two forms of dependence arises from the dimensionality of the dependence. In the time series case, dependence is unidimensional: the past influences the present, but the present does not influence the past. Cross-sectional spatial dependence, in contrast, is typically conceived of as multidimensional. In the diffusion case, neighbors influence the behavior of their neighbors *and vice versa*. In the case of attributional dependence, errors for neighboring observations exhibit simultaneous dependence. The simultaneous, multidimensional nature of spatial dependence leads to implications for inference that are distinct from the time series case.

1 This chapter draws on the presentation and notation in Anselin (1988c) and Anselin and Bera (1998).

This also significantly complicates estimation of spatial econometric models incorporating this spatial dependence.

3.2 SPATIAL VERSUS TEMPORAL AUTOCORRELATION

To understand the differing implications of spatial and temporal autocorrelation, it is helpful to consider Anselin's (1988c, 34) general spatial model for cross-sectional data:

$$y = \rho Wy + X\beta + \varepsilon$$
$$\varepsilon = \lambda W\varepsilon + \xi, \quad (3.2)$$

where y is an N by 1 vector of observations on the dependent variable; Wy is a spatially lagged dependent variable with spatial weights matrix W; X is an N by K matrix of observations on covariates; β is a K by 1 vector of parameters; ρ is the spatial autoregressive parameter for the spatially lagged dependent variable; ε is an N by 1 vector of error terms; $W\varepsilon$ is a spatially lagged error term with spatial weights matrix W; λ is the spatial autoregressive parameter for the spatially lagged error term; and $\xi \sim N(0,\Omega)$, where $\Omega_{ii} = h_i(z\alpha)$. When $\alpha = 0$, $h = \sigma^2$, and the errors are homoskedastic. The spatial lag model consistent with a diffusion process in the DGP results from setting λ equal to zero. The spatial error model consistent with attributional dependence results from setting ρ equal to zero. For simplicity's sake, we will first consider the case without $X\beta$ before returning covariates and their associated parameters to the model in Section 6.1.

Consider, first, the spatial lag model, where $\lambda = 0$. This bears some similarity to a time series model with a lagged dependent variable:

$$y_t = \rho y_{t-1} + \varepsilon_t, \quad (3.3)$$

where the lag in (3.3) is temporal rather than spatial, as it is in (3.2). In the time series case, ordinary least squares (OLS) is a biased but consistent estimator of ρ in the absence of serial correlation and other misspecification errors. Thus, although the OLS estimator should not be relied on in small samples, it can still be employed for asymptotic inference.

In contrast to the time series case, OLS estimates of the autoregressive parameter ρ in a spatial lag model will be biased and inconsistent, regardless of whether the errors exhibit dependence. The distinction between the spatial and temporal cases exists because of the multidimensional nature of spatial dependence. Consider first the bias of the OLS estimator of the spatial autoregressive parameter ρ. The expected value of the OLS estimator, $\hat{\rho}$, is

$$E(\hat{\rho}) = (y'W'Wy)^{-1}y'W'(\rho Wy + \varepsilon)$$
$$= \rho + (y'W'Wy)^{-1}y'W'\varepsilon. \quad (3.4)$$

As in the time series case, the expected value of the estimator will not equal the true value of ρ. In the spatial case, the sources of bias are twofold. Just as in the time series case, the complex nature of the matrix inverse induces a nonzero correlation with the error term. Unique to the spatial case, however, the expected value of $y'W'\varepsilon$ is also nonzero whenever $\rho \neq 0$ due to the multidimensional nature of spatial, as opposed to temporal, dependence.

The consistency of the OLS estimator in the time series case exists only because y_{t-1} is uncorrelated with ε_t when there is no serial correlation in the errors. This does not hold in the multidimensional spatial case. We can reformulate the spatial lag model in (3.2) as

$$y = (I - \rho W)^{-1}\varepsilon, \tag{3.5}$$

where $(I - \rho W)^{-1}$ is the Leontief inverse, which acts as a spatial multiplier, linking the spatially lagged dependent variable to the errors at all locations. In contrast to the unidimensional time-series case, in the multidimensional spatial case the matrix inverse is a full matrix, producing an infinite series, $(I + \rho W + \rho^2 W^2 + \ldots)\varepsilon$. As a result, Wy_i correlates not only with ε_i, but also with the errors at all other locations (Anselin and Bera 1998, 246–247).

Because of the simultaneous nature of spatial dependence, the OLS estimator $\hat{\rho}$ is not consistent, regardless of whether there is dependence in the error term or not. This can be seen via the probability limit:

$$\text{plim}\, N^{-1}(y'W'\varepsilon) = \text{plim}\, N^{-1}\varepsilon' W(I - \rho W)^{-1}\varepsilon, \tag{3.6}$$

where the error term takes a quadratic form and only when $\rho = 0$ does the probability limit equal zero (Anselin 1988c, 58).

If a diffusion process exists in the DGP and a spatially lagged dependent variable is omitted from the model altogether, the result is biased and inconsistent parameter estimates for the covariates in the model, reflecting omitted variable bias. Estimation of the spatial lag model incorporating the spatially lagged dependent variable must proceed via either maximum likelihood estimation or an instrumental variables specification.

The second principal spatial model is a spatial error model where now the dependence pertains to the error term, rather than to a spatially lagged dependent variable. The spatial error model bears a resemblance to a time series model with serially correlated errors. The implications of spatial error dependence are similar, though not identical, to those of serial correlation in time series. As in the time series case, OLS parameter estimates remain unbiased, but are no longer efficient. In the presence of spatial error dependence, standard error estimates will be biased downward, producing type I errors. The loss of information implicit in this spatial error dependence must be accounted for in estimation to produce unbiased standard error estimates. Similar to the case of a spatially lagged dependent variable, simultaneous autoregressive error dependence produces a nonzero covariance between the error terms at all

locations, via the spatial multiplier:

$$E[\varepsilon\varepsilon'] = \sigma^2(I - \lambda W)^{-1}(I - \lambda W')^{-1}, \tag{3.7}$$

with this covariance declining as the order of contiguity increases (Anselin and Bera 1998, 248).

In the unidimensional serial correlation case, iterative feasible generalized least squares (FGLS) estimators such as the Cochrane–Orcutt and Durbin estimators may be applied, producing consistent estimates of the autoregressive parameter for the serial dependence. These approaches are not applicable in the case of multidimensional spatial dependence. A direct spatial unidimensional analogue of the Cochrane–Orcutt estimator does not produce consistent estimates of the autoregressive parameter, λ (Anselin 1988c, 110). And as Kelejian and Prucha (1997, 108) demonstrated, λ is unidentified in a spatial analogue of the Durbin two-step method. As a result, estimation of the autoregressive spatial error parameter, λ, proceeds via maximum likelihood or generalized method of moments (GMM) estimation.

3.3 MONTE CARLO ANALYSIS

With a Monte Carlo analysis, we can examine how the OLS estimator performs when spatial dependence is present in the data but is ignored, as is the case in most applied research. The Monte Carlos are based on modified versions of the R code for omitted spatial error dependence in Anselin (2005). Recall from Section 3.2 the expected performance of the OLS estimator if spatial dependence in the data is ignored. If spatial autocorrelation consistent with a diffusion process exists in the DGP and a spatially lagged dependent variable is omitted from the OLS model, this will produce biased and inconsistent OLS parameter estimates for covariates in the model. Of course, the OLS estimate of the spatial autoregressive parameter for the lagged dependent variable will be biased and inconsistent if this term is included in the OLS model; estimation should instead proceed via maximum likelihood, instrumental variables, or GMM. However, given that a diffusion process is often implied by our theories and yet is often ignored in practice, it is critical to examine the performance of the OLS estimator for nonspatial covariates when this diffusion process is ignored. If, alternatively, the spatial autocorrelation pertains only to the errors, OLS will remain an unbiased estimator, but it will no longer be efficient. Standard error estimates will be biased downward in the presence of spatial dependence, producing type I errors.

In the Monte Carlos, the DGP for the case of spatial lag dependence takes the form

$$y = \rho Wy + \beta_0 + \beta_1 x_1 + \varepsilon, \tag{3.8}$$

where $\varepsilon \sim N(0,\sigma^2 I)$. The DGP for the case of spatial error dependence takes the form

$$y = \beta_0 + \beta_1 x_1 + \varepsilon$$
$$\varepsilon = \lambda W\varepsilon + \xi, \tag{3.9}$$

where $\xi \sim N(0,\sigma^2 I)$. In both cases, the independent variable, x_1, is normally distributed with a mean of 0 and a standard deviation of 3. I set $\beta_0 = \beta_1 = 1$. The OLS estimates for each experiment reflect a standard OLS specification that ignores the spatial lag or error dependence.

I examine the bias of the OLS estimates of β_1 when spatial lag and error dependence in the DGP are omitted from the OLS specification. I also examine the OLS estimates of the standard error of β_1 when spatial error dependence is omitted from the OLS specification. I examine the performance of OLS varying both the number of observations (and the corresponding spatial weights matrices) and the degree of spatial autocorrelation, as reflected in the autoregressive parameters ρ and λ. For each set of experiments, the observations are arrayed in regular square areals. Monte Carlos are performed for four different sizes of square areal structures: a 5 by 5 areal ($n = 25$), a 10 by 10 areal ($n = 100$), a 20 by 20 areal ($n = 400$), and a 30 by 30 areal ($n = 900$). In each case, a queen contiguity definition of neighbors is employed. The performance of OLS is examined for 10 values of both ρ and λ: −0.9, −0.7, −0.5, −0.3, −0.1, 0.1, 0.3, 0.5, 0.7, 0.9. For each combination of areal size and ρ or λ value, 1000 replications are performed.

3.3.1 Monte Carlo Results for Omitted Spatial Lag Dependence

Table 3.1 reports the bias of the OLS estimator of β_1 when spatial dependence consistent with a diffusion process exists in the DGP but is omitted from the OLS specification. As can be seen, OLS performs well at low levels of both positive and negative spatial autocorrelation. The bias of the OLS estimator, however, increases appreciably as $|\rho|$ increases to 0.5 and beyond. Moreover, there is an asymmetric effect, as bias is markedly more problematic at high levels of positive spatial autocorrelation. With an n of 25, the OLS estimator overstates the true value of β_1 by 15% when $\rho = 0.7$ and by 35% when $\rho = 0.9$. These results are consistent with the expectations from Section 3.2.

The bias of the OLS estimator can be seen graphically in Figure 3.1. This figure plots the bias in the OLS estimator for an n of 900 for each of the ten values of ρ. Here again is the pattern of negligible bias at low levels of ρ, increasing as both negative and positive spatial autocorrelations become more acute. Again, the bias in the OLS estimator is largest at high levels of positive spatial autocorrelation.

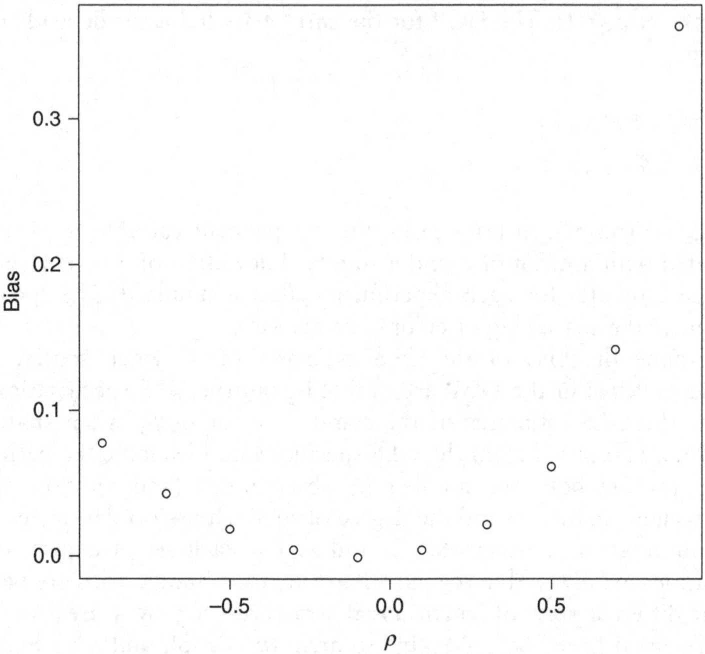

FIGURE 3.1. Bias of the OLS estimator with omitted spatially lagged dependent variable.

3.3.2 Monte Carlo Results for Omitted Spatial Error Dependence

In contrast to the Monte Carlo results with omitted lag dependence, the Monte Carlo experiments with omitted spatial error dependence show no appreciable bias in the OLS estimator. Employing proportional measures of bias, as in Table 3.1, there is no bias to two decimal places across the four different areal sizes and the ten values of λ. Consistent with expectations from Section 3.2, OLS remains an unbiased estimator of slope parameters even at high levels of positive and negative spatial error dependence.

As expected, however, OLS standard errors are unduly optimistic in the presence of spatial error dependence. Table 3.2 reports the ratio of the OLS standard errors to the true standard errors. At low levels of spatial error dependence, OLS standard errors remain unbiased. However, as both positive and negative error dependence increases in size, the standard errors reported by OLS increasingly understate the true standard errors. Similar to the case of omitted spatial lag dependence, the problem is particularly acute for high levels of positive spatial error autocorrelation. For example, with an n of 900 and a λ of 0.9, the OLS standard error is only 0.57 the size of the true standard error. In the presence of both positive and negative spatial error dependence, inference based on OLS is likely to lead to type I errors.

TABLE 3.1. *Bias of the OLS Estimator with Omitted Spatially Lagged Dependent Variable*

	ρ									
N	−0.9	−0.7	−0.5	−0.3	−0.1	0.1	0.3	0.5	0.7	0.9
25	0.09	0.05	0.02	0.01	0.00	0.01	0.03	0.07	0.15	0.35
100	0.12	0.07	0.04	0.01	0.00	0.00	0.01	0.04	0.11	0.29
400	0.11	0.06	0.04	0.02	0.00	0.00	0.01	0.04	0.09	0.25
900	0.08	0.04	0.02	0.00	0.00	0.00	0.02	0.06	0.14	0.36

TABLE 3.2. *Ratio of OLS Standard Error to True Standard Error with Spatial Error Dependence*

	λ									
N	−0.9	−0.7	−0.5	−0.3	−0.1	0.1	0.3	0.5	0.7	0.9
25	0.87	0.89	0.95	0.97	1.03	1.01	0.98	0.96	0.85	0.71
100	0.85	0.93	0.98	0.96	1.00	0.98	0.96	0.97	0.86	0.64
400	0.86	0.93	0.95	1.02	1.00	0.97	0.98	0.92	0.85	0.59
900	0.87	0.92	0.93	1.02	0.98	1.00	0.96	0.92	0.83	0.57

3.4 ADDITIONAL TOPICS

As the Monte Carlo results demonstrate, omitted spatial dependence poses consequential implications for inferences social scientists may draw from OLS regressions. Spatial dependence is also consequential for tests of violations of OLS assumptions. I examine the effects of spatial dependence on tests for incorrect functional form and heteroskedasticity, in turn, next.

A central assumption of OLS regression is that there is a linear relationship between the independent variables and the dependent variable. Greene (2003, 192) emphasizes incorrect functional form as a source of cross-sectional (though not explicitly spatial) autocorrelation in errors. The intuition of how an incorrect functional form can induce spatial error dependence is straightforward. Assume, for example, that the response variable is modeled as a linear function of the covariates. However, perhaps the correct functional form is an alternative function, such as a quadratic. If so, the misspecification is likely to produce correlated errors, and this is likely to particularly be the case at neighboring locations.

The issues of spatial dependence and functional form must be considered in tandem. Standard tests of functional form, such as the Box–Cox, typically assume no spatial autocorrelation in the DGP. Thus, it is

important to examine how spatial dependence may affect tests for functional form.

In a series of Monte Carlo experiments, Baltagi and Li (2001, 2005) examined the performance of four sets of test statistics – joint Lagrange multiplier (LM) tests, unidirectional LM tests, modified LM tests, and conditional LM tests – for functional form in the presence of either spatial lag or spatial error dependence. The joint LM tests test the joint null of no spatial lag (error) dependence and a particular functional form (a linear or a log-linear form, depending on the null). The simple unidirectional LM tests test the null of a linear or log-linear functional form, assuming no spatial lag or error dependence. Such simple LM tests, however, are not robust against the presence of the alternative form of spatial dependence (the presence of spatial lag dependence when error dependence is assumed to be absent, and vice versa). Under such misspecification of spatial dependence, the simple unidirectional LM test converges to a noncentral chi-square. The modified LM test developed by Bera and Yoon (1993) accounts for the noncentrality parameter, producing a test statistic that is robust to misspecification of the spatial autocorrelation (Baltagi and Li 2001, 200–202). Finally, Baltagi and Li also examined conditional LM tests of both linear and log-linear functional forms, given unknown autoregressive parameters, ρ and λ, for spatial lag and error dependence.

Baltagi and Li's Monte Carlos produce similar results whether spatial lag or spatial error dependence exists in the DGP. The joint LM tests for functional form overreject the null as both ρ and λ depart from zero. Similarly, overrejection increases in the modified LM tests as spatial lag or spatial error dependence increase. Perhaps somewhat surprisingly, the simple unidirectional LM tests are not sensitive to departures from the null of spatial randomness. Finally, the conditional LM tests both overreject the null as ρ and λ depart from zero. Clearly one must be sensitive to spatial dependence in the DGP when intrepreting tests for functional form.

Recently, Beck and Jackman (1998) have argued for the use of generalized additive models (GAMs) to model nonlinear functional forms. GAMs are more flexible than standard approaches such as the Box–Cox transformation, as they allow for local rather than global departures from linearity and model these departures nonparametrically. Spatial dependence, however, is typically not incorporated in standard GAMs. This is problematic, as spatial dependence in the DGP can produce concurvity (additive dependence) between the covariates in a GAM. Ramsay, Burnett, and Krewski (2003) demonstrated via a set of Monte Carlo experiments that this concurvity induced by spatial dependence can bias downward standard error estimates for linear parameters in a semiparametric GAM, producing type I errors. The bias increases as spatial dependence and concurvity increase. Thus, though often overlooked, spatial

dependence poses critical implications for inference, even when scholars are sensitive to questions of functional form.

Heteroskedasticity, nonconstant error variance, is a key violation of an OLS regression assumption, as OLS assumes constant error variance. In the presence of heteroskedasticity, OLS parameter estimates remain unbiased, but are inefficient, and standard error estimates are biased. The result often is type I errors in inference.

Heteroskedasticity is a particular problem given the aggregate areal data typically employed in spatial analyses. Often spatial data take the form of rates based on differing population sizes. Rates based on smaller population bases will tend to have larger error variances than rates based on larger population bases. This often results in spatial heteroskedasticity – nonconstant error variance that is related to units' spatial locations as units with similar population sizes will often be located near each other (e.g., neighboring sparsely populated rural counties). Heteroskedasticity may also occur in spatial data due to difficulties in measuring behaviors for particular areal objects.

In addition to the tendency toward heteroskedasticity induced by features of spatial data, heteroskedasticity is also induced by spatial data generating processes. As McMillen (1992) notes, just as phenomena of interest to social scientists are likely to vary spatially, so also are error variances likely to vary spatially. This is all the more likely because of the effects of spatial lag and spatial error dependence on error variances. Both types of spatial processes induce heteroskedastic errors, and this is true regardless of whether a spatial error process takes an autoregressive, moving average, or error components form (see Anselin and Bera 1998).

Standard tests of homoskedasticity such as the White and Breusch–Pagan tests do not incorporate spatial dependence. This is problematic, as Monte Carlo analyses by Anselin and Griffith (1988) demonstrated. Consistent with a common criticism of White's general test, Anselin and Griffith's Monte Carlos demonstrate that the test has consistently low power, in this case regardless of heteroskedasticity or error dependence. The power of the Breusch–Pagan test, they find, is more variable in response to levels of spatial error dependence. Specifically, they find that the power of the test declines as positive spatial error dependence increases in value, with the effects most pronounced as λ increases to 0.5 and above.

To reduce the probability of type II errors, Anselin and Griffith proposed a sequential test for heteroskedasticity and spatial autocorrelation. First, they suggest a joint test for spherical errors (against the joint existence of heteroskedastic and autocorrelated disturbances). This test is equivalent to the sum of a Breusch–Pagan LM test and an LM test for spatial error autocorrelation (LM diagnostics for spatial error dependence are discussed in detail in Chapter 5). A rejection of the joint null is then followed by separate tests for heteroskedasticity and spatial error autocorrelation.

3.4.1 Alternative Forms of Spatial Error Dependence

The spatial autoregressive form of error dependence in (3.2) is the typical form of spatial error dependence examined in spatial analysis. Less frequently examined is spatial moving average error dependence. In contrast to spatial autoregressive error dependence, spatial moving average error dependence takes the form

$$\varepsilon = \gamma W\xi + \xi, \tag{3.10}$$

where γ is the spatial moving average parameter and ξ is an independent error term. The principal distinction between spatial autoregressive and spatial moving average error dependence is the extent of the spatial error dependence implied by the two processes. Where the spatial autoregressive error process produces a nonzero covariance between the errors at all locations, the spatial moving average error process induces a much more localized form of error dependence in which only first-order and second-order neighbors exhibit error dependence. The error covariance matrix for the spatial moving average model takes the form

$$E[\varepsilon\varepsilon'] = \sigma^2(I + \gamma W)(I + \gamma W') = \sigma^2[I + \gamma(W + W') + \gamma^2 WW']. \tag{3.11}$$

As can be seen, only first-order neighbors $(W + W')$ and second-order neighbors (WW') exhibit spatial dependence in the spatial moving average error process (Anselin and Bera 1998, 250).

In contrast to the time series case, spatial moving average error processes have seen only limited application. As it turns out, most of the diagnostics for spatial error dependence presented in Chapter 5 have power against both spatial autoregressive and spatial moving average error forms of dependence (although Mur 1999 offers a diagnostic that distinguishes between the two forms of spatial error dependence). Interestingly, although there is a close mathematical relationship between spatial autoregressive error dependence and spatial autoregressive lag dependence (via the spatial Durbin model discussed in Chapter 5), this same relationship does not exist between spatial moving average error dependence and spatial autoregressive lag dependence.

Just as the spatial moving average error model implies a localized form of spatial error dependence, so also does the spatial error components model, a closely related spatial error model. The spatial error components model (Kelejian and Robinson 1995) separates the error process into two uncorrelated error components: a region-specific component incorporating a spatial spillover with neighboring error terms and a unit-specific error component:

$$\varepsilon = W\psi + \xi, \tag{3.12}$$

where ψ is the error term incorporating spillovers across neighboring locations, and ξ is the unit-specific error term. Generally, it is assumed that the two error components are normally distributed with means of zero, are homoskedastic, and are uncorrelated with each other.

The error covariance for the spatial error components model is

$$E[\varepsilon\varepsilon'] = \sigma_{\psi}^{2} I + \sigma_{\xi}^{2} WW'. \tag{3.13}$$

As can be seen from (3.13), the spatial dependence in the spatial error components model is even more limited than in the spatial moving average error model, now limited to the first-order and second-order neighbors in WW' (Anselin and Bera 1998, 250). Like the spatial moving average form of error dependence, work on the spatial error components form of error dependence is limited, although there have been some significant exceptions in the past two decades (Kelejian and Robinson 1993, 1995; Kelejian and Yuzefovich 2004; Anselin and Moreno 2003).

3.5 CONCLUSION

This chapter has examined how spatial lag and spatial error dependence affect analyses in the social sciences. Despite its similarity on first sight to the more familiar temporal dependence in time series analysis, spatial dependence is quite distinct from temporal dependence. This is due to the simultaneity, and resulting multidimensionality, of spatial as opposed to temporal dependence. (Unlike the time series case, OLS estimates of the autoregressive parameter ρ in a spatial lag model will be biased and inconsistent, regardless of whether the errors exhibit dependence. Also unlike the case of time series analysis, iterative FGLS estimators such as the unidimensional Cochrane–Orcutt estimator are not applicable in the case of spatial dependence.)

The consequences of ignoring either spatial lag or spatial error dependence in the model specification can be significant. Omission of spatial lag dependence from the model specification produces biased and inconsistent parameter estimators for the covariates in the model, reflecting omitted variable bias. Ignoring spatial error dependence results in biased standard error estimates and type I errors in inference.

These consequences of spatial dependence, combined with the fact that the units studied by social scientists are particularly predisposed toward spatial dependence due to the inherently social and spatial dimensions of their behaviors, argue strongly for the modeling of spatial dependence in the social sciences. The initial step in modeling this dependence is first diagnosing it in the absence of covariates. This diagnosis proceeds at both the global and local

levels, examining first whether a researcher's data as a whole exhibit spatial dependence and, subsequently, which units exhibit this dependence with their neighboring units. A variety of global and local tests for spatial autocorrelation have been developed. The next chapter examines these tests and discusses how they can be employed to diagnose spatial dependence in the social sciences.

4

Diagnosing Spatial Dependence

Before modeling either of the two alternative sources of spatial dependence inherent in Galton's problem via a spatial lag or spatial error model, the researcher first has to determine whether her data exhibit spatial dependence. Is there spatial autocorrelation in the behavior or process the social scientist is seeking to explain? The first step in a spatial analysis involving areal data is to diagnose this spatial dependence in the absence of covariates. A variety of tests exist to diagnose univariate spatial autocorrelation in the absence of covariates. This chapter examines these tests and demonstrates how social scientists can employ them in their research.

The chapter is structured as follows. First, I examine global tests for spatial autocorrelation, which diagnose dependence in the data as a whole. Next, I examine local tests for spatial autocorrelation, which diagnose the particular units that are spatially autocorrelated with their neighbors (where neighbors are defined utilizing a neighbor definition such as those discussed in Chapter 2). Here, a particularly important class of statistics for local spatial autocorrelation, local indicators of spatial association (LISA) statistics, is examined in detail. The spatial dependence diagnosed via global and local measures of spatial autocorrelation may not reflect true spatial dependence, but instead, a second type of spatial effect, spatial heterogeneity. This spatial heterogeneity, the topic of Chapter 7, is examined briefly. The chapter concludes by discussing the global and local tests for spatial autocorrelation examined in this chapter and previewing the modeling of spatial dependence in Chapter 5. Throughout the chapter, diagnostics for spatial dependence are demonstrated utilizing a set of empirical applications to civil wars, poverty rates, partisan voting, and legislative roll-call voting behavior.

4.1 GLOBAL MEASURES OF SPATIAL AUTOCORRELATION

Tests for spatial autocorrelation in areal data can proceed at either the global or local levels. Tests for global spatial autocorrelation examine whether the data

as a whole exhibit spatial autocorrelation (against a null of spatial randomness) as well as the strength and direction (positive or negative) of any spatial autocorrelation. Tests for local spatial autocorrelation (again, against a null of spatial randomness) identify particular observations that are autocorrelated with neighboring observations on the random variable of interest and also determine the strength and, depending on the statistic, also the direction of this spatial autocorrelation.

Tests for either global or local spatial autocorrelation in areal data proceed through the use of a Γ index. A Γ index consists of the sum of the cross products of the corresponding elements w_{ij}, v_{ij} in two matrices, W and V:

$$\Gamma = \Sigma_i \Sigma_j W_{ij} V_{ij}, \tag{4.1}$$

where W and V are, respectively, matrices of spatial (dis)similarity (a spatial weights matrix) and value (dis)similarity (Anselin 1995, 98). Measures of spatial autocorrelation are variants of this Γ index, with the v_{ij} elements in V reflecting how value (dis)similarity is conceptualized in the particular form of the Γ index.

4.1.1 Join Count Analysis

Global join count statistics are applicable when the random variable is dichotomous. By convention, units with a value of 1 on the binary variable are denoted as Black (B) and units with a value of 0 are denoted as White (W). There are then three possible types of joins: BB, BW, and WW. Assuming that the weights matrix, W, is symmetric, the number of BB, BW, and WW joins is, respectively,

$$BB = \frac{1}{2} \Sigma_i \Sigma_j w_{ij} y_i y_j, \tag{4.2}$$

$$BW = \frac{1}{2} \Sigma_i \Sigma_j w_{ij} (y_i - y_j)^2, \tag{4.3}$$

and

$$WW = A - (BB + BW), \tag{4.4}$$

where y_i and y_j are the observed values on the random variable at locations i and j and A is the number of joins in the data (Cliff and Ord 1973, 4). In contrast to the standard case for other spatial autocorrelation measures, W is unstandardized in join count analysis, producing a weights matrix that is symmetric and binary (Moran 1948). The observed frequencies of BB, BW, and WW joins are compared to the expected frequencies under the null of spatial randomness to determine whether the data are spatially autocorrelated (Cliff and Ord 1981).

Inference on a Γ index of spatial autocorrelation takes either of two approaches. If the random variable is normally distributed with a constant

variance, then the Γ indices are asymptotically normally distributed under the null. Inference then proceeds by comparing the observed *z*-value to its probability given the normal distribution.

Alternatively, one can apply a permutation approach. In the permutation approach for a Γ measure, the observed values on the random variable are randomly permuted across all locations. Note that this randomization with regard to spatial location corresponds to the null of spatial randomness. The appropriate Γ index is then calculated for each permutation to form an empirical reference distribution. The observed global spatial autocorrelation measure is then compared to the reference distribution to determine pseudo-statistical significance.

4.1.2 Application: Civil Wars

Both scholars and policymakers have become increasingly interested in the potential spread of civil wars from one country to neighboring countries (Ward and Gleditsch 2002; Salehyan and Gleditsch 2006; O'Loughlin and Wittmer 2005; see also Starr and Most 1983, 1985). Such spatial diffusion of intrastate conflict can destabilize regions and create humanitarian crises. The spatial diffusion of civil wars implies as a necessary condition that there be spatial dependence in the occurrence of these wars.[1] This application employs join count statistics to diagnose spatial dependence in civil wars among neighboring states.[2]

Before examining spatial dependence in civil wars, it is useful to examine the spatial distribution of civil wars. This application utilizes the period from 1991–2004 as the time frame for the analysis. This period allows for the examination of spatial dependence among states after the dissolution of the Soviet Union and the reunification of Germany. The data were obtained from the Peace Research Institute, Oslo (PRIO) Dataset on Armed Conflicts, Version 3-2005b (Gleditsch et al. 2002).

Figure 4.1 presents the occurrence of internal conflict within states from 1991 through 2004. States experiencing internal conflict during this period are mapped in gray while states not experiencing an internal conflict are mapped in white. As can be seen, internal conflict is not a rare occurrence in the international system. Overall, 35.8 percent of states experienced an internal conflict during this period. Visually, the map suggests some spatial patterning in these civil wars, with internal conflicts particularly common in Africa, Asia, and, to a lesser extent, South America.

1 Note that this spatial dependence does not, however, necessarily imply the existence of spatial diffusion, as the spatial dependence could be due to clustering in the causes of civil wars in neighboring, but atomistic, countries.

2 This analysis is based on work coauthored with Harvey Starr and Zaryab Iqbal (see Starr, Darmofal, and Iqbal, n.d.).

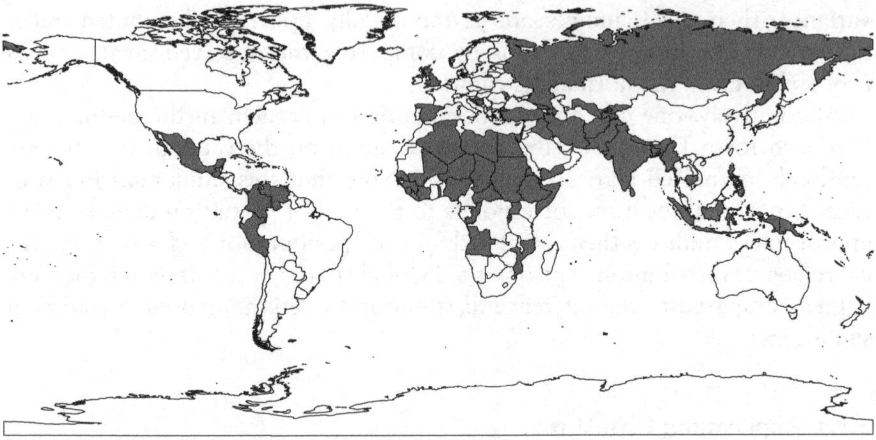

FIGURE 4.1. Internal conflict, 1991–2004.

This apparent spatial structure, however, may reflect apophenia, and thus we want to diagnose the existence of spatial dependence via a spatial diagnostic. In this case, because the presence or absence of internal conflict is a binary dependent variable, we need to employ join count statistics to determine whether there was spatial dependence in internal conflicts during this period.

In this application, neighbors are defined as contiguous states. That is, unit *i*'s neighbors are defined as all states that share a contiguous border with state *i* (i.e., a queen contiguity neighbor definition). For the purposes of this analysis, states are *B* units if they experienced an internal conflict in a given year and are *W* units if they did not. Thus, *BB* joins are those in which contiguous states both experienced a civil war in a given year. *BW* joins, in contrast, are those in which one country experienced an internal conflict and its neighboring state did not. Finally, *WW* joins are those in which both contiguous states did not experience civil wars in a given year.

Two principal questions animate this analysis. Is there spatial dependence in the *BB*, *BW*, and *WW* join counts among contiguous states in a given year? And if spatial dependence is diagnosed, what form does it take? Are the same values on the variable (*BB* and *WW* joins) more or less likely than we would expect under the null of spatial randomness? Are dissimilar values (*BW* joins) more or less likely than under the null of spatial randomness? Or are the frequencies of these joins consistent with the null of spatial randomness?

For each year from 1991 through 2004, the number of *BB*, *BW*, and *WW* joins for neighboring states was calculated and the frequency of these joins was compared to the expected number of joins if civil wars were spatially random. Rather than assuming normality, I employed the permutation approach, in which the occurrences and non-occurrences of civil wars in each year were

randomly permuted across states in the world. Again, this randomization with regard to spatial location corresponds to the null hypothesis of spatial randomness. I then calculated the number of *BB*, *BW*, and *WW* joins for each permutation, repeating the process for a total of 999 permutations. I thus created an empirical reference distribution under the null of spatial randomness and examined the observed numbers of joins for contiguous neighbors in the data to determine whether these counts differed from the expected value under the null.

Table 4.1 presents the results of the analysis. For each year, the table reports the observed number of each type of join for contiguous neighbors (in the Count column), the mean of the empirical reference distribution formed through the permutation process (in the Permutation Mean column) and the standard deviation of the reference distribution. Pseudo-significance is reported for two-tailed tests.

As Table 4.1 shows, civil wars exhibited spatial dependence in the period examined. In nine of the fourteen years examined, contiguous states exhibited spatial dependence in civil wars (the *BB* joins in the table). Moreover, in each of these years, the observed *BB* join counts were significantly larger than what we would expect to observe under the null of spatial randomness, the mean of the empirical reference distribution. In a majority of years examined, states were more likely to experience civil wars if their contiguous neighbors were also experiencing civil wars.

The positive spatial dependence in civil wars is also supported by the findings regarding the non-occurrence of civil wars. In twelve of the fourteen years, non-occurrences of civil wars (*WW* joins) also exhibited spatial dependence. Note, however, that in contrast to the occurrences of civil wars, the non-occurrences of civil wars were less likely than we would expect under the null of spatial randomness. Civil wars, in short, were more common than we would expect and the successful avoidance of civil wars was less common than we would expect among neighboring states if spatial location were irrelevant for internal conflict.

This finding of fewer "safe havens" from civil wars than would exist if geography were unimportant for internal conflict is reinforced by the findings regarding *BW* joins. Remember that *BW* joins reflect instances in which a state not experiencing a civil war was contiguous to a state that was in a civil war. There was an increased spatial patterning of such cases over time. In each of the final five years in the series, *BW* joins were more common than would be expected under spatial randomness. In only two earlier years was this the case. States that had successfully avoided internal conflict, in short, were increasingly finding themselves bordered by countries that were experiencing civil wars. This raises concerns that civil wars could spread over time to peaceful neighbors. At the same time, this trend also carries the possibility that states avoiding internal conflicts may have a pacifying effect on their conflict-riddled neighbors.

TABLE 4.1. *Join Count Results for Civil Wars, 1991–2004*

Year	Join Type	Count	Permutation Mean	Standard Deviation
1991	BB	20*	12.11	3.74
	BW	107	93.32	9.16
	WW	150*	171.57	10.50
1992	BB	18	11.36	3.36
	BW	103	91.47	9.78
	WW	157	175.17	10.93
1993	BB	18**	8.97	3.27
	BW	101	85.03	9.55
	WW	170*	195.00	10.67
1994	BB	19*	10.97	3.60
	BW	110*	91.20	9.94
	WW	160*	186.83	11.14
1995	BB	12	7.81	2.99
	BW	99*	80.62	9.31
	WW	178*	200.57	10.38
1996	BB	16**	7.27	2.85
	BW	94	78.17	9.59
	WW	179*	203.56	10.57
1997	BB	16**	7.15	2.86
	BW	83	78.25	9.57
	WW	190*	203.60	10.54
1998	BB	11	6.10	2.66
	BW	81	73.38	9.56
	WW	197	209.52	10.49
1999	BB	14**	5.61	2.55
	BW	87	70.93	9.26
	WW	188*	212.46	10.15
2000	BB	11**	4.73	2.29
	BW	89**	65.65	8.89
	WW	189**	218.62	9.65
2001	BB	11*	5.25	2.37
	BW	89*	68.26	8.83
	WW	189**	215.49	9.58
2002	BB	14**	4.75	2.29
	BW	82*	65.96	8.65
	WW	193**	218.29	9.36
2003	BB	7	3.51	1.96
	BW	76*	58.08	8.57
	WW	206*	227.41	9.08
2004	BB	6	3.82	2.06
	BW	84**	60.72	8.82
	WW	199**	224.46	9.45

* $p < 0.05$, ** $p < 0.01$, two-tailed tests.

4.1.3 Diagnostics for Continuous Variables

In contrast to the dichotomous case, the two principal global spatial autocorrelation measures for continuous variables are the Moran's I and Geary's c statistics. Again, both are Γ indices, with the two measures differing in their conception of value (dis)similarity. For the Moran's I, the value (dis)similarity in the v_{ij} elements of the V_{ij} matrix is measured as deviations from the mean. The global Moran's I is thus

$$I = \frac{N}{S}\frac{\Sigma_i \Sigma_j w_{ij}(y_i - \bar{y})(y_j - \bar{y})}{\Sigma_i (y_i - \bar{y})^2}, \quad (4.5)$$

where N is the number of observations, S is the sum of the weights, w_{ij} is an element of the spatial weights matrix W, y_i and y_j are the values on the random variable at locations i and j, and $\bar{y}$ is the mean on y. In a row-standardized weights matrix with no "island" cases (units without neighbors), $N = S$ and the initial term thus equals one.

A positive global Moran's I that differs significantly from the expected value under the null indicates positive spatial autocorrelation – the clustering of similar values on the random variable among neighboring observations. A negative global Moran's I that differs significantly from the expected value under the null indicates negative spatial autocorrelation – the clustering of dissimilar values on the random variable among neighboring observations. Note, however, that a null finding at the global level does not imply the absence of spatial dependence at the local level. The finding of no autocorrelation at the global level may instead reflect offsetting forms of local dependence, with negative spatial autocorrelation at some locations offset by positive autocorrelation at other locations. Thus, even if the null is supported at the global level, a subsequent examination of possible local spatial dependence is still warranted.

Although both the interpretation of the global Moran's I and the form of the measure suggest a correlation coefficient, Moran's I differs from a correlation coefficient in two key respects. The expected value of Moran's I under the null hypothesis is not zero, but instead, is $\frac{-1}{N-1}$, and thus is a function of the number of observations. As a consequence, the expected value of Moran's I under the null is negative, though it approaches zero asymptotically. Moreover, unlike a correlation coefficient, Moran's I is not bounded at ± 1. Instead, the bounds are a function of the data and will generally be narrower than ± 1 (Cliff and Ord 1981, 21).

Where the global Moran's I defines value (dis)similarity as deviations from the mean, the global Geary's c defines value (dis)similarity as the squared difference in values between neighboring observations:

$$c = \frac{N-1}{2S}\frac{\Sigma_i \Sigma_j w_{ij}(y_i - y_j)^2}{\Sigma_i (y_i - \bar{y})^2}, \quad (4.6)$$

where the notation is as in (4.5). Interpretation of Geary's c differs significantly from the interpretation of Moran's I. The expected value of Geary's c under the null is 1. A Geary's c that is significantly larger than 1 indicates negative spatial autocorrelation, while a Geary's c that is significantly smaller than 1 indicates positive spatial autocorrelation. Owing to the squared term in the numerator in (4.6), Geary's c gives greater weight to extreme values than does Moran's I (Cliff and Ord 1981, 14–15). As a consequence, the global Moran's I is generally preferred in practice.

4.1.4 Application: Poverty Rates

Poverty, as well as its causes and consequences, is a principal concern in a variety of disciplines in the social sciences. Wilson's (1987) influential study, for example, examined the growth of poverty, including deep poverty, in urban census tracts between 1970 and 1980. Wilson's study highlighted the spatial dimension of poverty and its focus on census tracts is part of a broader pattern of studies that examine poverty at the tract level. These studies range from those that directly extend Wilson's analysis, such as Massey, Gross, and Shibuya's (1994) analysis of the relationship between migration and the geographic concentration of poverty and the analysis of the effects of employment on the probability of single fathers marrying by Testa et al. (1989) to Ricketts and Sawhill's (1988) measurement of the underclass, the analysis of poverty's effects on child maltreatment by Coulton et al. (1995), and the analysis of its effects on premature mortality by Chen et al. (2006).

Given the prominence of tract-level analyses in studies of poverty, it is helpful to consider what census tracts are and why they were developed. The Census Bureau (1994, 10-1) defines census tracts as "small, relatively permanent geographic entities within counties (or the statistical equivalents of counties) delineated by a committee of local data users. Generally, census tracts have between 2,500 and 8,000 residents and boundaries that follow visible features. When first established, census tracts are to be as homogeneous as possible with respect to population characteristics, economic status, and living conditions."

Census tracts thus have several features that lead to their use as proxies for neighborhoods. Note that their size approximates that of neighborhoods and that they are defined by local committees who would be most likely to have knowledge of the boundaries of neighborhoods. Moreover, the boundaries of census tracts follow visible features such as "streets, roads, highways, rivers, canals, railroads, and high-tension power lines," and in certain cases, "pipelines and ridge lines" (U.S. Census Bureau 1994, 10-5). The connection between census tracts and neighborhoods is not an accident. The initial precursor to census tracts was an idea developed in 1906 by Dr. Walter Laidlaw, the Director of the Population Research Bureau of the New York Federation of Churches, as a tool for studying neighborhoods in New York City (U.S. Census Bureau

1994, 10-2). As a consequence, census tracts have been used as a proxy for neighborhoods since 1910 (see, e.g., U.S. Census Bureau 1994, 10-2, Clapp and Wang 2006).[3]

As proxies for neighborhoods, census tracts are likely to be susceptible to spatial dependence. First, neighborhood boundaries are unlikely to match perfectly with census tract boundaries. For example, census tracts are nested within counties and do not extend across county lines, though neighborhoods often do. Second, even where census tract boundaries do accurately proxy neighborhood boundaries, neighboring tracts are unlikely to be independent of each other. There are shared interactions across neighborhood and tract boundaries that produce spatial lag dependence. Neighboring tracts and neighborhoods also are likely to exhibit common attributes that shape their behaviors, producing potential spatial error dependence if we are not fully able to model the sources of this dependence. There is, in short, strong reason for suspecting spatial dependence in the analysis of poverty rates, even though this spatial dependence is rarely modeled.

This application examines the diagnosis of spatial dependence in census tracts' poverty rates. Specifically, in this application I examine the Moran's I test for global spatial dependence in poverty rates at the census tract-level. The data used in this application come from the 2000 census.

In this application, I examine spatial autocorrelation utilizing a variety of different census tract neighbor definitions. In all, I examine dependence for 8 different neighbor definitions: a rook contiguity definition, a queen contiguity definition, and six different k-nearest neighbor definitions (5, 10, 25, 100, 500, and 1000 nearest neighbors). For each, I employ the global Moran's I. The variable of interest is *Poverty Rate*, the percentage of the population in the census tract living in poverty. For each neighbor definition, I employed the random permutation approach for inference. Specifically, I employed 999 permutations to create an empirical reference distribution.

The results of the global Moran's I analyses are reported in Table 4.2. The table reports the neighbor definition, the Moran's I value, the mean of the empirical reference distribution, and the standard deviation of this distribution. In all cases, the expected value of the Moran's I under the null hypothesis of no spatial dependence was near zero, though negative (again, demonstrating the difference between the Moran's I and a correlation coefficient).

As we can see from the results in Table 4.2, there is a strong spatial clustering of poverty rates in the United States regardless of which of the neighbor definitions is employed. The global Moran's I's are positive and significant for each of the eight neighbor definitions. Poverty in the United States is not spatially random; geography matters for our understanding of poverty rates in this country as neighboring census tracts exhibit similar poverty rates.

3 See Krieger (2006) for an excellent discussion of the history of the use of census tracts in public health.

TABLE 4.2. *Global Moran's I Results for Census Tract-Level Poverty Rates in the United States*

Neighbor Definition	Moran's I	Mean	SD	p-value
Rook	0.6147	−0.0001	0.0025	0.001
Queen	0.6060	−0.0001	0.0025	0.001
5 Nearest	0.6206	−0.0000	0.0024	0.001
10 Nearest	0.5624	0.0000	0.0017	0.001
25 Nearest	0.4636	−0.0001	0.0011	0.001
100 Nearest	0.3093	−0.0000	0.0005	0.001
500 Nearest	0.1413	−0.0000	0.0002	0.001
1000 Nearest	0.0920	−0.0000	0.0002	0.001

As we can also see, however, the global Moran's estimates vary depending on the neighbor definition. Specifically, in this analysis, the global Moran's estimates decline as the number of nearest neighbors included in the neighbor definition increases. As the spatial neighborhood expands, the estimates become closer to zero in absolute terms, even though the pseudo-significance levels remain strongly robust at 0.001, the minimal pseudo-significance value for a permutation approach employing 999 random permutations.

This decline in the Moran's values as the k-nearest neighbor definition expands is as we would expect. Following Tobler's First Law of Geography, we would expect that as the neighbor definition expands that a more heterogeneous set of units becomes defined as unit i's neighbors. All else equal, we would expect unit i to exhibit less similarity with its neighbors as this set of neighbors broadens geographically. The results point again to the importance of neighbor definitions for spatial analysis and to the importance of theoretically motivated neighbor definitions.

4.2 LOCAL MEASURES OF SPATIAL AUTOCORRELATION

Often our interest lies not in determining whether the data as a whole exhibit spatial autocorrelation, but instead, in identifying the specific observations that exhibit spatial autocorrelation with their neighbors. Here, the researcher can examine local measures of spatial autocorrelation. The most widely used, LISA statistics, have the attractive feature that they are proportional to a corresponding global measure. As will be discussed, this relationship to a global measure makes LISA statistics particularly helpful in disaggregating global spatial autocorrelation.

4.2.1 Local Indicators of Spatial Association (LISA Statistics)

Anselin (1995, 94) defines a LISA statistic as any statistic satisfying the following two conditions: the LISA for each observation measures the extent

of significant spatial clustering of similar values around the observation, and the sum of LISAs for all observations is proportional to a corresponding global indicator of spatial association. Although Anselin defines a LISA in terms of the clustering of similar values, his definition is unnecessarily restrictive here. LISA statistics, like their global analogues, diagnose both positive and negative spatial autocorrelation. Formally, the second condition implies

$$\sum_i L_i = \gamma \Lambda, \tag{4.7}$$

where L_i are the LISA statistics for each observation, γ is a scale factor, and Λ is a corresponding global spatial autocorrelation measure. The sum of the LISAs is thus proportional to a global analogue up to a scaling factor.

The principal LISA statistics are the local Moran's I and the local Geary's c. The forms of the local Moran and local Geary are, respectively

$$I_i = \frac{\Sigma_j w_{ij}(y_i - \bar{y})(y_j - \bar{y})}{(y_i - \bar{y})^2} \tag{4.8}$$

and

$$c_i = \frac{\Sigma_j w_{ij}(y_i - y_j)^2}{(y_i - \bar{y})^2}, \tag{4.9}$$

where the notation is as in their global analogues in (4.5) and (4.6). Again, only the neighbors of i are incorporated in the LISA for i. The interpretation of values of the local Moran's I and local Geary's c is analogous to their global counterparts.

LISAs aid considerably in identifying local spatial dependence on the random variable. In addition to this identification of local spatial dependence, the correspondence between LISA statistics and global spatial autocorrelation measures carries significant additional advantage in decomposing the global measures. Through the estimation of LISA statistics, the researcher can identify which observations are consistent with the global pattern of positive or negative spatial autocorrelation and which observations run counter to this global pattern. Moreover, high leverage observations can also be identified. Often this follows a two-sigma rule: observations with LISAs that are more than two standard deviations from the mean can be examined to determine whether they are unduly influencing the global measure (Anselin 1995, 97).

Inference on LISA statistics proceeds in a manner analogous to global measures of spatial autocorrelation. On the one hand, the researcher can rely on asymptotics and assume a normal distribution. Alternatively, the researcher can employ a permutation approach in which the values on the random variable are randomly permuted across all locations. In contrast to the global approach, however, only as many observations as are in each observation's neighborhood set need be resampled from these permuted values. Repeated sampling with replacement produces an empirical reference distribution and the observed

local measure of spatial autocorrelation for each observation is compared to the distribution of spatially randomized values to determine statistical significance.

The identification of the particular form of clustering (i.e., is positive autocorrelation a reflection of values above or below the mean, is negative autocorrelation a reflection of a high value surrounded by lower values, or vice versa) is additionally aided through the use of a Moran scatterplot. A Moran scatterplot plots observed values on the random variable (along the x-axis) and the weighted average of the values in each observation's neighborhood set (along the y-axis) as standardized values. The result is a plot in four quadrants. Significant LISAs in the upper right quadrant denote positive local spatial autocorrelation above the mean on the random variable. Significant LISAs in the lower left quadrant denote positive local spatial autocorrelation below the mean. Significant LISAs in the upper left quadrant indicate negative local spatial autocorrelation in which observations have lower values than their neighbors' values. Significant LISAs in the lower right quadrant indicate negative local spatial autocorrelation in which observations have higher values than their neighbors' values. The observations' locations in the Moran scatterplot can then be combined with their significance on the local autocorrelation measure to map areas of positively autocorrelated values above or below the mean as well as observations exhibiting particular forms of negative local spatial autocorrelation.

4.2.2 Application: Blue States versus Red States?

Partisan polarization has become a prominent concern in both political science and in popular discussions of politics in recent years. Much of this interest in polarization began on election night in 2000, as popular commentators noticed that the election night maps on the television networks seemed to present a portrait of two distinct Americas. On the one hand were the Democratic, or "blue states," on the coasts, in the Northeast, and in the upper Great Lakes regions. On the other hand were the Republican, or "red states," in the South, Midwest, Plains, and Mountain regions. As the map was largely replicated in the 2004 election, interest in this apparent geographic partisan polarization grew.

In its strongest form, popular discussion of this blue state versus red state phenomenon has made two claims. On the one hand, popular observers argue that the map reflects distinct cultural and political outlooks in the two sets of states, with blue states decidedly more liberal on these dimensions than the red states. Moreover, these observers argue, this partisan polarization of the country into blue states and red states is a new phenomenon that began with the 2000 election and sets presidential elections since then apart from previous, less polarized elections.

Through the diagnosis of spatial dependence in partisan voting, we can examine the validity of these two arguments. Is there a state-level structuring of partisan voting that sets blue states apart from red states (beyond the fact that the former vote for Democratic candidates and the latter vote for Republican candidates)? And is any spatial structuring of partisan voting in the 2000 election distinct from what is commonly viewed as the previous, less polarized period?

Rather than assuming that partisan voting in presidential elections is structured at the state level, as the blue state and red state argument assumes, it is better to examine the possibility of spatial structuring at a more localized level. Counties are relevant units for presidential elections, as they are the units at which elections are administered. Moreover, voter turnout in presidential elections has exhibited a strong, positive spatial dependence at the county level since the beginning of mass voter participation in the 1820s (Darmofal 2006). Given the importance of counties for election administration and the spatial structuring of turnout at the county level, it is critical to examine spatial dependence in partisan voting at the county level.

In this diagnosis of spatial autocorrelation, I employ a queen contiguity neighbor definition, reflected in a row-standardized weights matrix. The variable for which I examine spatial dependence is *Margin*, which is the Democratic proportion of the vote in the presidential election minus the Republican proportion (both measured at the county level). *Margin* thus has a theoretical range from +1 (if the Democratic Party wins all of the votes in the county) to −1 (if the Republican Party wins all of the votes in the county). To examine the possibility of over time change in spatial dependence in *Margin*, I examine two presidential elections: the 1984 election in which Ronald Reagan won forty-nine of the fifty states and the 2000 presidential election which is generally seen as ushering in the new era of geographic partisan polarization. I use the permutation approach in diagnosing spatial dependence at both the global and local levels, employing 999 permutations for the analyses.

I first examine spatial autocorrelation in *Margin* at the global level in each election. Table 4.3 presents the results of the global Moran's *I* analyses for 1984 and 2000. The first column of results presents the global Moran's *I* estimates for 1984 and 2000, the next column presents the means of the empirical reference distributions created from the 999 permutations in each election, the third column presents the standard deviations of these reference distributions, and the fourth column presents the pseudo-significance levels for each of the elections.

The global Moran's estimate is 0.535 for 1984 and 0.585 for 2000. In both years, there is strong evidence of positive spatial dependence at the global level, as indicated by the pseudo-significance levels. With this positive spatial autocorrelation diagnosed at the global level in both elections, the next step is to examine spatial autocorrelation at the local level.

TABLE 4.3. *Global Moran's I Results for County-Level Margins of Victory in the 1984 and 2000 Presidential Elections*

Year	Moran's *I*	Mean	SD	Pseudo-significance level
1984	0.535	−0.001	0.010	0.001
2000	0.585	−0.001	0.011	0.001

I employ the local Moran's *I* statistic to examine spatial autocorrelation at the local level in the 1984 and 2000 elections. In both of the elections, significant percentages of counties exhibit positive local spatial autocorrelation, contributing to produce the global patterns of positive spatial autocorrelation. In 1984, 31.01 percent of counties evidence positive local spatial autocorrelation with their neighboring counties' presidential voting. Only 2.8 percent of counties exhibit negative local spatial autocorrelation in this election. In 2000, 32.82 percent of counties exhibit positive local spatial dependence in presidential voting. Only 2.61 percent of counties exhibit negative local spatial dependence in this election.

Thus far, positive spatial dependence has been diagnosed at both the global and local levels. Moreover, similar levels of positive spatial dependence are exhibited at the global and local levels in both the 1984 and 2000 elections. The latter is initial evidence against the argument that presidential voting has become more geographically polarized in recent elections. Thus far, however, we have not demonstrated that voting is not structured at the state level. That is, the positive spatial autocorrelation diagnosed at the county level may stop at the (state) border's edge, with counties within the same state exhibiting positive spatial autocorrelation while those at the border are unrelated to counties in neighboring states. Likewise, we have not determined whether any geographic patterning in local spatial dependence has changed over time. To examine these questions, it is helpful to combine the local Morans with the Moran scatterplot.

Figure 4.2 presents the Moran scatterplot for *Margin* in 1984. Along the x-axis are plotted the values for the units, as standardized z-values, measuring the number of standard deviations the observations are above or below the mean. Along the y-axis are plotted the weighted averages of the values for each unit's neighbors, again in standardized form. The positive spatial autocorrelation in 1984 is evidenced by the positive slope in the Moran scatterplot. Counties with values on the *Margin* variable above the national mean (counties that were more Democratic than the average county) tended to neighbor counties that were also above the mean, while counties below the mean tended to border counties below the mean.

By combining the significant LISAs with their locations in the Moran scatterplot, we can examine the local political geography of presidential voting in the 1984 and 2000 elections. Figure 4.3 plots the local spatial autocorrelation

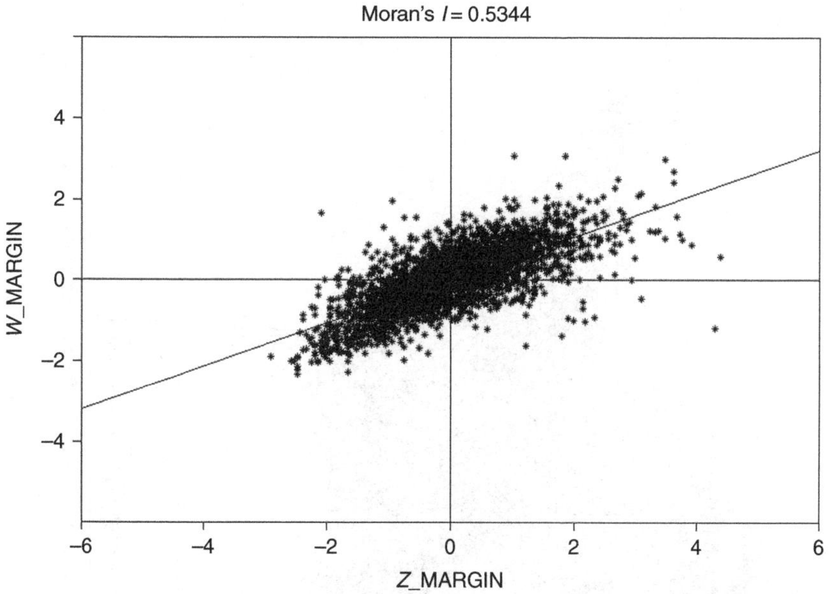

FIGURE 4.2. Moran scatterplot – county-level margin of victory in the 1984 presidential election.

in 1984 while Figure 4.4 plots the local spatial autocorrelation in 2000. In each of these figures, significant local Morans (at a $p < 0.05$ level) are plotted in four shades, depending on their location in the Moran scatterplot. Positively autocorrelated counties with values on *Margin* above the mean and with the weighted average of their neighbors above the mean are plotted in black and noted in the legend, for ease of exposition, as high–high cases. Positively autocorrelated counties below the mean with the weighted average of their neighbors below the mean are plotted in the lightest shade of gray and noted as low–low cases. The two types of negative autocorrelation cases are plotted in the two intermediate shades of gray. Counties above the mean with the weighted average of their neighbors below the mean are plotted in the darker of the two intermediate shades. Counties below the mean with the weighted average of their neighbors above the mean are plotted in the lighter of the two intermediate shades. Counties with insignificant local Morans are plotted in white.

Two features of the local spatial dependence are clear from these figures. First, in contrast to the blue states and red states thesis, presidential voting is not structured at the state level. Instead, the spatial structuring of partisan voting is much more localized, with neighboring counties reflecting pockets of Democratic or Republican strength. Thus states are not distinct, homogeneous Democratic or Republican entities.

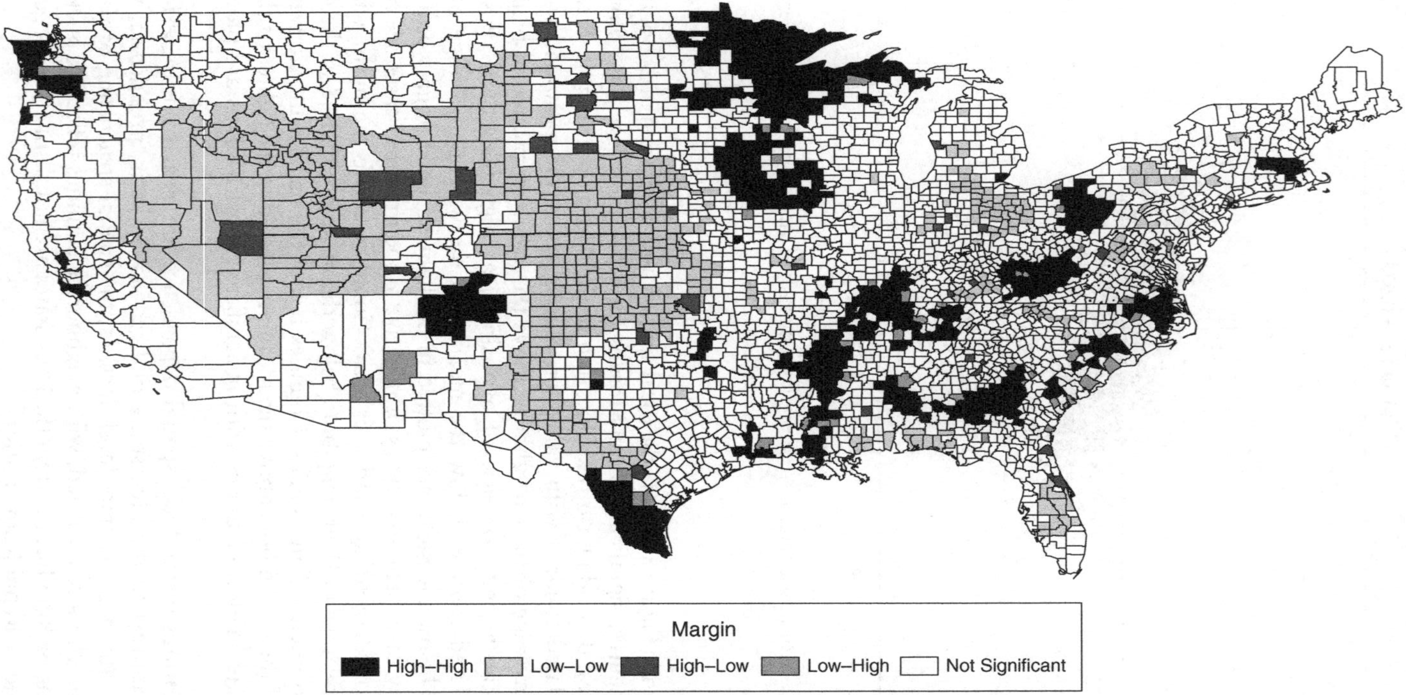

FIGURE 4.3. Local spatial autocorrelation – county-level margin of victory in the 1984 presidential election.

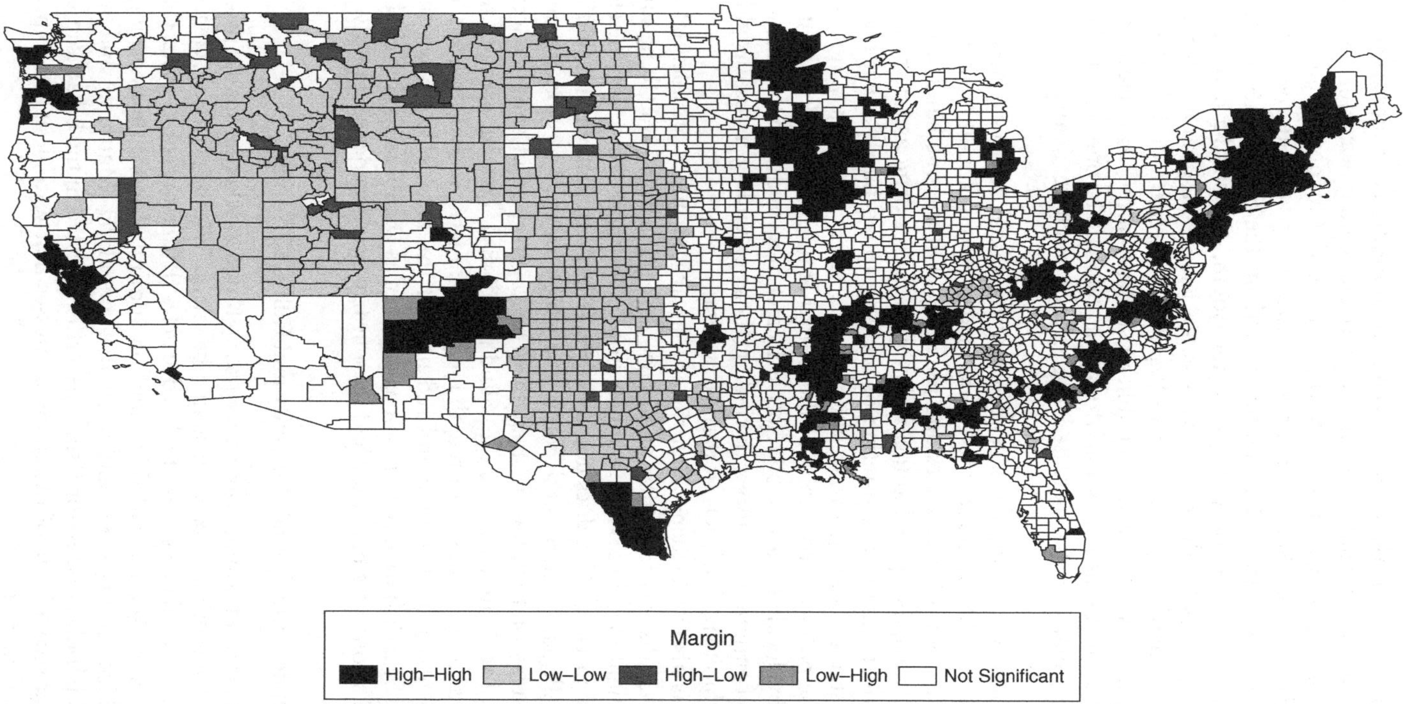

FIGURE 4.4. Local spatial autocorrelation – county-level margin of victory in the 2000 presidential election.

Perhaps most surprising given common conceptions of increased partisan polarization, the spatial structure of partisan voting was quite similar in the landslide 1984 presidential election and in the highly competitive 2000 presidential election. Areas of relative Democratic strength in the former were largely areas of relative Democratic strength in the latter. These include the "black belt" counties (Key 1949) in the South, the southern tip of Texas, southern counties bordering the Mississippi River, and counties in the upper Midwest. Similarly, areas of relative Republican strength in the 1984 election were largely areas of relative Republican strength in the 2000 election. These include counties in the Plains and Mountain regions. The one notable difference in the two maps is the increased Democratic strength in the Northeast in 2000.

This diagnosis of spatial dependence using global and local measures has allowed us to address the central claims made by popular commentators in the recent discussion of blue states and red states. On the one hand, contrary to popular claims, the spatial autocorrelation measures demonstrate that there is not a distinct state-level clustering of partisan voting into distinct blue states and red states. Homogeneous blue and red states are largely nonexistent; instead the political geography of the United States is better described as one marked by localized areas of relative Democratic and Republican strength in which contiguous counties (including those extending across neighboring states) exhibit similar levels of partisan voting.

There is also no evidence that the spatial structuring of presidential voting in 2000 was distinct from that of a previous, less polarized era. To be sure, the election night map in 2000 was much more dichromatic than was the election night map in 1984. This does not, however, reflect a fundamental reshuffling of partisan allegiances across the country in which areas of Democratic strength became areas of Republican strength or vice versa, as in some conceptions of political realignments (see, e.g., Sundquist 1983). Instead, areas of relative Democratic and Republican strength remained largely the same in 2000 as they had been in 1984. The blue and red map of the 2000 election was instead produced by a shift toward partisan parity, even as Democrats and Republicans remained strongest where they had been nearly two decades previously.

4.2.3 Application: Spatial Proximity and Roll-Call Voting

Both scholars and popular observers are interested in whether spatial proximity in legislative seating affects legislative behavior. Within political science, this interest is reflected in a series of related articles (Patterson 1959, 1972; Caldeira and Patterson 1987, 1988) that build on additional work on boardinghouse relationships (Young 1966) and legislative cue-taking (Matthews and Stimson 1975). In popular discussions, this interest is reflected in the bipartisan seating patterns at recent State of the Union addresses that were designed to promote comity in Congress.

We can employ spatial diagnostics to examine whether senators vote like senators who are seated near them and if so, which ones exhibit this spatial dependence. This application examines spatial dependence in voting behavior in the 26th Congress, which was in session from 1839 to 1841.[4] Figure 4.5 presents the seating chart for this Congress.

This application employs a "side by side" neighbor definition. That is, senators are treated as neighbors of Senator *i* if they sat next to Senator *i*. Senators who did not sit next to Senator *i* are treated as non-neighbors of Senator *i*. Consider, for example, Senator Daniel Webster's neighbors in the seating chart in Figure 4.5. According to this neighbor definition, Samuel L. Southard (in desk 16) and Samuel Prentiss (in desk 18) are treated as neighbors of Webster (in desk 17). This neighbor definition reflects the fact that Webster was most likely to interact personally with those senators who were most spatially proximate to him, those sitting directly next to him.[5]

The dependent variable in this analysis is the senator's first-dimension DW-NOMINATE score for this Congress. Based on multidimensional scaling of nearly all votes cast, NOMINATE provides an indicator of legislators' revealed preferences (Poole and Rosenthal 1997). Scores range from roughly -1 (liberal) to 1 (conservative), and tap into the primary dimension of conflict involving economic regulation.[6]

Consider, first, spatial dependence using the global Moran's *I*. The analysis diagnoses strong positive spatial dependence at the global level in NOMINATE scores. The global Moran's *I* for this variable was 0.496, with a *p*-value of 0.002 (with a two-tailed test). As a whole, the NOMINATE scores exhibit positive spatial autocorrelation, with senators more likely to share similar NOMINATE scores with those senators sitting next to them than one would expect if the NOMINATE scores were randomly distributed with regard to senators' seating locations.

Delving further into this spatial dependence via the local Morans, we see, however, that it was only a subset of the senators who produced this global spatial dependence. Only ten of the forty-two senators in this analysis exhibit spatially autocorrelated NOMINATE scores with their neighboring senators (at a $p < 0.10$ level). These ten senators with significant LISA statistics are Senators Nathan Dixon (desk 11), Thaddeus Betts (desk 12), John Spence (desk 13),

4 This application is based on work coauthored with Charles J. Finocchiaro (n.d.).

5 Note that because of the greater distance between desks across the aisle, this application does not treat senators across the aisle as neighbors of Senator *i*. Thus, for example, Senator John Robinson, in desk 24, is not treated as a neighbor of Senator William Merrick, in desk 23. Senator John Crittenden, in desk 22, is, however, treated as a neighbor of Merrick.

6 Senator William Preston and Senator John C. Calhoun of South Carolina are dropped from the analysis because of missing data. Senator Hugh White of Tennessee is also dropped from the analysis as he resigned at the beginning of the session over instructions from the Tennessee legislature to support the sub-Treasury bill and thus did not cast enough votes in this session to be scored by NOMINATE.

1.				
2. John C. Calhoun	12. T. Betts	22. J. J. Crittenden	32. Jno. Norvell	42.
3. Hugh L. White	13. J. S. Spence	23. Wm D. Merrick	33. Perry Smith	43.
4. Franklin Pierce	14.	24. Jno. M. Robinson	34. Wm Allen	44. Wm S. Fulton
5. Ruel Williams	15.	25. Alex. Mouton	35. Benj. Tappan	45. Silas Wright
6. R. C. Nicholas	16. S L. Southard	26. Bedford Brown	36. Thos. H. Benton	46. Garrett D. Wall
7. Wm H. Roane	17. Daniel Webster	27. Clemt C. Clay	37. H. Hubbard	47. James Buchanan
8. N. R. Knight	18. Samuel Prentiss	28. A. H. Sevier	38. Felix Grundy	48. Lewis F. Linn
9. R. M. Young	19. Thomas Clayton	29. Robt. Strange	39. Robt J. Walker	49 Jno Davis
10. O. H Smith	20 A. S. White	30. Wm R. King	40. Jno. Ruggles	50 Wm C. Preston
11. N. F. Dixon	21. S. L. Phelps	31. W. Lumpkin	41. A. Cuthbert	51. Henry Clay
				52.

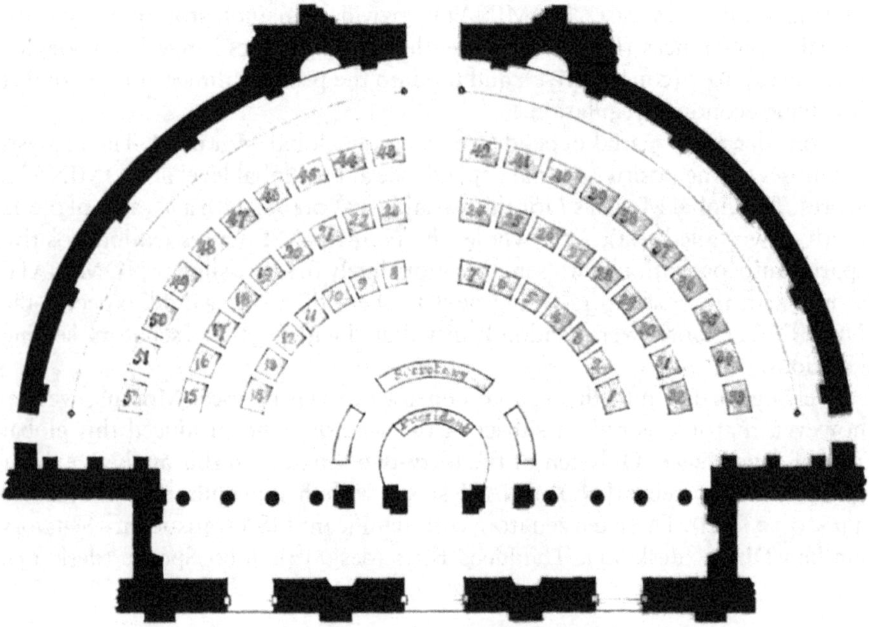

PLAN OF THE SENATE CHAMBER

1ST SESSION – XXVITH CONGRESS.

1840.

FIGURE 4.5. Seating chart – 26th Congress, 1839–1841.

Samuel Southard (desk 16), Daniel Webster (desk 17), Samuel Prentiss (desk 18), Thomas Clayton (desk 19), John Robinson (desk 24), Alexander Mouton (desk 25), and John Davis (desk 49). Nine of these ten exhibited positive spatial autocorrelation, while Davis exhibited negative spatial autocorrelation. In other words, nine of the ten exhibited greater similarity in NOMINATE scores with their neighbors than we would expect if these scores were randomly distributed in space; Davis exhibited greater dissimilarity to Senator Lewis Linn's NOMINATE score than we would expect at random.

Figure 4.6 displays the locations of the seats of these senators with significant local Morans. As can be seen, there's a particular clustering of significant LISAs on the left side of the Senate chamber. Importantly, however, the spatially autocorrelated senators represent only a minority of the members on even just this side of the chamber. A particular advantage of LISA statistics such as the local Moran's I is that they allow for this pinpointing of spatial dependence at the local level.

In summary, the global Moran's I's indicate that an assumption of spatial independence in roll-call voting behavior would be incorrect. The data as a whole indicate strong positive spatial autocorrelation. Importantly, only a subset of legislators produced this positive global spatial autocorrelation. One of the particular strengths of spatial analysis is that it allows us to identify which units exhibit spatial dependence. In this case, nine senators exhibited positive spatial autocorrelation in roll-call voting behavior with their neighboring senators. In the next chapter, I diagnose the form of this spatial dependence.

4.3 SPATIAL HETEROGENEITY

Once the researcher has diagnosed univariate spatial autocorrelation via global and local measures, the next step is to attempt to model this autocorrelation with covariates. In this step, the researcher estimates a standard (nonspatial) model and applies diagnostics to determine whether the covariates fully model the spatial dependence. If the diagnostics indicate that the covariates do not fully model this dependence, these diagnostics indicate whether a spatial lag or a spatial error model is in order.

An important consideration, however, merits attention at this step in the modeling process. The spatial dependence diagnosed via the global and local spatial statistics presented in this chapter may be the product of spatial heterogeneity in the effects of substantive covariates. Consider, for example, an analysis identifying significant local positive spatial autocorrelation in violent crime rates. This spatial dependence in crime rates may be produced by substantive covariates (e.g., unemployment rates, educational attainment) having particularly strong relationships to crime in certain neighboring locales and weaker relationships in other locales. If such behavioral heterogeneity

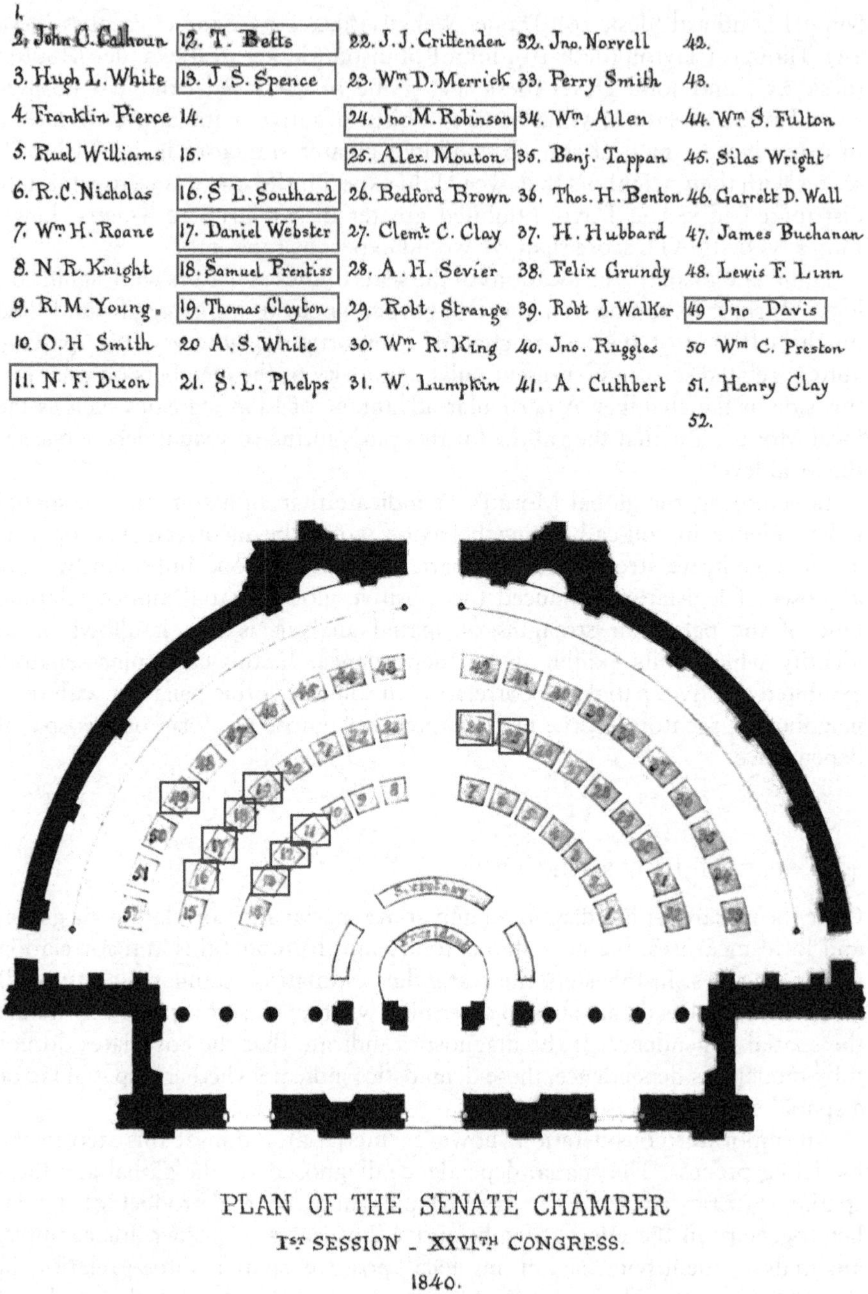

FIGURE 4.6. Significant local Moran's *I*'s for roll-call voting, 26th Congress, 1839–1841.

has produced any of the spatial autocorrelation that was diagnosed, this heterogeneity should be included in the model specification.

Several alternative approaches exist for modeling spatial heterogeneity in parameters. If the heterogeneity is of a discrete form, where a parameter or parameters are homogeneous within spatial subsets of the data and heterogeneous across these subsets, this may produce distinct spatial regimes in the data. Consider, for example, the comparative politics concepts of the global North and South, where relationships such as those between financial weakness and capital account liberalization or between globalization and welfare state spending differ in discrete spatial subsets of the data (Rudra 2002; Brooks 2004). In these cases, the researcher may wish to employ spatial switching regressions, where behavioral parameters are allowed to vary across these spatial regimes. Alternatively, one may posit continuous spatial heterogeneity in parameters, where the parameter values exhibit a continuous spatial drift as one moves across spatial dimensions. Such continuous parameter heterogeneity may be modeled via a spatial expansion model (where the behavioral parameters are modeled as a function of the x,y coordinates of the observations), or a geographically weighted regression (in which spatially proximate units are given greater weight in the calculation of the spatially varying parameters than more spatially distant units) (Fotheringham, Charlton, and Brunsdon 1998). Chapter 7 examines spatial heterogeneity and alternative approaches for modeling heterogeneity in detail. At this point, it is important to note that the spatial dependence diagnosed via the spatial tests discussed in this chapter points to the importance of examining possible spatial heterogeneity as a source of this dependence.

4.4 ADDITIONAL TOPICS

An alternative to LISA statistics for diagnosing local spatial autocorrelation are Ord and Getis' (1995) (see also Getis and Ord 1992) G_i and G_i^* statistics. Unlike LISA statistics, these statistics have no global spatial autocorrelation analogue. As a consequence, they are less frequently employed in practice than LISA statistics. This section, however, presents a brief introduction to these statistics for researchers interested in employing them. Additional information can be found in Getis and Ord (1992) and Ord and Getis (1995).

4.4.1 Ord and Getis Statistics

As originally developed (Getis and Ord 1992), the G_i and G_i^* statistics were expressly for the case of a distance-based neighbor definition and a symmetric, binary weight matrix. In a significant revision of the measures, Ord and Getis (1995) extended the statistics to the case of non–distance-based definitions of neighbors, and nonsymmetric, nonbinary weights matrices. I focus my discussion in this section on these revised G_i and G_i^* statistics. The G_i and

G_i^* statistics, respectively, take the forms

$$G_i = \frac{\Sigma_j w_{ij} y_j - \Sigma_j w_{ij} \bar{y}(i)}{s(i)([(n-1)S_{1i}) - (\Sigma_j w_{ij})^2]/(n-2))^{\frac{1}{2}}} \tag{4.10}$$

and

$$G_i^* = \frac{\Sigma_j w_{ij} y_j - (\Sigma_j w_{ij} + w_{ii})\bar{y}}{s([(nS_{1i}^*) - (\Sigma_j w_{ij} + w_{ii})^2]/(n-1))^{\frac{1}{2}}}, \tag{4.11}$$

where w_{ij} are the elements of the spatial weights matrix W corresponding to the units in the neighborhood set for unit i, w_{ii} is a nonzero weight in the case in which i is in its own neighborhood set, $\bar{y}(i)$ is the mean of the values on the random variable for the neighbors of i $\left(\frac{\Sigma_j y_j}{(n-1)}\right)$, $\bar{y}$ is the mean of the values on the random variable when i is in its own neighborhood set, $S_{1i} = \Sigma_j w_{ij}^2$, $S_{1i}^* = \Sigma_j w_{ij}^2 + w_{ii}^2$, and s^2 is the sample variance (Ord and Getis 1995, 289). G_i and G_i^* are thus standard normal variates, where G_i^* includes i in its own neighborhood set (thus incorporating a nonzero weight for w_{ii}) and G_i does not.

Note that common to other local spatial autocorrelation measures and unlike global measures, the Ord and Getis statistics incorporate only the neighborhood set for each observation. However, the incorporation of observations in their own neighborhood sets in the G_i^* statistic is nonstandard, running counter to the construction of most spatial weights matrices. This inclusion of i in its own neighborhood set can be seen as an inertial effect that impedes the influence of neighboring observations on i.

The interpretation of values on the G_i and G_i^* statistics is quite distinct from interpretation of Moran's I. Positive values on Moran's I indicate positive spatial autocorrelation. This includes both cases where high values on the random variable spatially cluster with other high values and cases where low values on the variable spatially cluster with other low values. Negative values on Moran's I, in contrast, indicate that observations with higher values on the random variable are neighbors of observations with lower values on the random variable, and vice versa. In contrast, positive values on the G_i and G_i^* statistics indicate that high values are spatially clustered with other high values on the random variable. Negative values on the G_i and G_i^* statistics indicate that low values are spatially clustered with other low values on the random variable. Negatively autocorrelated cases (those with negative values on Moran's I) will exhibit only weak, negative G_i and G_i^* values (Getis and Ord 1992, 198).

A key contribution of the G_i and G_i^* statistics, as with other measures of local spatial autocorrelation, is that they aid in identification of local pockets of spatial clustering. As stated earlier, such clustering may occur even in the absence of global spatial autocorrelation. In fact, in an application of the initial, distance-based forms of the G_i and G_i^* statistics, Getis and Ord identified five counties in North Carolina that exhibited significant local spatial

autocorrelation in sudden infant death syndrome (SIDS) rates despite the lack of a global structure to such death rates in the state as a whole (Getis and Ord 1992, 200). Local spatial autocorrelation can exist in the absence of global autocorrelation when the clustering at the local level is limited as a proportion of the overall number of observations or when local patterns are offsetting, producing no global pattern as a consequence. Clearly, a critical implication of Getis and Ord's analysis is that when scholars find spatial independence at the global level, they should still search for local spatial dependence or they risk overlooking potentially important local dependence in phenomena.

4.5 CONCLUSION

This chapter has examined statistics for the initial step in a spatial analysis, the diagnosis of univariate spatial autocorrelation in the absence of covariates. This chapter explored alternative global measures of spatial dependence as well as two classes of local measures, those without a global analogue, and LISA statistics, in which the measures of local spatial dependence are proportional to a global measure. The correspondence of LISAs to global measures, and the opportunities this affords for decomposing global (in)dependence into the local patterns producing it, make LISAs particularly attractive for the diagnosis of spatial dependence.

If spatial dependence is diagnosed at either the global or local levels using the measures examined in this chapter, the next step in the spatial analysis process is to attempt to model this dependence with substantive covariates. The next chapter examines this next sequential step and explores a set of diagnostics that can be employed by the researcher to diagnose any remaining spatial dependence in the presence of substantive covariates. Importantly, available diagnostics point to whether a spatial lag or spatial error model is indicated by the particular dependence in the researcher's data. As a consequence, these diagnostics help the researcher in modeling either of the two sources of spatial dependence posed by Galton via a spatial econometric alternative, if substantive covariates included by the researcher are not sufficient to model this dependence.

5

Diagnosing Spatial Dependence in the Presence of Covariates

When employing the spatial diagnostics examined in Chapter 4, social scientists will often find evidence of spatial autocorrelation (see, e.g., Eff 2004). As discussed in Chapter 1, this predisposition of social science data toward spatial autocorrelation often results from interdependence between the units studied by social scientists. In other cases, social science data exhibit spatial dependence not as a result of behavioral interdependence but as a consequence of spatial clustering in the sources of behaviors of interest to social scientists. The spatial dependence, in short, may be consistent with either a spatial lag model or a spatial error model.

Substantive theory will often lead scholars to believe that a spatial lag specification or a spatial error specification is more appropriate for their particular substantive application. Scholars may, for example, expect that a spatial diffusion process is at work and thus believe that a spatial lag model is warranted. Although such a specification may seem appropriate, such a theoretical expectation should not go untested. It would be inappropriate to estimate a diffusion model with a spatially lagged dependent variable if the spatial dependence diagnosed via, for example, the univariate Moran's *I*, is instead produced by spatial clustering in the sources of otherwise independent behaviors. This model misspecification will lead the researcher to inappropriate substantive inferences about the nature of the spatial dependence in her data.

Inappropriate spatial model specification is all the more problematic because of the close mathematical relationship between a spatial lag model and a spatial error model with spatial autoregressive error dependence. As this chapter will discuss, a spatial autoregressive error model can be rewritten as a spatial Durbin model with both spatially lagged dependent and independent variables if a set of nonlinear common factor constraints are valid. Because of this close relationship between spatial autoregressive dependence in a spatial lag model and spatial autoregressive dependence in a spatial error model, a significant

spatial parameter in a spatial lag model may reflect spatial clustering in omitted sources of the behavior of interest rather than true spatial lag dependence consistent with a diffusion process.

In short, although scholars may wish to trust in their theoretical expectation that a spatial lag or spatial error model is appropriate, they should verify this expectation via regression diagnostics. Happily, diagnostics have been developed that allow the researcher to determine whether any residual spatial dependence in a regression model is consistent with a spatial lag model or spatial error model. The most appropriate diagnostics for this purpose are the robust Lagrange multiplier (LM) diagnostics for spatial lag and spatial error dependence developed by Anselin et al. (1996). In this chapter, I argue for the use of these diagnostics combined with their nonrobust versions via a decision rule presented in this chapter to determine the appropriate form of spatial model that should be estimated.

Before examining these and other diagnostics for spatial dependence in regression models, we must first examine another practical reason for estimating a standard model with substantive covariates and applying diagnostics to examine whether any spatial dependence persists in the presence of these covariates. As stated in Chapter 3, if the spatial dependence diagnosed via the univariate diagnostics presented in Chapter 4 is consistent with spatial lag dependence, then standard estimation approaches such as ordinary least squares (OLS) cannot be employed. Instead, estimation must proceed via maximum likelihood, generalized method of moments, or instrumental variables estimation. If, however, spatial dependence is produced by spatial clustering in the sources of behavior (i.e., spatial lag dependence is absent), and these sources of behavior can be modeled fully such that no residual spatial dependence persists, then standard, nonspatial modeling approaches that are familiar to applied researchers can be employed. For example, if the dependent variable is continuous and spatial diffusion is absent, the researcher may employ OLS for estimation, if the sources of attributional spatial dependence can be fully modeled. Thus, estimating a standard model with substantive covariates serves as a critical first step in determining whether a spatial model is even required.

This chapter examines how spatial diagnostics can be applied to models for continuous dependent variables that are estimated with OLS. This chapter, in other words, examines the application of spatial diagnostics to OLS regression residuals. In all, six diagnostics are examined in this chapter, with a combination of robust and nonrobust LM diagnostics via a decision rule proposed by Anselin argued as the most effective diagnostic approach for assessing spatial dependence.

The first two diagnostics examined in this chapter are the Moran's *I* and Kelejian–Robinson (KR) diagnostics. These are unfocused diagnostics in that they merely diagnose the presence of spatial dependence and do not indicate whether this dependence reflects spatial lag or spatial error dependence. As a

consequence, their utility for diagnosing spatial autocorrelation is limited and scholars will typically wish to turn instead to focused diagnostics.

Next, I examine four focused diagnostics for spatial dependence which present a clear alternative hypothesis and thus point toward spatial lag or error dependence. The first of these are the LM diagnostic for lag dependence and the LM diagnostic for error dependence. Although these two diagnostics offer advantages over the unfocused Moran's *I* and KR diagnostics, they suffer from a lack of robustness to the presence of the alternative form of spatial dependence. Thus, for example, the LM diagnostic for spatial lag dependence will pick up spatial error dependence even in the absence of lag dependence and may as a consequence indicate the presence of spatial lag dependence even when it is absent. Similarly, the LM diagnostic for spatial error dependence may produce a false positive when lag rather than error dependence is present. The reason for the sensitivity of these diagnostics to the alternative form of dependence can be seen in the spatial Durbin model, which is examined here.

Given the sensitivity of the LM diagnostics to the alternative form of spatial dependence, scholars will often wish also to employ robust diagnostics. Here, I examine robust LM diagnostics for spatial lag dependence and for spatial error dependence. These diagnostics are often preferable to their nonrobust LM counterparts, as they account for the presence of the alternative form of spatial autocorrelation. After examining these robust diagnostics, I examine a decision rule developed by Anselin (2005) for diagnosing the particular form of spatial dependence that is present.

5.1 UNFOCUSED DIAGNOSTICS FOR SPATIAL DEPENDENCE IN OLS REGRESSIONS

The initial research on specification testing for spatial models emphasized Moran's *I*, an unfocused diagnostic for spatial dependence (see, e.g., Cliff and Ord 1972). In the case of an unfocused diagnostic, the null is simply the absence of spatial dependence; the alternative hypothesis is not explicitly specified to reflect either lag or error dependence, but instead, merely the presence of spatial dependence. Unfocused diagnostics are helpful for diagnosing the presence of spatial dependence. They are not prescriptive, however, in pointing toward whether a lag or error specification is more appropriate.

5.1.1 The Moran's *I* Diagnostic for Spatial Dependence

Given the wide familiarity with Moran's *I* as a diagnostic for univariate spatial autocorrelation, it is not surprising that it is the most frequently applied diagnostic for regression residuals. As a consequence, it is important to examine the properties and performance of this diagnostic, even though this chapter argues for the use of LM diagnostics rather than the Moran's *I* diagnostic

when diagnosing spatial dependence in the presence of covariates. Cliff and Ord (1972) provided the initial application of Moran's I to regression errors. In contrast to its univariate counterpart, the Moran's I in a regression context takes the form

$$I = \frac{N}{S}\frac{e'We}{e'e}, \tag{5.1}$$

where N is the number of observations, S is the sum of the weights, e are the residuals from an OLS regression, and W is the spatial weights matrix. As in (4.5), when the weights matrix is row standardized and there are no island cases, $N = S$ and the initial ratio equals 1.

Assuming no island cases, the Moran's I diagnostic for spatial autocorrelation is quite similar to the more familiar Durbin–Watson test for serial correlation in time series analysis. The Durbin–Watson statistic takes the form

$$d = \frac{e'Ae}{e'e}, \tag{5.2}$$

where e are again the regression residuals and, in its original formulation by Durbin and Watson (1951, 164), A is a real symmetric matrix:

$$A = \begin{bmatrix} 1 & -1 & 0 & \dots & \dots & \dots & 0 \\ -1 & 2 & -1 & \dots & \dots & \dots & \dots \\ 0 & -1 & 2 & \dots & \dots & \dots & \dots \\ \dots & \dots & \dots & \dots & \dots & \dots & \dots \\ \dots & \dots & \dots & \dots & \dots & \dots & 0 \\ \dots & \dots & \dots & \dots & \dots & 2 & -1 \\ 0 & \dots & \dots & \dots & 0 & -1 & 1 \end{bmatrix} \tag{5.3}$$

As Anselin and Bera (1998, 266) note, the Moran's I and Durbin–Watson statistics thus differ only in how the connectivities are specified in the W and A matrices, respectively. As discussed in Chapter 2, the connectivity matrix in spatial applications is typically row standardized and, unlike A, is thus asymmetric. Although Greene (2003, 192) recommends the use of a Durbin–Watson type test as a diagnostic for cross-sectional autocorrelation, Moran's I actually has some critical limitations as a diagnostic for spatial dependence in a regression context, as the discussion in this chapter will demonstrate.

Unlike the Durbin–Watson test, the exact distribution of the Moran's I statistic in small samples depends not only on X but also on W (Anselin and Rey 1991, 118). Tiefelsdorf and Boots (1995) demonstrated how the critical values of Moran's I can be computed for small samples via numerical integration (see Anselin and Bera 1998). In practice, however, this demanding computation is rarely employed, and instead inference typically proceeds by assuming normally distributed, independent, and homoskedastic errors and employing the asymptotic normal distribution developed for the statistic by Cliff and Ord

(1972, 1973). Clearly the assumptions of normal and homoskedastic errors may be restrictive in many of the applications that spatial researchers encounter. Kelejian and Prucha (2001) provide an important recent advancement in this regard in developing a new central limit theorem for Moran-type tests that allows for heteroskedasticity and non-normality.

As an alternative to Cliff and Ord's approach to inference, researchers sometimes employ a randomization approach similar to that discussed in Chapter 4. As Anselin and Rey (1991) note, however, this randomization approach is actually inappropriate for regression errors. The randomization approach is premised on the expectation that values will be equally likely to be observed at any location under the null. This expectation, however, is inappropriate because the regression errors are correlated by construction (Anselin and Rey 1991, 118). As Anselin and Rey note, moreover, using the randomization approach, the Moran's *I*'s empirical rejection frequency differs significantly from the nominal level and it does not follow a normal distribution under the null (see also Anselin and Rey 1990).

An attractive feature of the Moran's *I* diagnostic is that, unlike a Wald or likelihood ratio test, it does not require estimation of the alternative model. As a consequence, maximum likelihood estimation is not required. Instead, researchers can simply apply Moran's *I* to the residuals from a standard OLS regression that does not include any spatial terms. This feature of the Moran's *I* is shared by most of the diagnostics presented in this chapter.

A number of Monte Carlo studies have examined the small sample performance of Moran's *I*. These Monte Carlos primarily examine the size of the statistic (when the null of no spatial dependence is true) and the power of the statistic (when the null of no spatial dependence is false). On the question of empirical size, the Monte Carlo results are conflicting. Kelejian and Robinson (1998), for example, found that the Moran's *I* tends to underreject the null in the absence of spatial dependence. Conversely, however, Anselin and Florax (1995) found that when the weights matrix follows a rook contiguity definition (but not a queen contiguity definition), Moran's *I* exhibits bias in over-rejecting the null hypothesis of no spatial dependence. When the errors follow a log-normal distribution, however, Moran's *I* performs better than both standard and robust Lagrange multiplier diagnostics for error dependence to be examined shortly. Specifically, where these two LM diagnostics under-reject the null in three of four cases examined, Moran's *I* only under-rejects the null in the smallest sample ($n = 40$).

Clearly, in a spatial context, the implications of over-rejecting the null hypothesis in the absence of spatial dependence are more severe than the implications of under-rejecting the null in the absence of spatial dependence. If spatial autocorrelation is absent, a diagnostic that under-rejects the null hypothesis will simply lead the researcher to rely on standard, nonspatial OLS estimates. If, however, the researcher rejects the null hypothesis of no spatial

dependence when it is in fact true, she will employ a spatial model when it is not, in fact, warranted.

In examining the power of the Moran's *I* to detect spatial dependence, Kelejian and Robinson (1998) found that in the absence of heteroskedasticity, the Moran's *I* diagnostic has higher power than LM diagnostics and a KR diagnostic (KR_{SPHET}) for the case of heteroskedastic errors. However, in the presence of heteroskedasticity, the Moran's *I* diagnostic has less power than the KR_{SPHET} diagnostic for both spatial autocorrelation and/or heteroskedasticity. In fact, they find no evidence that Moran's *I* has power against heteroskedasticity. As a consequence, Kelejian and Robinson recommend that researchers employ the Moran's *I* diagnostic if they believe that heteroskedasticity is absent. However, if researchers believe that heteroskedasticity is present, they should employ the KR_{SPHET} diagnostic rather than the Moran's *I* diagnostic.

Anselin and Florax (1995) found that Moran's *I* performs better than other diagnostics in detecting spatial dependence when spatial error dependence is present. Specifically, in all cases examined in which the errors are normally distributed, Moran's *I* achieves higher power than all other diagnostics. It is important to note that all diagnostics exhibit low power against spatial error dependence in the smallest sample ($n = 40$). For example, Moran's *I* only achieves a 95% rejection frequency when $\lambda > 0.7$, though even in this smallest sample, its power is still greater than all of the other diagnostics examined.

They also find that the power of all diagnostics they examine, including Moran's *I*, against spatial moving average error dependence is much weaker than against spatial autoregressive error dependence. Although Moran's *I* does exhibit stronger power than the other diagnostics against spatial moving average error dependence, it remains quite weak in the smallest sample ($n = 40$). (Alternatively, Anselin and Rey [1991] found that the Moran's *I* diagnostic exhibits power against both autoregressive and moving average error dependence.) Stronger power is exhibited in larger samples ($n = 81$ and 127), though it remains less than in the spatial autoregressive error case. Morans' *I* performs well in detecting spatial dependence when moderate to high levels of lag dependence ($\rho > 0.6$) are present. However, its power against spatial dependence when spatial lag dependence is present in the data generating process is lower than a focused LM diagnostic for lag dependence to be examined shortly, especially at low levels of spatial autocorrelation.

Florax and de Graaff (2004) conducted a meta-analysis of previous Monte Carlo studies regarding the performance of Moran's *I*. They found that the power of Moran's *I* is not affected by departures from normality. The power of Moran's *I* is higher for irregular spatial weights matrices than for regular matrices. It is positively affected by the connectedness of the matrix and negatively affected by the density of the matrix. Note that, although density and connectedness are related (their correlation is 0.33 in Florax and de

Graaff's analysis), they measure different concepts. For example, as Florax and de Graaff note, the identical connectedness structure will result in a lower density as the sample size increases (53). Moran's *I* has greater power against first-order autocorrelation than higher order autocorrelation, whether the form of the dependence is spatial autoregressive error dependence, spatial moving average error dependence, or spatial lag dependence. As Kelejian and Robinson had found, Florax and de Graaff also find that Moran's *I* does not have power against heteroskedasticity. Its power is, however, increased by spatially correlated exogenous variables and decreased by systems endogeneity.

Anselin and Rey (1991, 124) also demonstrated that as the spatial weights matrix becomes more dense, and more units are treated as neighbors, Moran's *I* departs from the normal distribution under which it was developed. Specifically, they find that as one moves away from a rook contiguity neighbor definition to queen contiguity and distance-based contiguity (in which all units within three units of *i* are treated as neighbors of *i*), the Moran's *I* statistic departs from the normal distribution in small samples. Similarly, non-normal errors and heteroskedastic errors also lead to departures from normality. One thus should not invoke the asymptotic normal distribution for inference on Moran's *I* in small samples with dense weights matrices, or non-normal or heteroskedastic errors.

The principal drawback of the Moran's *I* diagnostic, however, results from its unfocused nature. The diagnostic does not present the researcher with an indication of whether spatial dependence diagnosed reflects spatial lag dependence or spatial error dependence. Unlike most of the diagnostics discussed in this chapter, the Moran's *I* test is an unfocused test in which the alternative hypothesis is simply the presence of spatial dependence, rather than the presence, specifically, of spatial lag or error dependence (Florax and de Graaff 2004, 30). As a consequence, Moran's *I* is quite limited as a specification diagnostic. Faced with a rejection of the null hypothesis of no spatial autocorrelation, which model should the researcher estimate next, a spatial lag model or a spatial error model? The Moran's *I* test provides no guidance, and as a consequence, researchers will typically favor more focused diagnostics for spatial lag or spatial error dependence.

5.1.2 The Kelejian–Robinson Diagnostic for Spatial Dependence

Kelejian and Robinson proposed an alternative, nonparametric diagnostic that does not assume linearity or normality. Like the Moran's *I* test, the KR diagnostic is an unfocused test in that it does not have a specific alternative hypothesis of lag versus error dependence and instead simply diagnoses the presence of spatial dependence. Unlike other diagnostics, the KR diagnostic does not require the specification of a weights matrix. However, the diagnostic does assume that the number of nonzero covariances is bounded and that this dependence is symmetric.

Formally, the KR diagnostic assumes that there is an ordering of observations such that the specification of the nonzero covariances, σ_{ij}, under the alternative hypothesis of spatial dependence is

$$\sigma_{ij} = Z_{ij}\gamma, \quad i < j, \quad i \in H_n \tag{5.4}$$

where Z_{ij} is a $1 \times k$ vector constructed from the independent variables X, γ is a k by 1 vector of parameters, and H_n is the set of units relating to i for which nonzero covariances are assumed (see Kelejian and Robinson 1992, 319–320; see also Anselin and Bera 1998, 268). Under the null hypothesis of spatial independence, the parameter vector $\gamma = 0$. Next, let C denote the $h_N \times 1$ vector of nonzero covariances σ_{ij}, $i < j$. With Z as the $h_N \times k$ matrix of values of Z_{ij}, a test of the null hypothesis of spatial independence (i.e., $\gamma = 0$) occurs by regressing C on Z. As the elements of C are unobserved, they are replaced by the cross product of OLS residuals, e_ie_j, with the resulting $h_N \times 1$ vector denoted by $\widehat{C}$ (Anselin and Bera 1998, 268).

Let $\widehat{\gamma} = (Z'Z)^{-1}Z'\widehat{C}$. Then the KR diagnostic takes the form

$$KR = \frac{\hat{\gamma}'Z'Z\hat{\gamma}}{\hat{\sigma}^4}, \tag{5.5}$$

where $\hat{\sigma}^4$ is a consistent estimator of σ^4. A consistent estimator is $\frac{(\widehat{C}-Z\widehat{\gamma})(\widehat{C}-Z\widehat{\gamma})}{h_N}$ (Anselin and Bera 1998, 268). The KR diagnostic is asymptotically distributed as a χ^2 statistic with k degrees of freedom, where k is, again, the number of regressors in Z.

As Kelejian and Robinson note, the KR diagnostic, unlike other approaches, does not require the construction of a weights matrix. Instead, as noted earlier, the researcher specifies an ordering of units expected to exhibit spatial dependence; following from this ordering, the researcher is also specifying units that are expected to be spatially independent of each other (this is thus in contrast to, for example, a distance-decay definition of neighbors with no cutoff, in which all units exhibit spatial dependence with unit i). However, in practice, the distinction from a weights matrix approach is not necessarily as beneficial as might be inferred. As Florax and de Graaff (2004, 36) note, if the researcher expects that contiguous units exhibit spatial dependence, then the information about the ordering of units is equivalent to a first-order contiguity weights matrix. A difference, however, is that the KR diagnostic is based on unique pairs of residuals, and thus assumes symmetric dependence. In essence, only half of the information that would be employed in a spatial weights matrix is employed. And as discussed earlier in the motivation of the row-standardized weights matrix as a weighted average of the effect of i's neighbors on i, the symmetry assumption runs counter to standard approaches to modeling spatial dependence and, indeed, much theory regarding spatial dependence.

The assumption of non-neighbors implicit in the ordering approach of Kelejian and Robinson also limits the applicability of many neighbor

definitions. As Florax and de Graaff note, a distance-decay approach is not applicable unless constraints are placed on the potential spatial dependence, for example, by limiting the number of units that may exhibit a nonzero correlation with unit *i* to the *k* neighbors of *i*, to allow for the existence of non-neighbors. And in such a case, any advantage in not defining a weights matrix is lost. Moreover, as Anselin and Moreno (2003) note (cited in Florax and de Graaff [2004, 37], the strict limitations placed on spatial dependence in the first-order contiguity, non-weights matrix approach of Kelejian and Robinson does not, in contrast to the first-order contiguity weights matrix approach, reflect how spatial dependence operates in an autoregressive process. As discussed in Chapter 3, a spatial autoregressive process (including for the first-order contiguity weights matrix case) implies spatial dependence throughout the observed spatial plane. That is, when one employs a first-order contiguity spatial weights matrix in an autoregressive model, one is implicitly allowing for spatial dependence throughout the spatial system. This type of dependence, however, is not accounted for in Kelejian and Robinson's non-weights matrix conception of an ordering of first-order spatial dependence. As Florax and de Graaff (2004, 37) note, ignoring this higher order spatial dependence may reduce the power of the KR test in diagnosing spatial dependence.

Anselin and Florax's Monte Carlo analysis examines the performance of the KR diagnostic. They find that the KR diagnostic exhibits more bias than several other diagnostics. For example, while all of the LM diagnostics are properly sized in the presence of a normal error distribution, the KR diagnostic over-rejects the null for two of the four cases examined (when $n = 81$ with either a queen or a rook contiguity matrix). Moreover, despite the fact that it is not dependent upon normality, KR performs very poorly when the errors follow a log-normal distribution. The KR diagnostic over-rejects the null hypothesis for all four cases of log-normal errors examined. In contrast, two diagnostics that assume normality in the errors perform considerably better. Moran's *I* under-rejects in only one of these cases and the LM_{Lag} and Robust LM_{Lag} (which is robust to error dependence) are properly sized in all four cases.

The KR diagnostic thus exhibits a tendency to over-reject the null hypothesis of spatial independence when it is true and thus lead to the unnecessary estimation of spatial models. Anselin and Florax propose two possible explanations for the poor performance of the KR diagnostic. On the one hand, it may not be robust to log-normal errors. Alternatively, and more likely they argue, the asymptotic properties of the KR diagnostic may not be reached in the small samples examined (*n*'s of 127 and smaller) (Anselin and Florax 1995, 36).

Just as the empirical size of the KR diagnostic is problematic in comparison to other diagnostics, so also is the power of the test. Regardless of the sample size, the KR diagnostic exhibits lower power against spatial error dependence

than Moran's *I* and the LM_{Error} diagnostic. Once again, the robustness of the KR diagnostic is called into question, as it does not exhibit greater power in the presence of log-normal errors than other diagnostics. The KR diagnostic also performs particularly poorly in detecting spatial moving average error dependence. The KR diagnostic also exhibits weaker power against spatial lag dependence than several other diagnostics. In all, the results of Anselin and Florax's Monte Carlo analysis are quite discouraging for the KR diagnostic.

Florax and de Graaff's meta-analysis finds that the KR diagnostic is sensitive to departures from normality where Moran's *I* is not. In contrast to Anselin and Florax's analysis, Florax and de Graaff find that the KR diagnostic has increased power in log-normal and mixed normal error distributions in comparison to the normal error distribution. Like Moran's *I*, KR has decreased power as the density of the weights increases and increased power as the connectedness of the weights increases. Like Moran's *I*, the power of the KR diagnostic is higher with irregular areals than with regular areals.

As with the Moran's *I* diagnostic, the KR diagnostic has more power against first-order spatial dependence than against higher order dependence. Like Moran's *I*, KR also has power against both spatial lag and error dependence, with slightly more power against first-order spatial autoregressive lag dependence than against first-order spatial autoregressive error dependence. Like Moran's *I*, KR also has more power against spatial autoregressive error dependence than against spatial moving average error dependence. Unlike Moran's *I*, KR has power against heteroskedasticity. The KR diagnostic also exhibits less power than Moran's *I* against first-order spatial autoregressive error dependence and first-order spatial moving average error dependence.

In summary, the standard KR diagnostic performs poorly in comparison to other diagnostics in terms of empirical size and power. More generally, however, the KR diagnostic suffers from the same limitation as the Moran's *I* diagnostic. As an unfocused test, the KR diagnostic does not point toward a clear alternative specification. After diagnosing spatial autocorrelation with either the Moran's *I* or KR diagnostic, the researcher has no guidance as to whether a spatial lag or spatial error model should be employed. Given this critical limitation, researchers will instead often wish to employ focused diagnostics for spatial dependence instead. The next section examines these diagnostics, first discussing the focused LM diagnostic for spatial lag dependence.

5.2 FOCUSED DIAGNOSTICS FOR SPATIAL DEPENDENCE IN OLS REGRESSIONS

The critical advantage offered by focused diagnostics for spatial dependence is the guidance they provide as to whether a spatial lag or spatial error model is more appropriate. This specification guidance is critical for drawing valid inferences. Consider, for example, the implications if one erroneously

estimates a spatial error model when a spatial lag model is required. As discussed in Chapter 3, the consequences of ignoring a diffusion process in the data generating process are biased and inconsistent parameter estimates, reflecting omitted variable bias. Thus, although theory should always guide model specification, the use of specification diagnostics is necessary for drawing valid inferences. The unfocused diagnostics explored in the previous section will take the researcher only so far in indicating that a spatial model is appropriate, but not indicating which form of spatial dependence must be modeled.

This section examines four focused diagnostics for spatial dependence: the LM diagnostic for spatial lag dependence, the LM diagnostic for spatial error dependence, the robust LM diagnostic for spatial lag dependence, and the robust LM diagnostic for spatial error dependence. Note that each of these four diagnostics takes the form of an LM test rather than the asymptotically equivalent Wald or likelihood ratio (LR) tests.[1] Although the three tests are asymptotically equivalent, Lagrange multiplier tests have the advantage over the Wald and LR tests in that the former only require OLS estimation of the model under the null hypothesis rather than the full estimation of the alternative model as is required for the Wald and LR tests.

Typically the researcher estimates all four of the LM diagnostics and then employs a decision rule (Anselin 2005) for guidance as to the proper alternative specification if spatial dependence is diagnosed. I first consider the unidirectional LM tests for spatial lag dependence and spatial error dependence. Neither of these unidirectional tests is robust to the presence of the alternative form of spatial dependence. That is, the LM diagnostic for spatial lag dependence assumes the absence of spatial error dependence while the LM diagnostic for spatial error dependence assumes the absence of spatial lag dependence. As we will see, this assumption of the absence of the alternative form of spatial dependence is problematic for the performance of the unidirectional LM tests, as they may reject the null hypothesis of no spatial dependence when only the alternative form of spatial dependence is present. That is, the LM diagnostic for spatial lag dependence may reject the null even when lag dependence is absent if spatial error dependence is present. Similarly, the LM diagnostic for spatial error dependence may reject the null even when error dependence is absent if spatial lag dependence is present.

As a consequence of the lack of robustness of the standard LM diagnostics, researchers may instead wish to employ robust LM diagnostics. As a consequence, following the next two sections, I next examine the robust LM diagnostics for spatial lag dependence in the presence of spatial error dependence and spatial error dependence in the presence of spatial lag dependence. These diagnostics relax the assumption of the absence of the alternative form of spatial dependence and are robust to the presence of this alternative form of dependence.

1 See Long (1997) for an introduction to LM, Wald, and likelihood ratio tests.

5.2.1 LM Diagnostic for Spatial Lag Dependence

Following Anselin and Rey's (1991, 119) notation, the unidirectional LM diagnostic for spatial lag dependence takes the form

$$LM_{Lag} = [Ne'Wy/e'e]^2[N(WX\hat{\beta})'M(WX\hat{\beta})/e'e + \mathrm{tr}(W'W + W^2)]^{-1}, \quad (5.6)$$

where N is the number of observations, e are the OLS residuals, $M = I - X(X'X)^{-1}X'$, $\hat{\beta}$ is the OLS estimate of β, tr is the matrix trace operator, and W is the spatial weights matrix for the spatially lagged dependent variable. The LM test is distributed as a χ^2 statistic with 1 degree of freedom. Like the Moran's I diagnostic, the LM diagnostic for spatial lag dependence (like the other LM diagnostics to be discussed) is based on the assumption that the errors are normally distributed.

Anselin and Rey (1991) find that the LM_{Lag} test performs more poorly than the Moran's I diagnostic in terms of empirical size when the errors are normally distributed. Where the size of the Moran's I diagnostic does not differ significantly from the nominal 0.05 level for any of the six sample sizes and three weights structures examined when the errors follow a normal distribution, this is not the case for the LM_{Lag} diagnostic. The LM_{Lag} does perform effectively for sparse weights matrices that follow either a queen or rook contiguity neighbor definition. However, as the number of connections increases, with a distance-based neighbor definition, the LM_{Lag} significantly under-rejects the null.

The Lagrange multiplier lag diagnostic, however, exhibits much more robustness to departures from normality than does the Moran's I diagnostic. The Moran's I diagnostic is more likely than the LM_{Lag} test to significantly under-reject the null when the errors follow a log-normal or exponential distribution. Neither the Moran's I nor the LM_{Lag} diagnostic performs well in terms of empirical size when the errors are heteroskedastic.

In a separate Monte Carlo analysis, Anselin and Florax (1995) found that the LM_{Lag} diagnostic outperforms the Moran's I diagnostic in terms of empirical size regardless of the error distribution. When the errors follow a normal distribution and the spatial weights matrix takes the form of a rook contiguity definition, the LM_{Lag} is properly sized while Moran's I exhibits a tendency to overreject the null hypothesis of no spatial dependence. In fact, Anselin and Florax (1995) found no evidence of bias for the Lagrange multiplier spatial lag diagnostic in small samples. For both normal and log-normal error distributions, the empirical size matches the nominal level for each of four sample sizes, ranging from an n of 40 to an n of 127. The LM_{Lag} diagnostic outperforms both the Moran's I and Kelejian–Robinson diagnostics in terms of empirical size.

Anselin and Rey also find that the LM_{Lag} test reflects its χ^2 distribution when the errors are normally distributed and exhibits less sensitivity to the choice of weights matrix in this regard than does the LM_{Error} test. The LM_{Lag}

test is also robust in its distribution when the errors follow an exponential distribution and is less affected by log-normal errors than either the Moran's *I* or LM_{Error} diagnostics. The LM_{Lag} test, like the LM_{Error} test, does not reflect a χ^2 distribution, however, when the errors are heteroskedastic.

Anselin and Rey found that the LM_{Lag} test exhibits significant power against spatial error dependence, although less than the LM_{Error} test. This power of the LM diagnostic to the alternative form of spatial dependence is, as we will see, a critical limitation of the nonrobust LM diagnostics. The LM_{Lag} diagnostic exhibits significantly more power against spatial lag dependence than does the LM_{Error} diagnostic. Anselin and Florax also found that the LM_{Lag} test exhibits power against spatial autoregressive error dependence. As in Anselin and Rey's Monte Carlo analysis, the LM_{Lag} test exhibits less power against error dependence than does the LM_{Error} test. Still, the power exhibited by the LM_{Lag} diagnostic against the spatial error alternative raises concerns about the capacity of the unidirectional LM_{Lag} test to point toward the proper alternative model. Interestingly, the LM lag diagnostic exhibits considerably less power against spatial moving average error processes. As Anselin and Florax (1995, 40) note, the power of the LM_{Lag} diagnostic against spatial autoregressive error dependence as opposed to spatial moving average error dependence likely follows from the stronger similarity between spatial autoregressive error and spatial autoregressive lag processes, a subject to be discussed shortly in the context of a spatial Durbin model.

The LM diagnostic for spatial lag dependence is the most powerful diagnostic against spatial lag dependence in Anselin and Florax's Monte Carlos. As they note, the test reaches a 95% rejection level for $\rho > 0.3$ in a sample of $n = 40$, and for $\rho > 0.1$ at $n = 127$ (41). The diagnostic thus exhibits considerable power against spatial lag dependence, even in samples quite a bit smaller than those encountered in many social science applications.

Florax and de Graaff's (2004) meta-analysis found that the LM diagnostic for spatial lag dependence has less power against first-order autoregressive or moving average error dependence than Moran's *I*, the standard Kelejian–Robinson diagnostic, and the LM diagnostic for spatial error dependence. At the same time, the LM_{Lag} diagnostic exhibits more power against spatial lag dependence than either of these three diagnostics. Importantly, however, the LM_{Lag} diagnostic exhibits less power against spatial lag dependence than does the robust LM diagnostic for lag dependence, again pointing to the utility of a robust approach to specification testing.

5.2.2 LM Diagnostic for Spatial Error Dependence

Burridge (1980) provides the initial consideration of an LM approach to diagnosing spatial error dependence. As Burridge demonstrates, when the errors follow a normal distribution, the Moran's *I* diagnostic is equivalent to an LM test for a spatial autoregressive or moving average error process

with an unscaled denominator. Anselin (1988a) built on Burridge's analysis by formulating a score form of the test.

Anselin's one-directional LM diagnostic for spatial error dependence takes the form

$$LM_{Error} = [Ne'We/e'e]^2[\mathrm{tr}(W'W + W^2)]^{-1}, \quad (5.7)$$

where, as in (5.6), N is the number of observations, e are the OLS residuals, tr is the matrix trace operator, and W is now the spatial weights matrix for the spatially lagged errors. As with the Lagrange multiplier diagnostic for lag dependence, the LM_{Error} diagnostic is based on the assumption that the errors are normally distributed and is distributed as a χ^2 statistic with 1 degree of freedom.

It is important to note that the LM error test is equivalent for either spatial autoregressive or spatial moving average error dependence. The spatial autoregressive error and spatial moving average error models are locally equivalent alternatives (LEA) because the score is identical under the null hypothesis for both processes (see Godfrey 1988; Anselin and Moreno 2003, 598). As a consequence, a finding of significant spatial error dependence does not indicate whether this dependence is limited to first- and second-order neighbors (as in a moving average error process) or extends throughout the observed spatial plane (as in a spatial autoregressive error process) (see Anselin and Bera 1998, 270–271). Importantly, this equivalence does not hold between the moving average error process and the spatial error components process, which also induces localized spatial error dependence. As a consequence, LM tests can be used to distinguish between these two localized alternatives.

In terms of its empirical size, Anselin and Rey (1991) found that the LM_{Error} test performs poorly in comparison to the LM_{Lag} test. Unlike the LM_{Lag} test, the LM_{Error} test significantly under-rejects the null hypothesis in small samples when the errors follow a normal distribution. Where the LM_{Lag} test is robust to departures from normality in terms of log-normal and exponential error distributions, the LM_{Error} diagnostic significantly under-rejects the null when the errors follow either the log-normal or exponential distributions. As with the LM_{Lag} diagnostic, the LM_{Error} diagnostic exhibits a tendency to significantly over-reject the null when the errors are heteroskedastic. When the errors are heteroskedastic, the LM_{Error} diagnostic also does not follow a χ^2 distribution.

As with the LM_{Lag} diagnostic, Anselin and Florax's (1995) Monte Carlo analysis found that the LM_{Error} diagnostic exhibits the proper empirical size in all four cases examined with normally distributed errors. However, where the LM_{Lag} diagnostic exhibits robustness to a log-normal distribution, this does not hold for the LM_{Error} diagnostic. In three of the four cases examined in which the errors follow a log-normal distribution, the LM diagnostic for spatial error dependence under-rejects the null hypothesis. As stated earlier, the consequences of under-rejection of the null when it is, in fact true, are not particularly problematic as this simply prevents the researcher from estimating

a spatial model when it is not indicated. Still, the LM_{Error} diagnostic does exhibit some nonrobustness in comparison to the LM_{Lag} diagnostic.

The LM_{Error} diagnostic exhibits good power against spatial autoregressive error dependence, though interestingly it consistently places second to the Moran's *I* diagnostic. This is interesting because the Moran's *I* is more powerful than the LM_{Error} diagnostic against spatial autoregressive error dependence despite the fact that the former is an unfocused diagnostic while the latter is a focused diagnostic for spatial error dependence. Kelejian and Robinson (1998) also found that the LM_{Error} diagnostic exhibits less power than Moran's *I*. They also conclude that the LM_{Error} diagnostic has no power against heteroskedasticity. As a consequence, when heteroskedasticity is absent (and thus a heteroskedastic-robust diagnostic is not indicated), they recommend use of the Moran's *I* rather than the LM_{Error} diagnostic.

In contrast to its performance against the Moran's *I* diagnostic, the LM_{Error} diagnostic consistently outperforms the Kelejian–Robinson diagnostic in detecting spatial autoregressive error dependence. The LM_{Error} diagnostic also outperforms the LM_{Lag} diagnostic in detecting spatial autoregressive error dependence, though the latter, again, does exhibit power against this error dependence. Interestingly, the LM_{Error} diagnostic exhibits less power against spatial moving average error dependence than spatial autoregressive error dependence in Anselin and Florax's diagnostics. This is particularly the case in the smallest samples, leading Anselin and Florax to conclude that the LM_{Error} diagnostic, like other diagnostics, is not particularly well suited to detecting spatial moving average dependence in the smallest samples (40). The LM_{Error} diagnostic also exhibits considerable power against spatial lag dependence, though always less than the LM_{Lag} diagnostic.

Florax and de Graaff's meta-analysis finds that the LM_{Error} diagnostic exhibits more power against spatial autoregressive error dependence and spatial moving average error dependence than the LM_{Lag} diagnostic. It also exhibits more power against both forms of spatial error dependence than the standard KR diagnostic. Interestingly, however, the LM_{Lag} and Moran's *I* diagnostics are statistically indistinguishable from each other in their detection of autoregressive error dependence and the Moran's *I* diagnostic actually exhibits more power against spatial moving average error dependence than the LM_{Error} diagnostic. This is consistent again with the strong power found for the Moran's *I* diagnostic in the literature.

Florax and de Graaff also found that the LM_{Error} diagnostic exhibits less power against spatial autoregressive lag dependence than the LM_{Lag} diagnostic. Its power against spatial lag dependence is also slightly less than Moran's *I* and the standard KR diagnostic. In all, Florax and de Graaff's meta-analysis indicates that the LM_{Lag} diagnostic is preferred over the LM_{Error} diagnostic for detecting spatial lag dependence and that the unfocused Moran's *I* diagnostic is comparable to the LM_{Error} diagnostic in diagnosing autoregressive error dependence and is preferred for diagnosing moving average error dependence.

In general, the LM_{Error} diagnostic does not fare as well in terms of power against the type of spatial dependence it was designed to diagnose as the LM_{Lag} diagnostic.

5.2.3 Spatial Durbin Model

The sensitivity of the LM_{Lag} diagnostic to spatial autoregressive error dependence and of the LM_{Error} diagnostic to spatial autoregressive lag dependence is a product of the close relationship between the two forms of autoregressive dependence. Consider the spatial autoregressive error model:

$$y = X\beta + \varepsilon$$
$$\varepsilon = \lambda W\varepsilon + \xi, \tag{5.8}$$

where y is an $N \times 1$ vector of observations on the dependent variable, X is an $N \times K$ matrix of observations on the independent variables, β is a $K \times 1$ vector of regression parameters, λ is the spatial autoregressive parameter for the spatially lagged error terms $W\varepsilon$, and ξ is an $N \times 1$ vector of i.i.d. error terms. As Anselin (1988c, 227) notes, the spatial autoregressive error model can be alternatively expressed as

$$y = X\beta + (I - \lambda W)^{-1}\xi. \tag{5.9}$$

If both sides of (5.9) are premultiplied by $(I - \lambda W)$ and the spatial lag is moved to the right side, the result is the spatial Durbin model:

$$y = \lambda Wy + X\beta - \lambda WX\beta + \xi, \tag{5.10}$$

where λ is the spatial autoregressive parameter from the spatial error model, now applied to the spatially lagged dependent variable, Wy, and to the spatially lagged independent variables, WX, with corresponding parameter vector β, and the remaining terms are as in (5.8). For (5.10) to be a spatial autoregressive error model, however, a set of common factor constraints must be met. Specifically, the product of the parameters for Wy and X, that is, $\lambda \times \beta$ must equal the negative of the parameters for the spatially lagged independent variables, WX $(\lambda\beta)$. With a row-standardized weights matrix, this produces $K - 1$ nonlinear constraints (that is, one less than the number of regressors in the model, as the two constant terms cannot each be separately identified) (Anselin 1988c, 227). It is important to note that this close relationship with spatial autoregressive lag dependence does not exist for spatial moving average error dependence, and thus diagnostics against spatial autoregressive lag dependence do not exhibit as much power against spatial moving average error dependence as they do against spatial autoregressive error dependence.

Because of the correspondence between spatial autoregressive lag and spatial autoregressive error dependence in the spatial Durbin model, researchers should not assume that a diagnosis of spatial autoregressive lag or error

dependence via the unidirectional LM diagnostics is valid. The diagnostic for spatial lag (error) dependence may reject the null when only spatial error (lag) dependence is present. Researchers instead will wish to examine robust diagnostics that take into account the possible presence of the alternative form of autoregressive dependence if the unidirectional LM diagnostic suggests the presence of spatial autocorrelation. The next section examines robust LM diagnostics that meet this condition.

5.2.4 The Robust LM Diagnostic for Spatial Lag Dependence

When the alternative form of spatial dependence is present, the simple unidirectional LM tests converge to a noncentral χ^2 distribution featuring an additional noncentrality parameter. Recognizing this, Bera and Yoon (1993) developed modified LM tests that account for the noncentrality parameter, and are, as a consequence, robust to misspecification of the form of spatial dependence. Anselin et al. (1996) subsequently extended Bera and Yoon's modified LM tests to the diagnosis of spatial lag and spatial error dependence in OLS specifications. In essence, the spatial lag dependence is estimated in the diagnostic for lag dependence by accounting for spatial error dependence that may exist. Likewise, spatial error dependence is estimated in the diagnostic for error dependence by accounting for spatial lag dependence that may exist. The robust LM diagnostic for spatial lag dependence developed by Anselin et al. (1996, 83) as an extension of the Bera and Yoon modified LM test takes the form

$$\text{Robust LM}_{\text{Lag}} = \frac{(e'Wy/s^2 - e'We/s^2)^2}{N\tilde{J}_{\rho\cdot\beta} - t}, \tag{5.11}$$

where $s^2 = \frac{e'e}{N}$, and $N\tilde{J}_{\rho\cdot\beta} = [t + (WX\beta)'M(WX\beta)/s^2]$, with $M = I - X(X'X)^{-1}X'$, and $t = \text{tr}(W'W + W^2)$.

Anselin and Florax (1995) examined the size of the Robust LM_{Lag} diagnostic via a set of Monte Carlos.[2] They found that the Robust LM_{Lag} diagnostic, like the standard LM lag diagnostic, is properly sized for all four weights configurations they examine and for both normal and log-normal errors. The empirical size differs little across the two diagnostics in their Monte Carlos.

Anselin et al. (1996) also examined the size of the Robust LM_{Lag} diagnostic against the nonrobust LM_{Lag} test via a set of Monte Carlos. For the case of normally distributed errors, there is little difference in the empirical size of the two tests regardless of sample size or neighbor definition. Moreover, neither of these diagnostics exhibits bias when the errors are normally distributed. The two diagnostics also perform similarly when the errors follow a log-normal distribution. In all but one case, the diagnostics do not exhibit bias. The

[2] Although the diagnostic was most fully developed in Anselin et al. (1996), Anselin and Florax's chapter thus provides an initial Monte Carlo assessment of the diagnostic.

one exception is with the largest sample size ($n = 127$ with an irregular areal structure based on regionalizations in the Netherlands). Here, the Robust LM_{Lag} diagnostic exhibits a slight tendency to over-reject the null in the absence of spatial dependence where the nonrobust form of the diagnostic does not.

Both Anselin and Florax's and Anselin et al.'s Monte Carlos demonstrate, however, that the Robust LM_{Lag} diagnostic outperforms the nonrobust LM_{Lag} when spatial autoregressive error dependence is present. Anselin and Florax found that where the standard lag diagnostic exhibits considerable power against error dependence, particularly for high values of λ, the Robust LM_{Lag} diagnostic exhibits much lower empirical rejection frequencies in comparison. Although the power of the standard LM lag diagnostic is lower against first order spatial moving average error dependence than in the autoregressive error case, the Robust LM_{Lag} diagnostic again outperforms the standard LM lag diagnostic when spatial moving average error dependence is present. The empirical rejection frequencies for the Robust LM_{Lag} diagnostic are nearly always lower than for the standard LM lag diagnostic, as was also the case when the errors reflected autoregressive dependence.

Importantly, the Robust LM_{Lag} diagnostic also exhibits little loss in terms of power against spatial autoregressive lag dependence as a consequence of the robustification of the diagnostic. The empirical rejection frequencies for the Robust LM_{Lag} diagnostic are quite close to those of the standard LM lag diagnostic and are indistinguishable when $\rho > 0.3$ except in the smallest dataset. Thus, little power is lost correcting for spatial error dependence when it is in fact absent.

Anselin and colleagues' Monte Carlos also demonstrate that the correction for spatial error dependence in the Robust LM_{Lag} diagnostic works well. Specifically, the Robust LM_{Lag} diagnostic exhibits little power against spatial autoregressive error dependence when the errors follow a normal distribution. This is in contrast to the nonrobust LM_{Lag} diagnostic, which has high empirical rejection frequencies at high values of λ. Thus, when only spatial error dependence is present, the nonrobust LM_{Lag} diagnostic exhibits a markedly higher probability of invalidly diagnosing spatial lag dependence than does the Robust LM_{Lag} diagnostic. The Robust LM_{Lag} diagnostic also exhibits less power against spatial moving average errors than the nonrobust LM_{Lag} diagnostic, though the empirical rejection frequencies in the presence of moving average error dependence for the latter are generally smaller than in the presence of autoregressive error dependence.

Although the nonrobust LM_{Lag} diagnostic exhibits slightly more power against spatial autoregressive lag dependence than does the Robust LM_{Lag} diagnostic, especially for low levels of lag dependence, the differences are not large. As a consequence, the penalty for robustness against spatial error dependence when error dependence is absent is very small. Given the advantage of the Robust LM_{Lag} diagnostic when only error dependence is present, Anselin

and colleagues' Monte Carlos as a whole point toward the use of the Robust LM_{Lag} diagnostic over the nonrobust LM_{Lag} diagnostic.

Florax and de Graaf's meta-analysis finds that the Robust LM_{Lag} diagnostic exhibits greater power against spatial lag dependence than its nonrobust alternative. At the same time, the nonrobust LM diagnostic for lag dependence exhibits more power against spatial autoregressive or moving average error dependence than does the Robust LM_{Lag} diagnostic. As a consequence, the use of the nonrobust LM_{Lag} diagnostic may find spatial dependence when only error dependence and not lag dependence is present. In all, the Monte Carlo evidence argues for the use of the Robust LM_{Lag} over the standard LM_{Lag} diagnostic when spatial error dependence is present.

5.2.5 The Robust LM Diagnostic for Spatial Error Dependence

The robust LM diagnostic for spatial error dependence in an OLS model takes the form

$$\text{Robust } LM_{Error} = [e'We/s^2 - t(N\tilde{J}_{\rho\cdot\beta})^{-1}(e'Wy/s^2)]^2/[t - t^2(N\tilde{J}_{\rho\cdot\beta})^{-1}]. \tag{5.12}$$

Anselin and Florax's Monte Carlos demonstrate that the Robust LM_{Error} diagnostic, like the nonrobust LM_{Error} diagnostic, is properly sized when the errors follow a normal distribution. However, unlike their spatial lag counterparts, neither the robust nor the standard LM diagnostic for error dependence perform well in terms of size when the errors follow a log-normal distribution. Both the robust and standard LM error diagnostics under-reject the null when the errors are log-normally distributed. Again, not rejecting the null when, in fact, spatial dependence is absent, is not particularly problematic in practical terms as it merely means than an unnecessary spatial model is not estimated.

Anselin and colleagues' Monte Carlo analysis found that their robust LM diagnostic for spatial error dependence performs similarly to the nonrobust diagnostic in terms of empirical size. Both the robust and nonrobust LM error diagnostics are properly sized, exhibiting no bias when the errors follow a normal distribution. A log-normal error distribution, however, affects the size of both diagnostics, with both behaving similarly, and generally poorly in the presence of log-normal errors. Both diagnostics under-reject the null in three of the four cases examined. Again, however, an under-rejection of the null when spatial dependence is in fact absent carries little practical negative consequence.

Anselin and Florax's Monte Carlos demonstrate that the Robust LM_{Error} diagnostic exhibits strong power against spatial autoregressive error dependence, although the loss of power in comparison to the nonrobust version is slightly more discernible than was the case for the LM lag analogues. The loss of

power, however, is less noticeable in larger sample sizes than in smaller sample sizes. The same pattern holds for spatial moving average error dependence. In contrast, Florax and de Graaff's (2004) meta-analysis found that the robust LM diagnostic for spatial error dependence exhibits the same power against either first-order autoregressive or first-order moving average error dependence as the nonrobust LM error diagnostic. Anselin (1988a) also developed an alternative robust LM diagnostic for spatial error dependence in the presence of lag dependence. Unlike Anselin and colleagues' (1996) robust LM diagnostic, Anselin's robust LM diagnostic requires maximum likelihood estimation of the spatial lag model. Unlike the case of Anselin's robust LM lag diagnostic, Anselin et al. find that Anselin's robust LM error diagnostic performs similarly to their robust LM error diagnostic. Given that the latter requires only OLS estimation, however, it is preferred.

Anselin and colleagues' Monte Carlos also demonstrate that the nonrobust LM diagnostic for error dependence exhibits slightly greater power than their robust LM error diagnostic against either autoregressive or moving average error dependence. The difference, however, is very minor. The advantage of the Robust LM_{Error} diagnostic over its nonrobust alternative is generally demonstrated in the Monte Carlos. For three of the four areal structures examined, the Robust LM_{Error} diagnostic exhibits little tendency to diagnose spatial dependence when only lag rather than error dependence is present. This is in stark contrast to the nonrobust LM error diagnostic, which exhibits high empirical rejection frequencies when only lag dependence is present. The lone exception to the strong performance of the Robust LM_{Error} diagnostic is for a queen areal structure with an n of 81. Here, the Robust LM_{Error} diagnostic exhibits a strong tendency to diagnose spatial dependence for high values of ρ. Even here, however, the Robust LM_{Error} diagnostic performs better than its nonrobust alternative, which has higher empirical rejection frequencies for all values of ρ examined. In all, Anselin and colleagues' Monte Carlos argue for the use of the Robust LM_{Error} diagnostic over the nonrobust LM_{Error} diagnostic.

5.3 DECISION RULE FOR STANDARD AND ROBUST LM DIAGNOSTICS

Anselin (2005, 198–199) proposed a multistep decision rule for the use of the standard and robust LM diagnostics against spatial lag and spatial error dependence. The first step is to consider the nonrobust LM_{Lag} and LM_{Error} diagnostics. Remember that the potential drawback to these diagnostics is that they may lead to a diagnosis of spatial dependence when only the alternative form of spatial dependence is present. In some circumstances, however, they may have a slight advantage of slightly stronger power than their robust forms when the alternative form of spatial dependence is absent.

If neither the LM_{Lag} nor the LM_{Error} tests diagnose spatial dependence in the presence of covariates, the researcher can employ the OLS estimates. If one of the two nonrobust LM diagnostics diagnoses spatial dependence while the other does not, the researcher should estimate the indicated spatial model. For example, if the LM_{Lag} diagnostic indicates spatial dependence while the LM_{Error} diagnostic does not, the researcher should next estimate a spatial lag model. Note that the problem with erroneously diagnosing spatial dependence (e.g., erroneously assuming lag dependence when only error dependence is present) is minimized by the joint use of both the standard LM_{Lag} and LM_{Error} diagnostics. If the alternative diagnostic does not indicate the presence of that form of spatial dependence, the researcher should feel comfortable estimating the model indicated by the diagnostic that rejects the null.

The drawback of using the standard LM diagnostics arises when both diagnose spatial dependence. In this case, the researcher cannot be confident which form of spatial dependence is present. As a consequence, she will wish to estimate the Robust LM_{Lag} and Robust LM_{Error} diagnostics. Here the researcher should employ the model indicated by the significant robust LM diagnostic. If both robust LM diagnostics are significant, she should choose the model indicated by the larger test statistic.

5.4 APPLICATION: DIAGNOSING SPATIAL DEPENDENCE IN POVERTY RATES USING LM DIAGNOSTICS

In Chapter 4, I diagnosed spatial dependence in poverty rates at the census tract-level utilizing 2000 census data. I return now to that application, focusing in this section on poverty rates in California. The question now is whether an OLS specification is able to capture the spatial dependence in these rates. If not, which model do the LM diagnostics suggest is appropriate?

Consider first the diagnosis of spatial dependence in California census tracts' poverty rates in the 2000 census in the absence of any covariates. Does the spatial autocorrelation diagnosed for the country as a whole in Chapter 4 exist also in the California subset of these data? As in Chapter 4, a queen contiguity neighbor definition was utilized for this analysis. Table 5.1 presents the results from a global Moran's I test for spatial autocorrelation utilizing 999 random permutations.

As Table 5.1 shows, the global Moran's I is positive and strongly significant. The pseudo p-value of 0.001 is the smallest possible p-value with 999 random permutations. There is, in short, strong evidence that neighboring census tracts exhibited similar poverty rates in the 2000 census.

Table 5.1 also shows that the expected value of the Moran's I statistic for these data under the null hypothesis of spatial randomness is not 0, but instead is -0.0001. This matches the mean for the empirical reference distribution produced by the 999 random permutations that simulate spatial

TABLE 5.1. *Global Moran's I Results for California Poverty Rates*

Moran's *I*	0.6339
E[I]	−0.0001
Mean	−0.0001
SD	0.0071
Pseudo *p*-value	0.001

randomness. The standard deviation of this empirical reference distribution is 0.0071.

In summary, the Moran's *I* test demonstrates that there is spatial dependence in poverty rates. If we can model this spatial autocorrelation fully with substantive covariates, we have no need to subsequently estimate a spatial lag or spatial error model. If, however, we are not able to model fully the sources of the spatial autocorrelation, we will want to estimate the appropriate spatial model that is indicated by the LM diagnostics.

I model poverty rates in California census tracts utilizing a set of tract-level covariates. *Urban Proportion* is a measure of the proportion of the population that lived in the urbanized portion (if any) of the tract. *African American Proportion* measures the proportion of the census tract's population that was African American. *Hispanic Proportion* is a measure of the proportion of the tract's population that was Hispanic. *Immigrant Proportion* is a measure of the proportion of the census tract's population that was foreign-born. *Female Proportion* measures the proportion of the tract's population that was female. *Median Year* is a measure of the median year in which housing structures in the tract were built. The dependent variable in this model is *Poverty Rate*, the proportion of the population living in poverty in 2000.

The results from an OLS estimation are reported in Table 5.2. As we can see, each of the covariates has a significant effect on poverty rates. California census tracts with higher values on *African American Proportion*, *Hispanic Proportion*, and *Immigrant Proportion* all had significantly higher poverty rates in 2000. Census tracts with larger proportions of females, conversely, had lower poverty rates. Tracts with larger proportions of their populations living in urban portions of tracts had lower poverty rates. Finally, *Median Year* was positively related to poverty rates, though one has to go out to the fifth decimal place to find this positive effect in the coefficient. Note also that all of these covariates were strongly significant. Each of the covariates in the model reaches statistical significance at a $p < 0.0000001$ level. We will return to these strong significance levels in the next chapter.

Do these highly significant covariates capture the spatial dependence that was diagnosed via the Moran's *I* test? Table 5.3 reports the results of the

TABLE 5.2. *OLS Estimates for California Poverty Rates*

Urban Proportion	−0.049**
	(0.005)
African American Proportion	0.283**
	(0.009)
Hispanic Proportion	0.217**
	(0.006)
Immigrant Proportion	0.102**
	(0.008)
Female Proportion	−0.142**
	(0.023)
Median Year	0.000**
	(0.000)
Intercept	0.034*
	(0.016)
$N = 6922$.	
Adjusted R^2	0.44.
Log-likelihood	7135.64.
AIC	−14257.3.

OLS estimates are given with standard errors in parentheses below.
* $p < 0.05$, ** $p < 0.0000001$, two-tailed tests.

TABLE 5.3. *Spatial Diagnostics, California Poverty Rates*

Lagrange multiplier spatial error	5179.754	.000
Lagrange multiplier spatial lag	4032.575	.000
Robust Lagrange multiplier spatial error	1147.49	.000
Robust Lagrange multiplier spatial lag	.310	.578

Column 1 = Diagnostic value; column 2 = p-value.

four LM diagnostics. As we can see, both the standard LM error and lag tests are significant, although the spatial error diagnostic is slightly larger than the lag diagnostic. With both of these diagnostic tests significant, the decision rule presented in Section 5.3 tells us to turn to the robust LM diagnostics. Here, we can see that a spatial error model is appropriate. The robust LM error test is strongly significant where the robust LM lag test is not significant. In short, the OLS estimates presented in Table 5.2 do not fully capture the spatial dependence diagnosed in Table 5.1. The remaining spatial autocorrelation reflects spatial error dependence consistent with omitted covariates. In Chapter 6, I present the results of the spatial error model recommended by these diagnostics.

5.5 APPLICATION: DIAGNOSING SPATIAL DEPENDENCE IN ROLL-CALL VOTING USING LM DIAGNOSTICS

In Chapter 4, I diagnosed spatial dependence in roll-call voting behavior in the 26th Congress at both the global and local levels using the global Moran's *I* and the local Moran's *I*. I return to this application here, examining whether this spatial dependence can be modeled via substantive covariates and, if not, diagnosing the sources (i.e., spatial lag vs. spatial error) of continued spatial dependence.

I model this spatial dependence using four common covariates in studies of roll-call voting (see, e.g., Kau and Rubin 1979; Kalt and Zupan 1990; Levitt 1996; Stratmann 2000; Ansolabehere, Snyder, and Stewart 2001; Lee, Moretti, and Butler 2004; and Rogowski and Sinclair 2012). These variables are *Population* (the state's population in the 1840 census), *Presidential Vote* (1 – the Democratic share of the two-party vote), *Manufacturing* (the percentage of the population in the state employed in manufacturing and trades), and *Seniority* (the senator's total years of Senate service). The dependent variable is, again, *NOMINATE*, the senator's score on the first dimension of the scaled NOMINATE measure. The model was estimated once again using the side by side neighbor definition.

The OLS estimates for the side-by-side–based analysis are reported in Table 5.4. For the spatial analysis, the critical question is whether the covariates in the OLS model are sufficient to capture the spatial dependence diagnosed via the global and local tests for spatial dependence. To determine this, I employed the LM error and LM lag diagnostics, along with their robust versions, to diagnose whether spatial dependence persists in the presence of the covariates in the OLS specification. The results of these four diagnostics for the side-by-side analysis are reported in Table 5.5.

As can be seen, both the standard LM error and lag diagnostics indicate the continued presence of spatial dependence. However, the LM lag statistic is much larger than the LM error statistic. Following the decision rule presented in this chapter, we next examine the robust LM diagnostics. Here we can see that the robust LM lag diagnostic is statistically significant while the robust LM error diagnostic isn't. This indicates the presence of spatial dependence consistent with behavioral diffusion between legislators. I model this spatial lag dependence in the next chapter.

5.6 APPLICATION: DIAGNOSING SPATIAL DEPENDENCE IN TURNOUT USING LM DIAGNOSTICS

As an additional example of how spatial diagnostics can be utilized to diagnose spatial autocorrelation in the presence of covariates in an OLS model, I employ the focused LM diagnostics for spatial lag dependence and for spatial error dependence as well as their robust forms to diagnose spatial dependence in

TABLE 5.4. *OLS Estimates for Roll-Call Voting, Side-by-Side Analysis*

Covariate	Estimate
Population	−0.00
	(0.00)
Presidential Vote	2.80*
	(0.71)
Manufacturing	5.30*
	(1.28)
Seniority	0.00
	(0.01)
Intercept	−1.75*
	(0.34)

$N = 42$, Adj. $R^2 = 0.45$.
OLS estimates are shown with standard errors in parentheses below.
* $p < 0.01$, two-tailed tests.

TABLE 5.5. *Spatial Diagnostics for Roll-Call Voting, Side-by-Side Analysis*

Lagrange multiplier spatial error	2.93	0.09
Lagrange multiplier spatial lag	7.16	0.01
Robust Lagrange multiplier spatial error	0.98	0.32
Robust Lagrange multiplier spatial lag	5.21	0.02

Column 1 = Diagnostic value; column 2 = p-value.

turnout in the U.S. presidential election of 1828. The 1828 presidential election, featuring a rematch of President John Quincy Adams and his challenger from 1824, Andrew Jackson, was one of the most consequential presidential elections in U.S. history.

Jackson's supporters had believed that their candidate had been cheated out of the presidency in 1824 because of a "corrupt bargain" between John Quincy Adams and Henry Clay. Although Jackson had won a plurality of the electoral college (and popular) votes in 1824, he did not win the presidency. Instead, because no candidate had a majority in the Electoral College, the election was decided in the House of Representatives. Adams was elected by the House despite Jackson's plurality lead in the Electoral College. The corrupt bargain thesis posits that Clay delivered the votes of several states in the House of Representatives in exchange for becoming Adams' Secretary of State. Recent evidence argues against the notion of a corrupt bargain, as House

members appear to have voted sincerely for Adams over Jackson (Jenkins and Sala 1998). At the time, however, Jackson's supporters had not forgotten the outcome of the 1824 election. They turned out in strong numbers for Jackson in 1828, ensuring his election and ushering in Jacksonian democracy and its accompanying high levels of popular participation in presidential elections.

I model county-level turnout in the 1828 presidential election as a function of several covariates. *African American Percent* measures the percentage of the county-level population that was African American in 1828 while *Foreign-Born Percent* measures the percentage of the county-level population that was foreign born in 1828. *Rural* is a dummy variable that takes on a value of 1 if the county was a rural county in 1828 and a value of 0 otherwise. *South* likewise is a dummy variable that has a value of 1 if the county was in the South and a value of 0 otherwise. *African American Percent* × *South* is an interaction term with the two components of this term as defined previously. *Average Margin* is a moving average of the absolute value of the margin in presidential elections in the county over three presidential elections. *Average Minor Party Percentage* is a moving average of the support for minor parties in presidential elections in the county over three presidential elections. *Registration Law* is a dummy variable with a value of 1 if there was any voter registration law in the state in 1828 and a value of 0 otherwise. *Property Requirement* is a dummy variable with a value of 1 if there was a property requirement in the state in 1828 and a value of 0 otherwise. The dependent variable in the analysis is *Turnout*, a measure of the county-level turnout in the 1828 presidential election.

First, we'll examine spatial dependence in county-level turnout at the global level using the global Moran's I. With a queen contiguity neighbor definition, the global Moran's I is 0.6857 and has a pseudo p-value of 0.001 utilizing the permutation approach to inference and 999 permutations. The expected value of the Moran's I under the null is −0.0014. The empirical reference distribution has a mean of −0.0018 and a standard deviation of 0.0276. In summary, there is strong evidence of positive spatial dependence in turnout using the permutation approach. We thus will want to examine whether an OLS model is able to account for all of this spatial dependence.

The results of the OLS estimation are presented in Table 5.6. Two-tailed tests are employed for all covariates. Many of the covariates had statistically significant effects on county-level turnout in the 1828 presidential election. For example, somewhat counterintuitively, more competitive counties had lower turnout rates. Counties with larger shares of minor party support also had lower turnout. The main effect of *African American Percent* was significant and positive while the main effect of *South* was insignificant and their interaction term, *African American Percent* × *South* was significant and negative.

Once again, however, the most important results for this example are those for the four LM diagnostics, which are reported in Table 5.7. Employing

TABLE 5.6. *OLS Estimates for Turnout in the 1828 Presidential Election*

Covariate	Estimates
Intercept	0.64**
	(0.01)
African American Percent	0.19**
	(0.06)
Foreign-Born Percent	0.22
	(0.13)
Rural	0.02
	(0.01)
South	−0.01
	(0.03)
African American Percent × South	−0.38**
	(0.08)
Average Margin	−0.06*
	(0.02)
Average Minor Party Percentage	−1.27**
	(0.37)
Registration Law	−0.17**
	(0.03)
Property Requirement	−0.12**
	(0.02)

$N = 730$.
Adjusted $R^2 = 0.34$.
AIC = −685.00.
* $p < 0.05$, ** $p < 0.01$.

TABLE 5.7. *Diagnostics for Spatial Dependence in OLS Model of Turnout in the 1828 Presidential Election*

Test	Value	*p*-Value
LM_{Lag}	300.94	0.0000
LM_{Error}	307.65	0.0000
Robust LM_{Lag}	22.58	0.0000
Robust LM_{Error}	29.29	0.0000

Anselin's decision rule, the LM diagnostics point toward the appropriateness of a spatial error specification. Looking first at the nonrobust tests, we can see that both the LM_{Lag} and LM_{Error} tests are statistically significant, with the LM_{Error} diagnostic having a larger value. Turning next to the robust LM tests, we see that both of the robust LM diagnostics are also statistically significant.

However, the Robust LM_{Error} diagnostic has the larger value. As a consequence, the researcher should employ a spatial error specification.

5.7 CONCLUSION

It is critically important for social scientists to employ spatial diagnostics to ensure that they are adopting the appropriate spatial model specifications in their analyses. Spatial models should always be informed by theory, including by expectations that a spatial lag or spatial error process is more likely to be at work for a particular phenomenon. However, the theoretical expectation that a spatial lag or spatial error specification is appropriate should never go untested with diagnostics. Too often in applied spatial research, diagnostics are not employed and scholars rush instead directly to specifying a spatial lag or spatial error model. The result is often spatial model misspecification, limiting our understanding of how behavioral diffusion or attributional dependence affect the phenomena of interest to us.

Six diagnostics in total were examined in this chapter: the Moran's *I* diagnostic, the Kelejian–Robinson diagnostic, the LM lag and error diagnostics, and the robust LM lag and error diagnostics. A variety of Monte Carlo tests of these diagnostics were examined. The tests point toward the use of the focused LM diagnostics over their unfocused alternatives. A decision rule developed by Anselin was presented to provide guidance for the choice of whether a spatial lag model or a spatial error model is the proper model. In Chapter 6, I present estimation methods for these spatial models.

6

Spatial Lag and Spatial Error Models

If the ordinary least squares (OLS) diagnostics discussed in the previous chapter indicate the existence of spatial lag or spatial error dependence, the researcher will wish to model the type of dependence indicated by these diagnostics. If the OLS diagnostics indicate the presence of a diffusion process, the researcher will wish to estimate a spatial lag model via maximum likelihood (ML) estimation or an instrumental variables specification incorporating instruments for the spatially lagged dependent variable. Alternatively, if the OLS diagnostics indicate the existence of spatial error dependence, the researcher may choose to estimate a more fully specified OLS model to model the spatial dependence or may choose to employ a ML or generalized method of moments (GMM) approach incorporating the spatial dependence in the errors.

The spatial dependence diagnosed via the diagnostics discussed in Chapter 5 may alternatively be produced by spatial heterogeneity in the effects of covariates. If this is the only source of spatial dependence, modeling this heterogeneity will be sufficient to capture the spatial dependence. As a consequence, any specification search should also consider the possibility of spatial heterogeneity, which is the focus of Chapter 7. This chapter will first, however, examine alternative approaches for modeling spatial dependence if spatial heterogeneity is not present.

This chapter begins by examining ML estimation of spatial lag models that derives from Ord (1975). Next, I explore alternative instrumental variables and GMM estimators for spatial lag dependence. Next, I turn to approaches for estimating spatial error models. I conclude by considering areas of concern in the estimation of spatial models. These include estimators for large sample sizes and diagnostics for continued spatial dependence.

6.1 MAXIMUM LIKELIHOOD SPATIAL LAG ESTIMATION

The mixed regressive, spatial autoregressive model, or spatial lag model, extends the pure spatial autoregressive model considered in Section 3.2 to include also the set of covariates and associated parameters:

$$y = \rho W y + X\beta + \varepsilon, \tag{6.1}$$

where X is again an N by K matrix of observations on the covariates, β is a K by 1 vector of parameters, and the remaining notation is as discussed in Section 3.2. As discussed in Chapter 3, if spatial lag dependence exists in the data generating process (DGP), OLS estimates of the spatial autoregressive parameter, ρ, will be biased and inconsistent, regardless of whether spatial dependence exists in the error term or not. As a result, if the researcher assumes that the errors are normally distributed, she may wish to estimate ρ via ML estimation.

A critical difficulty in obtaining ML estimates for spatial lag models is the Jacobian term $|I - \rho W|$, which must be evaluated at each value of ρ (Smirnov and Anselin 2001, 302). As Smirnov and Anselin (2001, 302) note, this is computationally problematic in even moderately sized samples, as the determinant pertains to an n by n matrix. However, as Ord (1975) noted, a computationally simpler approach can be employed using the eigenvalues of the spatial weights matrix W. Ord's approach has become the principal approach to ML estimation in applied spatial research.

Consider the spatial lag model outlined by Ord (1975, 121), in which the intercept is suppressed to simplify the exposition:

$$Y = \rho W Y + \varepsilon, \tag{6.2}$$

where

$$\varepsilon = AY, \tag{6.3}$$

with

$$A = I - \rho W. \tag{6.4}$$

Then, if the errors are normally distributed with a mean of zero and constant variance, the log-likelihood function for ρ, σ^2 is

$$l(\rho, \sigma^2) = -(n/2)\ln(2\pi\sigma^2) - (1/2\sigma^2)y'A'Ay + \ln|A|. \tag{6.5}$$

As Ord (1975, 121) notes, from (6.5) the ML estimators are

$$\hat{\sigma}^2 = n^{-1}y'A'Ay, \tag{6.6}$$

and $\hat{\rho}$, where $\hat{\rho}$ is the value of ρ that maximizes (Mead [1967]):

$$l(\rho, \hat{\sigma}^2) = \text{constant} - (n/2)\ln(\hat{\sigma}^2|A|^{-2/n}). \tag{6.7}$$

Whittle (1954) had proposed a large sample ML estimation approach in his development of the spatial lag model. As Ord (1975, 121) notes, however, Whittle's approach is problematic either in small samples or in cases of irregular areals. The latter limitation is particularly problematic as nearly all applications of spatial areal models are to irregular areals.

Ord's approach is instead to exploit the eigenvalues of the spatial weights matrix. As Ord (1975, 121) notes, if W has eigenvalues $\omega_1, \ldots, \omega_n$ then

$$|\omega I - W| = \prod_{i=1}^{n} (\omega - \omega_i) \tag{6.8}$$

and therefore

$$|I - \rho W| = \prod_{i=1}^{n} (1 - \rho\omega_i), \tag{6.9}$$

where ω_i are the eigenvalues of the weights matrix, W. The critical advantage of this approach is that the ω_i need be determined only once, with $\hat{\rho}$ then the value of ρ that minimizes

$$\left[\prod_{i=1}^{n} (1 - \rho\omega_i)\right]^{-2/n} (y'y - 2\rho y'y_L + \rho^2 y'_L y_L), \tag{6.10}$$

where $y_L = Wy$ (Ord 1975, 121).

Ord's estimation approach eases computation considerably, in replacing the repeated evaluation of the determinant for each value of ρ with a one-time calculation of the eigenvalues. Ord (1975, 122) also extended his eigenvalues-based ML approach to the more interesting case of the mixed regressive, spatial autoregressive model that also includes substantive covariates. As Anselin and Bera (1998) demonstrated, employing the eigenvalues-based approach, the log-likelihood for this model then takes the form

$$L_{Lag} = \sum_i \ln(1 - \rho\omega_i) - \frac{n}{2}\ln(2\pi) - \frac{n}{2}\ln(\sigma^2) - \frac{(y - \rho Wy - X\beta)'(y - \rho Wy - X\beta)}{2\sigma^2}, \tag{6.11}$$

where the terms are as defined previously (Anselin and Bera 1998, 255). As Anselin and Bera (1998, 256) showed (see also Anselin 1988c, 181–182), by substituting the ML estimates for β

$$\beta_{ML} = (X'X)^{-1} X'(I - \rho W)y \tag{6.12}$$

and σ^2

$$\sigma^2_{ML} = \frac{(y - \rho Wy - X\beta_{ML})'(y - \rho Wy - X\beta_{ML})}{n}, \tag{6.13}$$

the likelihood function can be expressed as a concentrated log-likelihood function of the spatial autoregressive parameter, ρ

$$L^c_{Lag} = -\frac{n}{2}\ln\left[\frac{(e_O - \rho e_L)'(e_O - \rho e_L)}{n}\right] + \sum_i \ln(1 - \rho\omega_i), \tag{6.14}$$

where e_O and e_L are, respectively, the residuals from OLS regressions of y on X and from W_y on X (Anselin 1988c, 181). The ML estimate of ρ is then found from the optimization of this concentrated log-likelihood function (Anselin and Bera 1998, 256).

The ML estimator for the spatial lag model has the attractive properties of consistency, asymptotic efficiency, and asymptotic normality when several conditions hold (see, e.g., Bates and White 1985 and Heijmans and Magnus 1986a, 1986b, 1986c, cited in Anselin [1988c, 60]). As Anselin (1988c, 60) states, these conditions are "the existence of the log likelihood for the parameter values under consideration (i.e., a non-degenerate log-likelihood); continuous differentiability of the log likelihood (to the second or third order, and for parameter values in a neighborhood of the true value); boundedness of various partial derivatives; the existence, positive definiteness and/or non-singularity of covariance matrices; and the finiteness of various quadratic forms. A further requirement...is that the number of parameters should be fixed and independent of the number of observations...[for spatial lag models], the various conditions are typically satisfied when the structure of spatial interaction, which is expressed jointly by the autoregressive coefficient and the weight matrix, is nonexplosive." As Anselin (1988c, 60) notes, it is typically clear when these conditions are not met in practice as the usual warning signs such as nonconvergence in the optimization routine occur when the model is estimated.

By employing a one-time calculation of the eigenvalues of the weights matrix, Ord's approach simplifies ML estimation of the spatial lag model considerably. However, Ord's approach is not a panacea for problems with ML estimation for large samples. Specifically, the precision of the calculation of the eigenvalues declines as the sample size increases. The accuracy of the eigenvalue calculation in large samples is greater for symmetric weights matrices than for nonsymmetric weights matrices (Bell and Bockstael 2000). Often, however, weights matrices are nonsymmetric, particularly due to the row standardization of these weights matrices. Smirnov and Anselin (2001, 302) argued that eigenvalue calculation becomes unstable for sample sizes larger than 1000 while Kelejian and Prucha (1998, 120) reported finding that eigenvalue computation can become inaccurate for nonsymmetric weights matrices in samples as small as 400. As a consequence, scholars employing ML estimation in large samples may often wish to employ one of the approaches exploiting the sparsity of many spatial weights matrices discussed later in this chapter.

Recently, Lee (2004) has proposed a quasi-maximum likelihood estimator (QMLE) for the spatial lag model. As Lee (2004, 1900) notes, "The QMLE is appropriate when the estimator is derived from a normal likelihood but the disturbances in the model are not truly normally distributed." Lee (2004, 1901) motivates the QMLE estimator using the spatial lag model

$$Y_n = X_n\beta + \rho W_n Y_n + V_n, \tag{6.15}$$

where V_n is a vector of independent and identically distributed disturbances with a mean of zero. The log-likelihood function for this spatial lag model is then

$$\ln L_n(\theta) = -\frac{n}{2}\ln(2\pi) - \frac{n}{2}\ln\sigma^2 + \ln|S_n(\rho)| - \frac{1}{2\sigma^2}V_n'(\delta)V_n(\delta), \tag{6.16}$$

where $\theta = (\beta', \rho, \sigma^2)'$, $S_n(\rho) = (I_n - \rho W_n)$, and $V_n(\delta) = Y_n - X_n\beta - \rho W_n Y_n$, with $\delta = (\beta', \rho)'$ (Lee 2004, 1901–1902). The QMLE of β is then

$$\hat{\beta}_n(\rho) = (X_n'X_n)^{-1}X_n'S_n(\rho)Y_n, \tag{6.17}$$

the QMLE of σ^2 is

$$\begin{aligned}\hat{\sigma}_n^2(\rho) &= \frac{1}{n}[S_n(\rho)Y_n - X_n\hat{\beta}_n(\rho)]'[S_n(\rho)Y_n - X_n\hat{\beta}_n(\rho)] \\ &= \frac{1}{n}Y_n'S_n'(\rho)M_nS_n(\rho)Y_n,\end{aligned} \tag{6.18}$$

and the concentrated log-likelihood function of ρ is

$$\ln L_n(\rho) = -\frac{n}{2}(\ln(2\pi)+1) - \frac{n}{2}\ln\hat{\sigma}_n^2(\rho) + \ln|S_n(\rho)|, \tag{6.19}$$

where $M_n = I_n - X_n(X_n'X_n)^{-1}X_n'$ and the remaining notation is as defined previously. The QMLE of ρ is then the estimator, $\hat{\rho}_n$, that maximizes (6.19) (Lee 2004, 1902).

Lee examines the properties of the QMLE. Importantly, the analysis finds that the QMLE may not have the $\sqrt{n}$-rate of convergence assumed of ML estimators. The consistency of the QMLE estimator is found to depend on the form of asymptotics that are assumed. In the case of increasing-domain asymptotics, in which asymptotics occur with the expansion of the observed spatial plane outward, the QMLE is found to be a consistent estimator. However, in the case of infill asymptotics, in which the number of observations grows as observed areal objects are subdivided into an increasing number of smaller units, the QMLE is found to be inconsistent (Lee 2004, 1917).

6.1.1 Application: Spatial Lag Model of Roll-Call Voting Behavior

In Chapter 4, I diagnosed spatial dependence at the global level in roll-call voting behavior in the 26th Congress. An examination at the local level

TABLE 6.1. *OLS and ML Spatial Lag Estimates for Roll-Call Voting, Side-by-Side Analysis*

Covariate	(1)	(2)
Population	−0.00	−0.00
	(0.00)	(0.00)
Presidential Vote	2.80*	2.19*
	(0.71)	(0.61)
Manufacturing	5.30*	4.93*
	(1.28)	(1.06)
Seniority	0.00	0.00
	(0.01)	(0.01)
Intercept	−1.75*	−1.41*
	(0.34)	(0.30)
ρ		0.33*
		(0.11)
$N = 42$		

OLS estimates are shown in column 1, ML spatial lag estimates in column 2, with standard errors in parentheses below.
* $p < 0.01$, two-tailed tests.

diagnosed nine senators who exhibited positive spatial dependence with their neighbors' voting behavior in this Congress. Diagnostics presented in Chapter 5 demonstrated that a standard OLS specification was unable to model this spatial dependence. Indeed, diagnostics demonstrated that the observed spatial dependence reflected spatial lag dependence and that a spatial lag model was appropriate. In this section, I estimate a spatial lag model to model this dependence.

Table 6.1 presents the results of the OLS estimation from Chapter 5 (column 1) as well as the results of a ML estimation of a spatial lag model (column 2). The ρ parameter captures the spatial lag dependence that was excluded from the OLS model specification. As expected given the significant spatial lag dependence diagnosed in Chapter 5, the ρ estimate is statistically significant. This estimate is positively signed, consistent with positive spatial dependence resulting from behavioral diffusion between senators.

The estimates for the remaining covariates and their statistical significance are little affected by the inclusion of the spatially lagged dependent variable. In this particular application, there is little evidence that the omission of the significant spatial lag effect biased the estimates for the other covariates in the model. Yet, the OLS model is fundamentally misspecified nonetheless, assuming atomistic senators where spatial dependence consistent with behavioral diffusion was operating. In short, we need to include the spatially lagged dependent

variable to accurately model the interdependence between senators in the 26th Congress.

6.2 ML SPATIAL ERROR ESTIMATION

The diagnostics for OLS models discussed in the preceding chapter may, alternatively, point not to spatial lag dependence but rather to the existence of spatial error dependence. The regressive model with autoregressive error dependence takes the form

$$y = X\beta + \varepsilon$$
$$\varepsilon = \lambda W\varepsilon + \xi, \tag{6.20}$$

where the notation is as in (3.2). As discussed in Chapter 3, OLS estimates of the autoregressive parameter, λ, will not be consistent. As a result, if the researcher cannot model the spatial error dependence with covariates in a more fully specified OLS model, she will wish to employ either an ML approach or a GMM approach to the estimation of the spatial error model.

Consider, first, the ML approach to estimation of the spatial error model. As Anselin and Bera (1998, 257) note, spatially autocorrelated errors can be thought of as special cases of nonspherical errors, with $E[\varepsilon\varepsilon'] = \sigma^2\Omega(\theta)$, where θ is a vector of parameters. In the spatial autoregressive error case, then

$$\Omega(\lambda) = [(I - \lambda W)'(I - \lambda W)]^{-1}, \tag{6.21}$$

where I is an identity matrix and λ and W are as defined previously (Anselin and Bera 1998, 257).

Magnus (1978) formulated a ML approach to the estimation of generalized least squares models with unknown parameters in their error covariance matrices. Magnus (1978, 294) showed that under very general conditions, his ML estimator is consistent, asymptotically efficient, and asymptotically normally distributed. Clearly, the spatial error model is a particular case of Magnus's more general framework and Anselin and Bera (1998) demonstrate how Magnus's approach can be applied to the model with spatial autoregressive errors. As Anselin and Bera (1998) show, the log-likelihood takes the form

$$L_{\text{Error}} = -\frac{1}{2}\ln|\Omega(\lambda)| - \frac{N}{2}\ln(2\pi) - \frac{N}{2}\ln(\sigma^2) - \frac{(y - X\beta)'\Omega(\lambda)^{-1}(y - X\beta)}{2\sigma^2}. \tag{6.22}$$

The GLS estimates for β are then

$$\beta_{\text{ML}} = [X'\Omega(\lambda)^{-1}X]^{-1}X'\Omega(\lambda)^{-1}y, \tag{6.23}$$

where $\Omega(\lambda)^{-1} = (I - \lambda W)'(I - \lambda W)$ in the case of spatial autoregressive errors and the ML estimates in this case are equivalent to OLS applied to the spatially filtered dependent and independent variables in

$$(I - \lambda W)y = (I - \lambda W)X\beta + \xi. \tag{6.24}$$

As Anselin and Bera (1998, 257) note, "an explicit optimization of the likelihood function must be carried out. One approach is to use the iterative solution of the first-order conditions in Magnus (1978, 283):

$$\text{tr}\left[\left(\frac{\partial\Omega^{-1}}{\partial\lambda}\right)\Omega\right] = e'\left(\frac{\partial\Omega^{-1}}{\partial\lambda}\right)e \tag{6.25}$$

where $e = y - X\beta$ are GLS residuals. For a spatial autoregressive error process, $\frac{\partial\Omega^{-1}}{\partial\lambda} = -W - W' + \lambda W'W$." As Anselin and Bera (1998, 257–258) note, the solution of condition (6.25) can be obtained by numerical means or the log-likelihood function can be expressed as a concentrated log-likelihood function of the single autoregressive parameter λ (similar to the spatial lag case) by substituting the GLS expression for β and the solution of the first-order conditions for σ^2 into the log-likelihood function. If one uses Ord's (1975) eigenvalues-based approach for the spatial error model, the concentrated log-likelihood function then takes the form:

$$L^c_{\text{Error}} = -\frac{N}{2}\ln\left[\frac{e'e}{N}\right] + \sum_i \ln(1 - \lambda\omega_i), \tag{6.26}$$

where $e'e$ is the residual sum of squares from the regression of the spatially filtered variables, $y - \lambda Wy$ and $X - \lambda WX$ (Anselin 1992a, 210).

6.2.1 Application: Spatial Error Model of Poverty Rates

In Chapter 5, I diagnosed residual spatial error dependence in an OLS estimation of census tract poverty rates in California in 2000. The robust LM error diagnostic was strongly significant where the robust LM lag diagnostic was not. Recall also that each of the substantive covariates was highly significant in the OLS estimation, reaching significance at a $p < 0.0000001$ level. Because spatial error dependence can produce type I errors in inference, we need to examine the effects of the covariates in a model that accounts for the spatial dependence.

Table 6.2 presents the results from the OLS estimation in Chapter 5 as well as the results from a ML spatial error model estimation. Of most note is the change in the effect of *Female Proportion*. This covariate had a strongly significant effect in the model that ignored the spatial dependence in the data. As we can see from the spatial error model estimates in column 2, this reflects a type I error in inference. Once we account for the spatial dependence in the data, the proportion of the population in the census tract that is female has no effect on the tract's poverty rate.

TABLE 6.2. *OLS and ML Estimates for California Poverty Rates*

Covariate	(1)	(2)
Urban Proportion	-0.049^{***}	-0.014^{**}
	(0.005)	(0.005)
African American Proportion	0.283^{***}	0.294^{***}
	(0.009)	(0.013)
Hispanic Proportion	0.217^{***}	0.183^{***}
	(0.006)	(0.008)
Immigrant Proportion	0.102^{***}	0.185^{***}
	(0.008)	(0.011)
Female Proportion	-0.142^{***}	−0.028
	(0.023)	(0.018)
Median Year	0.000^{***}	0.000^{***}
	(0.000)	(0.000)
Intercept	0.034^{*}	−0.015
	(0.016)	(0.013)
λ		0.765^{***}
		(0.010)
$N = 6922$		
Log-likelihood	7135.64	8977.37
AIC	−14257.3	−17940.7

1 = OLS estimates with standard errors below.
2 = Spatial error ML estimates with standard errors below.
* $p < 0.05$, ** $p < 0.01$, *** $p < 0.001$, two-tailed tests.

The statistical significance of the *Urban Proportion* covariate is also diminished in the spatial model, reaching only a $p < 0.01$ level of significance in this model where it was significant to a $p < 0.0000001$ level in the OLS estimation. The strong positive spatial error dependence in the data is captured in the significant λ parameter estimate of 0.765. In all, these estimates show the importance of modeling spatial error dependence in our data. Had we not modeled this dependence, we would have concluded that the proportion of a tract's population that is female has a significant effect on its poverty rate. The smaller Akaike information criterion (AIC) value for the spatial error ML model in comparison to the OLS model also suggests the superiority of the spatial error ML model.

6.2.2 Application: Spatial Error Model of Voter Turnout

Chapter 5 presented an application of LM diagnostics to the diagnosis of spatial dependence in county-level turnout in 1828. The LM diagnostics for the OLS model in that application indicated that a spatial error model was the preferred

TABLE 6.3. *OLS and ML Spatial Error Estimates for Turnout in the 1828 Presidential Election*

Covariate	OLS Estimates	ML Error Estimates
Intercept	0.64**	0.62**
	(0.01)	(0.02)
African American Percent	0.19**	0.16*
	(0.06)	(0.08)
Foreign-Born Percent	0.22	−0.05
	(0.13)	(0.11)
Rural	0.02	0.00
	(0.01)	(0.01)
South	−0.01	−0.14**
	(0.03)	(0.04)
African American Percent × *South*	−0.38**	−0.09
	(0.08)	(0.10)
Average Margin	−0.06*	−0.01
	(0.02)	(0.02)
Average Minor Party Percentage	−1.27**	0.16
	(0.37)	(0.30)
Registration Law	−0.17**	−0.18**
	(0.03)	(0.04)
Property Requirement	−0.12**	−0.09**
	(0.02)	(0.03)
λ		0.66**
		(0.03)
$N = 730$.		
AIC	−685.00	−976.48

* $p < 0.05$, ** $p < 0.01$.

specification. In this section, I apply the spatial error model using the same set of covariates and data as in Chapter 5.

The results of both this analysis and the OLS estimation in Chapter 5 are presented in Table 6.3. As can be seen, the inferences drawn from the spatial error ML estimation are quite different than those drawn from the OLS estimation that ignored the spatial dependence in the data. The OLS estimates indicated that features of partisan competition influenced voting behavior in 1828, with more competitive counties and those with larger levels of minor party support exhibiting lower turnout. These features of partisan competition in the county have no effect on turnout in the spatial error ML estimates. Where the main effect of *South* was insignificant and the interaction of *African American Percent* × *South* was significant in the OLS estimates, these are reversed in the spatial error ML estimates. The strong positive spatial error dependence in the data is evidenced by the statistical significance of the λ

parameter that captures this dependence. The AIC values for the two models also point toward the superiority of the spatial error model. In all, these estimates point to the importance of modeling spatial error dependence when it is present in our data.

6.3 ESTIMATION FOR LARGE NUMBERS OF OBSERVATIONS

A critical drawback of ML estimation of spatial models is the required computation of determinants and inverses of n by n matrices, where n refers to sample size. These computations require $O(n^3)$ operations, which can quickly prove prohibitive for large sample sizes. Ord's (1975) approach of using a single calculation of the eigenvalues of the spatial weights matrix to ease ML estimation of the spatial lag model is helpful in easing computational limitations in moderately sized datasets. However, the eigenvalues-based approach can become problematic even in samples as small as 400 with nonsymmetric weights matrices due to inaccuracy in the computation of the eigenvalues. As a consequence, scholars working with moderate to large datasets may prefer an alternative approach to ML estimation. In recent years, a variety of approaches have been proposed for overcoming these computational difficulties, often focusing on exploiting the sparseness of many spatial weights matrices.

Pace (1997) offers an approach to the computation of the determinant that reduces the computational cost of the $O(n^3)$ operations (see also Pace and Barry 1997). Many spatial weights matrices are quite sparse, with few nonzero elements. This is particularly the case for k-nearest neighbor and contiguity-based matrices. Because the number of operation counts depends only on the number of nonzero elements in the weights matrix, the sparsity of weights matrices can be exploited to speed computation. Sparse weights matrix methods achieve this computational saving by storing only the nonzero elements of the weights matrix and discarding the non-neighbors (Pace 1997, 286). The result is a great increase in speed of computation. Sparse matrix methods are now, in fact, employed in most spatial estimation packages. Methods exploiting sparse matrix storage operate effectively for most estimation applications assuming that neighbor definitions do reflect sparseness or the n is not unusually large. If neither of these conditions is met, researchers may instead wish to employ the characteristic polynomial approach developed by Smirnov and Anselin (2001).

Recently, Pace and LeSage (2002) have proposed a semiparametric ML modeling approach. Their approach employs upper and lower bounds to the ML function as well as small matrices that do not increase in size with the number of observations. Pace and LeSage demonstrated the utility of their semiparametric approach in large datasets, though it has not yet received extensive use in practice.

Although much attention has been paid to maximizing the log-likelihoods of spatial models, much less attention has been paid to the calculation of the

variances of the coefficient estimates, which also suffers from the computational complexities associated with large datasets. An important exception is Smirnov's (2005) approach to computing and inverting the information matrix to produce the asymptotic variance matrix. Once again, computing the inverse of the information matrix involves $O(n^3)$ computations. Smirnov's approach exploits the sparseness of most spatial weights matrices via a sparse conjugate gradient method for computing the inverse of the information matrix. Smirnov finds that this approach exhibits strong performance both in terms of numerical stability and computational requirements and thus can provide effective computation of variance estimates for large datasets.

6.4 INTERPRETING SUBSTANTIVE EFFECTS IN THE SPATIAL LAG MODEL

Interpreting substantive effects in a spatial lag model is much more complex than in a nonspatial model (or in a spatial error model) because of the presence of the spatial multiplier that links the independent variables to the dependent variable. As Ward and Gleditsch (2008, 45) note, the expected value of the dependent variable in the spatial lag model is

$$E(y) = (I - \rho W)^{-1} X\beta, \tag{6.27}$$

and thus the equilibrium effect of x depends on the spatial multiplier $(I - \rho W)^{-1}$. Thus, even though the lag pertains to the dependent variable, the interpretation of substantive effects of independent variables in the simultaneous spatial autoregressive model must incorporate units' effects on neighboring units. As a consequence, where the effect of a one-unit change in x_i in a nonspatial model is simply $\beta \Delta x_i$, the effect of a one-unit change in x_i in a spatial lag model is $(I - \rho W)^{-1} \beta \Delta x_i$. Thus, to examine the equilibrium effect of a one-unit change in a covariate, we must premultiply the vector Δx_i by $(I - \rho W)^{-1} \beta$, holding the values for all other units constant (Ward and Gleditsch 2008, 45).

In the nonspatial model, it does not matter which unit is experiencing the change on the independent variable. The effect of a change is constant across all observations. This is not the case in the spatial lag model, where the substantive effects of covariates vary by observation as a result of the differing neighbors for each unit in the data (Ward and Gleditsch 2008, 45).

An important implication of the spatial multiplier therefore is that even where parameters are assumed homogeneous in a spatial lag model and are not allowed to vary by spatial location, the equilibrium effects of substantive covariates still vary depending on the spatial locations of the units. (Models for spatial heterogeneity such as the spatial regimes model and geographically weighted regressions [GWR], examined in the next chapter, relax the assumption of homogeneous parameters altogether and directly model variation in the β parameters in a regression context.) Note that because the

spatial multiplier in a spatial error model pertains only to the errors, substantive covariates do not vary in their equilibrium effects based on the spatial locations of the observations in a spatial error formulation.

There are two components to the effects of covariates in a spatial lag model. There is a direct, local effect on unit *i* itself. In contrast to nonspatial models or spatial error models, there is also an indirect or spillover effect of the covariate through the spatial multiplier. The total effect of a covariate is thus the combination of the direct and indirect effects.

Just as the independent variables influence values on the dependent variable in neighboring units owing to the spatial autoregressive structure of the spatial lag model, so also do neighbors' values on the dependent variable directly influence each other's values via the spatially lagged dependent variable. Clearly this also depends on the neighbor structure in *W*. Ward and Gleditsch (2008, 48–49) raise the important point that this direct diffusion effect between unit *i* and unit *j* varies when *W* is row standardized depending on how many neighbors unit *j* has. For example, if *j* has few neighbors (of which *i* is one), then neighboring unit *i*, all else equal, will exert a larger relative effect on unit *j*'s behavior than if *j* had many additional neighbors. For example, the spatial diffusion effect on fertility rates in inland U.S. counties (see, e.g., Tolnay 1995) will typically, all else equal, be smaller than for coastal counties, as the former typically have more neighbors than the latter.

6.5 APPLICATION: STATE SPENDING ON HIGHER EDUCATION

In this section, I examine how to substantively interpret the results of spatial lag models using an example of state spending on higher education. State commitments to higher education spending are of interest in a variety of social science disciplines. Typically, however, we do not examine how changes in features of one state spill over to affect spending in other states. We can do so through a spatial lag model.

The dependent variable in this analysis is *Higher Education Share*, which measures the share of the state's budget that went to higher education in the state.[1] I model these higher education spending shares as a function of five covariates in addition to a spatially lagged dependent variable. The five covariates are *Poverty Rate*, which measures the state's poverty rate; *State NOMINATE*, Berry and colleagues' (2010) widely used State NOMINATE scores, which are used as a proxy measure for the ideology of state governments; *Minimum Wage*, the state's minimum wage; *Union Density*, the density of union membership in the state; and *Health Share*, the share of the state's

1 The data for this variable come from the U.S. Census Bureau's Annual Survey of State and Local Government Finances. See Witko and Newmark (2010) for a more detailed discussion of these data.

TABLE 6.4. *Estimates for Spatial Lag Model of Higher Education Spending*

Covariate	Estimates
Poverty Rate	−0.282*
	(0.143)
State Ideology	−0.000
	(0.000)
Minimum Wage	−0.003
	(0.005)
Union Density	−0.003**
	(0.001)
Health Share	−0.800*
	(0.355)
Intercept	0.196**
	(0.040)
ρ	0.428**
	(0.143)

* $p < 0.05$, ** $p < 0.01$, two-tailed tests.

budget that went to health care spending. The data for this application are for 1994. A queen contiguity weights matrix was employed for the analysis.

The results from the spatial lag ML estimation are reported in Table 6.4. As can be seen, *Poverty Rate*, *Union Density*, and *Health Share* all had statistically significant effects on states' spending on higher education. All have negative coefficients, suggesting that increases in these covariates were associated with lower spending levels on higher education. Note also that the autoregressive parameter for the spatially lagged dependent variable, ρ, is statistically significant, indicating the potential for strong spatial spillover effects in these covariates on the dependent variable.

We can get a better sense of the substantive effects of one of these three covariates, *Poverty Rate*, on higher education spending by altering the value on this covariate for one of the states and examining how this affects higher education spending in this and other states. For this example, I changed Ohio's value on the poverty rate variable from 14.1 percent to the maximum value in the data, Louisiana's poverty rate of 25.7 percent. What would be the effects on higher education spending from this single switch of changing Ohio's poverty rate so that it matched Louisiana's? The results of this analysis are presented in Table 6.5.

Table 6.5 presents the predicted percentage point change in each state's share of spending devoted to higher education as a result of Ohio's poverty rate increasing from 14.1 percent to 25.7 percent (the states are listed in their order in the shapefile used for the analysis). As expected, the strongest effect

TABLE 6.5. *Substantive Effects from Spatial Lag Model of Higher Education Spending*

State	Difference in Higher Education Spending
Washington	0.699
Montana	0.296
Maine	2.869
North Dakota	0.346
South Dakota	−0.157
Wyoming	−0.626
Wisconsin	−0.929
Idaho	0.258
Vermont	2.025
Minnesota	−0.504
Oregon	.070
New Hampshire	1.722
Iowa	−0.040
Massachusetts	1.584
Nebraska	0.010
New York	1.680
Pennsylvania	−0.021
Connecticut	1.670
Rhode Island	2.660
New Jersey	−0.112
Indiana	−1.079
Nevada	−0.248
Utah	−0.209
California	0.725
Ohio	−4.597
Illinois	−1.225
Delaware	1.153
West Virginia	−0.309
Maryland	−0.453
Colorado	−0.629
Kentucky	−1.128
Kansas	−0.903
Virginia	−0.126
Missouri	−0.452
Arizona	−1.123
Oklahoma	−0.704
North Carolina	−0.187
Tennessee	−0.268
Texas	−0.410
New Mexico	−1.294
Alabama	0.536
Mississippi	−0.797
Georgia	−0.288
South Carolina	0.616
Arkansas	−0.138
Louisiana	0.244
Florida	−0.844
Michigan	−2.285

TABLE 6.6. *Direct, Indirect, and Total Effects of Covariates in Spatial Lag Model of Higher Education Spending*

Covariate	Direct	Indirect	Total
Poverty Rate	−0.297	−0.195	−0.492
State Ideology	−0.000	−0.000	−0.000
Minimum Wage	−0.003	−0.002	−0.005
Union Density	−0.003	−0.002	−0.005
Health Share	−0.843	−0.555	−1.398

was on Ohio's own education spending rate. Ohio's higher education spending share is predicted to have declined by over 4.5 percentage points as a result of this change in one covariate. The effect on higher education spending is by no means limited to Ohio, however. Michigan's spending is predicted to have declined by more than 2 percentage points as a result of the increased poverty in the neighboring state of Ohio. Illinois, a neighbor of a neighbor, is predicted to have a more than one percentage point decline in its higher education spending share as a result of Ohio's increased poverty.

The spatial spillover effect ripples throughout the states. Note, also, that not all of these spending effects are negative. Many of the effects in the Northeast are positive. Maine's spending share on higher education is predicted to have increased by nearly 3 percentage points as a result of the change in Ohio's poverty rate. New York's spending share is predicted to have increased by more than 1.5 percentage points. In short, in the presence of a significant spatial lag effect it is clear that what happens in one state does not stay confined to that one state.

These effects are instructive. However, we might be interested in what the effects are on average for a particular covariate. As stated earlier, the effect of a covariate is the sum of two particular effects: a direct, local effect of the covariate in that unit and an indirect, spillover effect due to the spatial lag. We can estimate the average direct, indirect, and total effects of our covariates. These results are presented in Table 6.6.

As we can see, nearly 40 percent of the effect of poverty rates on higher education spending are spatial spillover effects. Likewise, nearly 40 percent of the effect of health care spending is not a localized one, but instead is an indirect spillover effect. In applications in which we think our data are likely to exhibit spatial lag dependence, it is clearly important to consider both the direct and indirect effects of our covariates.

6.6 GOODNESS OF FIT STATISTICS

Scholars are often interested in assessing how well the specified model fits the data. The most familiar and frequently used measure of fit in empirical models

is the R^2. However, as is well known, the R^2 measure is not appropriate when assessing model fit for models employing ML estimators. In an OLS context, the R^2 measure makes some sense, given that it captures the residual sum of squared errors. In an ML context, however, the ML estimator maximizes the likelihood of producing the observed data, a fundamentally different estimation criterion. As a consequence, the R^2 measure isn't applicable for either spatial lag or spatial error ML models. Even an R^2 analogue, in the form of a pseudo-R^2 measure, doesn't necessarily make intuitive sense in an ML context, given the different estimation criteria for these estimators. If one is interested, however, in employing a pseudo-R^2 measure, Anselin (1992a, 190) proposed two principal alternatives. The first of these pseudo-R^2 measures is the ratio of the variance of the predicted values on the dependent variable divided by the variance of the observed values on this variable. The second is the squared correlation between the predicted and the observed values on the dependent variable, which, as Anselin (1988c, 244) notes, has the positive attribute that it "still provides a measure of linear association (or in-sample predictive ability) that is between zero and one, although it no longer is related to the variance decomposition."

The R^2 measure is often used, inappropriately, as a measure of model fit for instrumental variables models. However, as with other instrumental variables models, R^2 should not be used as a model fit measure for the spatial lag model estimated via instrumental variables, as the resulting R^2 cannot be guaranteed to be non-negative (Pesaran and Smith 1994, 705). The problem, as Pesaran and Smith (1994, 705–707) note, is that the the instrumental variables residuals are employed to calculate the R^2 instead of the prediction errors. As a consequence, Anselin (1992a, 202) proposed the use of the two pseudo R^2 measures also applicable for the MLE spatial lag model.

As Anselin (1988c, 243) notes, as with other models for nonspherical errors, the spatial error model may not have a mean of zero, and as a consequence, the R^2 is no longer a measure of the proportion of the total variance that is explained by the model. Anselin (1992a, 210) proposed three alternatives to the standard R^2 measure for spatial error models. The first two are the pseudo R^2 measures already discussed. The third measure is a pseudo R^2 with adjustments to the standard R^2 suggested by Buse (1973) applied to the case of spatial error dependence (Anselin 1992a, 210). As Anselin (1992a, 210) shows, this pseudo R^2 takes the form

$$R_B^2 = 1 - (e - \lambda We)'(e - \lambda We)/(y - \iota y_w)'(I - \lambda W)'(I - \lambda W)(y - \iota y_w) \quad (6.28)$$

where

$$y_w = (\iota - \lambda W\iota)'(y - \lambda Wy)/(\iota - \lambda W\iota)'(\iota - \lambda W\iota) \quad (6.29)$$

with ι an $N \times 1$ vector of ones. As Anselin (1988c, 244) notes, "When the weight matrix is row-standardized, the numerator in y_w becomes $N(\lambda - 1)^2$, since $W\iota = \iota$."

6.6.1 Information Criteria

Information criteria are often used as comparative measures for model choice across a set of possible model specifications. The three principal information criteria used by applied researchers are the AIC, the small sample corrected version of the Akaike information criterion (AICc), and the Bayesian information criterion (BIC). Each of these information criteria has seen applications to spatial models.

The AIC takes the form

$$\text{AIC} = -2\log L + 2k, \tag{6.30}$$

where $\log L$ is the maximized log likelihood and k is the number of parameters in the model. The AIC is thus a measure of model fit combined with a penalty for overfitting the model via the inclusion of a large number of covariates. As with other information criteria, the AIC is a comparative measure of model choice, pointing not to the best model, but rather to the preferred model among a set of possible model specifications that need not be nested. As with other information criteria, smaller values of the AIC are preferred over larger values.

When n is small or the ratio of the number of observations to the number of parameters estimated $\left(\frac{n}{k}\right)$ is small, the AIC tends to underpenalize for overfitting models. As a consequence, scholars often use the small sample corrected version of the AIC, the AICc, when either the sample size is small or the ratio of the sample size to the number of parameters is small. (As Lee and Ghosh [2009, 96] note, Burnham and Anderson [2002] suggest that the AICc should be used when the ratio $\frac{n}{k} < 40$ for the model with the largest number of parameters examined.) As n approaches infinity, the AIC and AICc converge to the same value, and thus little is lost by being conservative and employing the AICc as the information criterion. The AICc takes the form

$$\text{AICc} = \text{AIC} + \frac{2k(k+1)}{n-k-1}, \tag{6.31}$$

where the notation is as defined previously.

The third frequently used information criterion is the BIC. The BIC penalizes overfitting more strongly than does the AIC, generally resulting in more parsimonious model specifications (Lee and Ghosh 2009, 96). The BIC takes the form

$$\text{BIC} = -2\log L + k\log(n). \tag{6.32}$$

As with the other criteria, the model with the smallest BIC is chosen as the preferred model specification.

Although often applied to spatial models, the AIC, AICc, and BIC each were developed under the assumption of spatial independence. We know little about how spatial dependence in areal data affects the performance of these information criteria. In a recent analysis, however, Lee and Ghosh (2009)

employed Monte Carlos to examine the performance of these information criteria to geostatistical data. They found that the information criteria vary in their performance depending on the stationarity of the data and whether the data are isotropic or anisotropic. A spatial process is said to be isotropic if the spatial correlation between two locations depends only on the distance between the locations. A spatial process is anisotropic when the spatial correlation depends also on direction (see Cressie 1993; Lee and Ghosh 2009). They find that generally, however, the information criteria are more likely to choose the correct model as sample size increases (Lee and Ghosh 2009, 105).

6.7 ADDITIONAL TOPICS

If diagnostics such as the Jarque-Bera indicate that the errors are not normally distributed, or if the researcher is concerned about computational difficulties in large samples, she may wish to employ an alternative approach to estimation rather than ML. An instrumental variables model is one approach to obtaining estimates of the spatial autoregressive parameter, ρ. One advantage of an instrumental variables approach is that researchers comfortable and familiar with standard nonspatial estimation routines in standard statistical software can employ these routines to estimate spatial lag models using instrumental variables.

Remember from Chapter 3 that OLS is not a consistent estimator of ρ because of the correlation between the spatially lagged dependent variable, Wy, and the errors, ε, that results from the multidimensional nature of spatial, as opposed to temporal, dependence. The logic of an instrumental variables estimator of ρ is to find variables, that is, instruments, that correlate with the spatially lagged dependent variable, Wy, but are asymptotically uncorrelated with the error term. If the proper instruments are found, the instrumental variables estimator will be a consistent estimator.

A variety of instruments have been suggested for Wy. Anselin (1988cc, 85) suggests spatially lagged predicted values of the dependent variable as well as spatial lags of the covariates in the model as instruments for the spatially lagged dependent variable. In the development of their GMM diagnostic for spatial error components, Kelejian and Robinson (1993, 302) prove the consistency of this estimator when first-order spatially lagged covariates (WX) and higher order spatially lagged covariates (W^2X, W^3X) are employed as instruments and note that the efficiency of the estimator may be improved by including more of the higher order terms (see also Anselin and Bera 1998, 260). Clearly, however, such an approach is likely to suffer from multicollinearity. Land and Deane (1992, 246) stress the importance of the R^2 as a guide in the choice of instruments, arguing that the R^2 for the first-stage regression should be higher than the R^2 for the second-stage regression in the two stage least squares approach.

The instrumental variables estimator will generally be consistent if the proper instruments are chosen for *Wy*. In a recent analysis, however, Kelejian and Prucha (2002) demonstrated an important exception to this general rule. As they showed, the two-stage least squares estimator will not be consistent if the weights matrix is row standardized and has equal weights for all units and only a single cross section of data is available. (Kelejian and Prucha [2002, 692] demonstrate, however, that when the weights matrix is row standardized with equal weights for all units and at least two panels of data are available, the two-stage least squares estimator is consistent.) As a consequence, if these conditions are met (e.g., when using a *k*-nearest neighbors definition with no island cases), one should employ an alternative estimator.

Regardless of the structure of the spatial weights matrix, the instrumental variables estimator generally will not be the most efficient estimator and may, as a consequence, have a larger mean squared error than the biased OLS estimator (Anselin 1988c, 85). As Lee (2007, 490) notes, the IV estimator will be consistent only if all of the exogenous covariates in the spatial lag model are not jointly irrelevant, that is, they are not all jointly equal to zero. Moreover, as he notes, the joint significance of the exogenous covariates cannot be tested using the instrumental variables approach, unlike the case with the ML approach (see also Kelejian and Prucha 1998). The efficiency of the IV estimator depends on the instruments chosen for the spatially lagged dependent variable (Anselin 1988c, 84; Anselin and Bera 1998, 259). Moreover, like the OLS estimator, the IV estimator may produce an explosive estimate of the spatial autoregressive parameter, ρ. This lack of stability for the estimated spatial process is not possible in the ML estimate, in which ρ is constrained to be a nonexplosive parameter. (See Lee and Yu [2007] for a discussion of near unit roots for spatial autoregressive processes.) Given these limitations, researchers may often prefer the ML approach over the instrumental variables approach for modeling spatially lagged dependent variables when the assumption of normality is supported. If large samples are a concern, researchers may also wish to consider one of the approaches for ML estimation with large datasets discussed later in this chapter.

Generalized method of moments (GMM) estimators are attractive for the estimation of spatial models due to their relative computational ease in comparison to ML estimators. As Lee (2001, 2) notes, "The GMM method has been noted for its possible use with the estimation of spatial models in the presence of exogenous variables" in a variety of publications including Anselin (1988c), Land and Deane (1992), and others. Importantly, however, the GMM estimators suggested in these studies are, as Lee (2001, 23) notes, "either linear IV, 2SLS, or generalized 2SLS methods. The validity of those methods relies exclusively on the presence of exogenous variables in the model to construct their IVs. Those methods cannot be applied to (pure) SAR processes as there are no relevant exogenous variables in the processes."

Kelejian and Prucha (2001) provide the initial development of a method of moments estimator for a spatial autoregressive lag model, demonstrating that their estimator is nearly as efficient as a QMLE. Lee (2001) exploits nonlinear moment conditions to develop several GMM estimators for the pure spatial autoregressive lag model and demonstrates that his GMM estimators are consistent and asymptotically normally distributed.

More recently, Lee (2007) has extended this GMM estimation framework to the mixed regressive, spatial autoregressive lag model. Lee demonstrates that the GMM estimators are consistent and asympotically normally distributed. Moreover, Lee's best GMM estimator has the advantage over the two-stage least squares (2SLS) estimator in that the former is as efficient as the ML estimator whereas the latter is not.

Lee (2007, 501) examined the performance of the GMM estimators in small ($n=49$) and moderate ($n=245$ and $n=490$) samples via a set of Monte Carlos using the following spatial lag model:

$$Y_n = \rho W_n Y_n + X_{n1}\beta_1 + X_{n2}\beta_2 + X_{n3}\beta_3 + \varepsilon_n. \tag{6.33}$$

Lee examined the performance of three GMM estimators as well as the performance of the 2SLS estimator and the ML estimator. The first of the three GMM estimators is an unweighted estimator that, as Lee (2007, 501) notes, uses "$Q_n = (X_n, W_n X_n, W_n^2 X_n)$ for linear moments and W_n and $W_n^2 - (\mathrm{tr}(W_n^2)/n)I_n$ for quadratic moments (with an identity matrix as the distance matrix)." The second GMM estimator examined is the optimum GMM estimator, with, as Lee (2007, 501) notes, "$Q_n = (X_n, W_n X_n, W_n^2 X_n)$ for linear moments and W_n and $W_n^2 - (\mathrm{tr}(W_n^2)/n)I_n$ for quadratic moments (with the inverse of their (estimated) variance matrix as the distance matrix)." The final GMM estimator is the best optimum GMM estimator that, as Lee (2007, 501) states, uses "X_n and $(I_n - \hat{\rho}_n W_n)^{-1} X_n \hat{\beta}_n$ for the linear moments, and $W_n(I_n - \hat{\rho}_n W_n)^{-1} - (1/n)\mathrm{tr}[W_n(I_n - \hat{\rho}_n W_n)^{-1}]I_n$ for the quadratic moment, where $(\hat{\rho}_n, \hat{\beta}_n)$ is an initial consistent estimate." The two-stage least squares estimator uses X_n, $W_n X_n$, and $W_n^2 X_n$ as its instruments. The spatial autoregressive parameter, ρ, is set at 0.6 in all cases.

Lee (2007, 502–503) found that the estimators vary in their performance for the estimation of ρ but not for the β's in the model. The three GMM estimators outperform the 2SLS estimator as they exhibit smaller biases and standard deviations of their empirical distributions than the latter. The 2SLS estimator performs particularly poorly for models with low R^2's. The optimum GMM estimator and the best optimum GMM estimator are as efficient as the ML estimator in the two moderate sample sizes examined. In all, these two GMM estimators are found to perform well and may be preferred over the ML estimator given their computational advantage over the latter.

Kelejian and Prucha (1999) proposed a GMM estimator for a spatial autoregressive error model.[2] As with other GMM estimators, Kelejian and Prucha's estimator exhibits advantages over the ML estimator. The GMM estimator is more computationally feasible in large samples than the ML estimator. The estimator also does not rely on an assumption of normality.

In a Monte Carlo analysis, Kelejian and Prucha (1999) found that their GMM spatial error estimator performs similarly to the ML estimator and is superior to the OLS estimator. Specifically, they find that the average absolute biases for the ML and GMM estimator are smaller than for the OLS estimator. The root mean squared error (RMSE) for the ML and GMM estimator are also similar and smaller than for the OLS estimator. Kelejian and Prucha (1999, 511) concluded, importantly, that their GMM estimator is "virtually as efficient" as the ML estimator.

Conley (1999) proposed an alternative GMM estimator for modeling spatial dependence. Conley's approach follows Newey and West's (1987) similar approach in time series analysis. Conley's estimator has the advantage over the ML estimator in not requiring parametric assumptions. However, as Fleming (2004, 162) notes, Conley's estimator is limited in its applicability to spatial processes as the standard spatial autoregressive error process does not meet the covariance stationarity requirements necessary for Conley's GMM approach.

6.8 CONCLUSION

The valid estimation of behavioral parameters of interest is typically the principal goal of most research in the social sciences. Given the ubiquity of spatial dependence in social science data, researchers in the social sciences must be attentive to modeling spatial dependence diagnosed via the diagnostics for spatial dependence discussed in Chapter 4 and the diagnostics for spatial dependence in the presence of covariates discussed in Chapter 5. If spatial dependence exists in the DGP and is not modeled, the result will either be biased and inconsistent parameter estimates or inefficient parameter estimates and standard error estimates that are biased, depending on the form that the spatial dependence takes.

This chapter has examined approaches for estimating models of spatial dependence. The chapter has explored models for spatial lag dependence and spatial error dependence. The chapter has also examined ML, instrumental variables, and GMM estimators for spatial models. These spatial models and estimation approaches are of critical importance for scholars interested in validly estimating the behavioral parameters of interest.

[2] Kelejian and Prucha's estimation approach is available via the `spdep` package in R.

Often, the models discussed in this chapter will be the best approach for modeling the spatial dependence that is diagnosed by social scientists. Scholars should, however, be attentive to the possibility that the dependence they have diagnosed may be produced by heterogeneity in the behavioral parameters of interest. Consider, for example, a case in which sociologists are interested in the incidence of divorce across the United States. Scholars may find that divorce rates are higher in some neighboring locales than in other neighboring locales. This spatial dependence in divorce rates may occur because covariates that affect the incidence of divorce vary in their effects across the United States. Religious beliefs, for example, may have differing effects on divorce rates in different areas of the country. If so, the spatial dependence diagnosed by researchers is actually produced by spatial heterogeneity in the effect of a covariate. It may well be that once heterogeneous effects such as this are modeled, the spatial dependence that has been diagnosed will be modeled fully as well, and thus spatial lag or spatial error models will be unnecessary.

Thus, although social scientists will often principally be interested in the models and estimation approaches discussed in this chapter, they should also consider the possibility of spatial heterogeneity in their datasets. In practice, scholars often ignore this possibility and do not consider models for spatial heterogeneity. The next chapter examines several different approaches for the modeling of spatial heterogeneity.

7

Spatial Heterogeneity

Spatial autocorrelation that is diagnosed may be produced neither by a diffusion process nor by an attributional process. Instead, it may be produced by behavioral heterogeneity. Within a modeling context, this will take the form of spatial heterogeneity in parameters. If this parameter heterogeneity is not modeled, spatial dependence will persist in the presence of covariates. Residual spatial dependence in a multivariate model may also be produced by another undiagnosed form of spatial heterogeneity – functional form heterogeneity. Depending on the modeling strategy employed to account for spatial heterogeneity in parameters or functional form, a spatial econometric specification may not be required to model the spatial heterogeneity. Instead, the researcher may choose to model the spatial heterogeneity via standard econometric approaches.

7.1 SPATIAL HETEROGENEITY IN PARAMETERS

The intuition of how spatial heterogeneity in parameters may produce univariate spatial autocorrelation is straightforward. If a covariate differs in its effects on the phenomenon of interest to social scientists across observations, and if the effects are similar among neighboring observations, this may produce similar values on the dependent variable. I examine three sets of approaches for modeling spatial heterogeneity in parameters – spatial random coefficients models, spatial switching regressions models for discrete parameter heterogeneity, and spatially varying coefficients models for continuous parameter heterogeneity – in turn next.

7.2 SPATIAL RANDOM COEFFICIENTS MODELS

Random coefficients models have received extensive use in econometrics as an approach for modeling heterogeneity in parameters (Swamy 1970; Hsiao

1975). The standard, nonspatial random coefficients specification takes the following form:

$$y_i = X_i\beta_i + \varepsilon_i$$
$$\beta_i = \beta + \mu_i, \tag{7.1}$$

where β_i is no longer assumed constant, but instead is allowed to vary across observations as a function of a mean, β, and a stochastic term, μ_i. The random coefficients model induces heteroskedasticity, which is modeled via feasible generalized least squares (FGLS).

In the standard random coefficients model, the stochastic variation, μ_i, around the common mean, β, is assumed to be random with regard to the spatial locations of observations. In contrast, in the spatial random coefficients approach, there is spatial dependence in this variation around the mean. As a result, the spatial random coefficients specification takes the form

$$y_i = X_i\beta_i + \varepsilon_i$$
$$\mu_i = \beta_i - \beta \tag{7.2}$$

with

$$\mu_i = \lambda \Sigma_j w_{ij}(\beta_j - \beta) + \xi_i \tag{7.3}$$

or

$$\mu_i = \lambda \Sigma_j w_{ij}\mu_j + \xi_i, \tag{7.4}$$

where μ_i are the stochastic variations around the common mean, ξ are i.i.d. error terms, λ is the spatial autoregressive parameter for the stochastic dependence around the common mean, and w_{ij} are the elements of the spatial weights matrix, W, for the neighborhood set of i (Anselin and Cho 2002, 283). The simultaneous spatial dependence induces heteroskedasticity and a nonzero covariance between the errors for all observations. Ignoring this heteroskedasticity and spatial dependence will produce inefficient estimates of the common mean, β, and biased estimates of the variance (Anselin and Cho 2002). Thus, the spatial dependence in the error terms must be accounted for in estimation of spatial random coefficients models and the explicitly spatial econometric form of these models differs from other approaches for modeling spatial heterogeneity in parameters or functional form.

7.3 SPATIAL SWITCHING REGRESSIONS

Discrete spatial heterogeneity in parameters occurs when a parameter is homogeneous within spatial subsets of the data and heterogeneous across these subsets. The concept of discrete spatial heterogeneity in parameters can be found in many social science theories. Consider, for example, studies of racial

interactions, American voting behavior, or policy diffusion where behavioral parameters are hypothesized to operate differently in the South versus the non-South. Or consider the comparative politics concepts of the global North and South where relationships such as those between financial weakness and capital account liberalization or between globalization and welfare state spending differ in discrete spatial subsets of the data (Brooks 2004; Rudra 2002).

Tests on such structural instability in parameters are well known in the time series literature where Chow tests are often employed to diagnose structural breaks in parameters over time. We can adapt the Chow test to the case of spatial structural instability via a spatial switching regression specification, also known as a spatial regimes model. Here, in contrast to the standard time series approach, where the subsets of the data reflect discrete temporal periods, the subsets of the data are instead spatially indexed:

$$\begin{bmatrix} y_i \\ y_j \end{bmatrix} = \begin{bmatrix} X_i & 0 \\ 0 & X_j \end{bmatrix} \begin{bmatrix} \beta_i \\ \beta_j \end{bmatrix} + \begin{bmatrix} \varepsilon_i \\ \varepsilon_j \end{bmatrix}, \tag{7.5}$$

where i,j index discrete spatial subsets of the data. The spatial Chow test then proceeds as a test of the null that $\beta_i = \beta_j$ via an F test

$$C = [(e_R'e_R - e_U'e_U)/K][e_U'e_U/(N-2K)] \sim F_{K,N-2K}, \tag{7.6}$$

where e_R and e_U are the (OLS) residuals from a restricted model (with the equality restriction imposed) and from an unrestricted model, N is the number of discrete spatial subsets in the data, and K is the number of regressors (Anselin 1990b, 192).

If the switching regression specification models fully the sources of univariate spatial autocorrelation, a spatial econometric specification is not required. If, however, spatial lag or spatial error dependence remains after the spatial heterogeneity in parameters has been modeled, the researcher will wish to employ either an instrumental variables specification or a spatial econometric specification incorporating both spatial heterogeneity and spatial autocorrelation.

A critical related concern is the effect of spatial dependence on Chow tests. Anselin (1990b) demonstrated that spatial error dependence can invalidate spatial Chow tests for spatial structural instability in parameters. Consider the spatial autoregressive error process:

$$\varepsilon = (I - \lambda W)^{-1}\varepsilon. \tag{7.7}$$

In this case, a common spatial autoregressive process extends across the spatial regimes, allowing for the use of a single spatial weights matrix, W. When such an autoregressive error process exists, the correct form for the spatial Chow test becomes

$$C_{err} = [e_R'(I - \lambda W)'(I - \lambda W)e_R - e_U'(I - \lambda W)'(I - \lambda W)e_U]/\sigma^2 \sim \chi^2_K. \tag{7.8}$$

In a series of Monte Carlo experiments, Anselin demonstrated that a spatial autoregressive error process can inflate both the size and power of standard spatial Chow tests. There is, however, a noteworthy asymmetry to these effects. Overrejection of the null increases markedly as λ reaches 0.5 for certain spatial regime layouts. In contrast, negative spatial autocorrelation has little effect on the size of the standard spatial Chow. Negative spatial autocorrelation does tend to produce a modest reduction in the power of the standard spatial Chow, but this reduction in power is much less severe than the inflation of the power of the test in the case of positive spatial autocorrelation.

Given that positive, rather than negative, spatial autocorrelation is likely to predominate in social science data, scholars should be keenly aware of the implications of positive spatial error dependence for measures of spatial structural instability in parameters. Scholars should thus first estimate spatial dependence via global and local measures of spatial autocorrelation. Given a finding of spatial dependence, scholars should then incorporate this dependence in their spatial Chow tests. This will produce more valid estimates of both forms of spatial effects than considering only spatial heterogeneity or spatial dependence in isolation.

7.4 APPLICATION: SPATIAL SWITCHING REGRESSION MODEL OF SPATIAL HETEROGENEITY IN THE SOURCES OF VOTING BEHAVIOR DURING THE NEW DEAL REALIGNMENT

I employ data on voting behavior during the New Deal realignment to examine how spatial dependence and spatial heterogeneity can be diagnosed and modeled. Theory predicts spatial dependence in voting behavior during such critical realignments. Realignment theory emphasizes emerging issue concerns as the impetus for changes in voting behavior (Sundquist 1983). Voters in neighboring electorates are likely to share similar policy concerns; as a consequence, we should expect similar shifts in voting behavior in neighboring electorates in response to these shared concerns. Such shifts, moreover, may reflect a diffusion process. For example, shared social networks that transcend local electorates may promote shared changes in voting behavior in response to these emergent policy concerns. Indeed, in an analysis that did not employ spatial analysis, Nardulli (1995) found that neighboring counties exhibit similar changes in voting behavior during realignments.

I examine changes in county-level support for the Democratic Party between the 1928 and 1932 presidential elections. Change in the Democratic vote between the Al Smith and Franklin D. Roosevelt candidacies is measured as a proportion of the eligible electorate $\left(\frac{\text{Democratic Vote}_{1932}}{\text{Eligible Electorate}_{1932}} - \frac{\text{Democratic Vote}_{1928}}{\text{Eligible Electorate}_{1928}}\right)$. This reflects the argument by Andersen (1979) that the mobilization of non-voters, rather than the conversion of active partisans, may have played a critical role in producing the increased support for the Democrats during this period.

Again, the first step in assessing spatial dependence in changes in Democratic support between the 1928 and 1932 elections is diagnosing this dependence in the absence of covariates via global and local measures of spatial autocorrelation. The global Moran's *I* for the changes in Democratic support is 0.67 ($p < 0.01$, employing the randomization approach with a queen contiguity neighbor definition). The global Moran's *I* thus diagnoses strong positive global spatial autocorrelation. At the local level, more than 40 percent of the counties exhibit significant positive spatial autocorrelation with their neighbors, as estimated by the local Moran's (also employing the randomization approach and a queen contiguity neighbor definition). The strong global spatial dependence reflects a common local pattern and is not the product of a few outlying cases.

An analysis of this local spatial autocorrelation shows a strong spatial patterning of changes in aggregate partisan voting in 1932 that was focused in the Plains and in the South (see Figure 1 in Darmofal 2008). There was a strong shift toward the Democrats in the Plains, where the Dust Bowl had hit between the two elections (an average increase in Democratic support of 24 percentage points in positively autocorrelated Plains counties). In contrast, much of the South evidenced much smaller movement toward the Democrats, unsurprising given the Democratic dominance that already existed in the South (an average increase of only 4 percentage points in positively autocorrelated southern counties). Given these discrete spatial subsets of the data, a spatial regimes model in which the behavioral parameters are allowed to vary between the Plains and the South is indicated.

Given the findings of significant positive global and local spatial autocorrelation and the indication of potential behavioral heterogeneity, the next step is to attempt to model this spatial dependence and spatial heterogeneity with covariates. I modeled changes in county-level support for the Democrats between 1928 and 1932 as a function of six county-level covariates suggested by the literature on voting behavior during the New Deal realignment. $\textit{Republican Vote}_{1928}$ measures the Republican vote in the county in the 1928 presidential election (again, as a proportion of the eligible electorate) and accounts for changes from Republican support to Democratic support between the 1928 and 1932 elections. $\textit{Non-Voting}_{1928}$ measures the non-voting population in the county in the 1928 presidential election as a proportion of the eligible electorate and reflects Andersen's thesis that the increase in Democratic support resulted from the mobilization of previous non-voters. *Foreign-Born* is the proportion of foreign-born individuals in the county in 1932 and reflects Andersen's (1979) argument that immigrants played a pivotal role in producing the increase in Democratic support. *Rural* is a dichotomous variable coded 1 if the county was a rural county and 0 otherwise. This covariate examines Brown's (1991) argument that the surge in Democratic support was disproportionately a rural phenomenon, rather than the urban phenomenon suggested by Andersen and others.

I also included two interaction terms to assess the effects of interactions between electoral and demographic features of local electorates. The interaction term *Non-Voting*$_{1928}$ $*$ *Foreign-Born* examines whether shifts toward the Democrats were promoted by the joint presence in a county of two groups likely to have weak prior attachments to the political parties, non-voters and immigrants. The interaction term *Republican Vote*$_{1928}$ $*$ *Foreign-Born* examines whether shifts toward the Democrats were promoted or impeded by the joint presence of immigrants and prior Republican supporters. Such prior Republican support may have discouraged movement toward the Democrats or encouraged it through the interaction of conversion and mobilization.

Table 7.1 presents the estimates from an OLS spatial regimes model. The OLS estimates indicate that in both the Plains and the South, shifts to the Democrats in 1932 were stronger where Republicans had run stronger in 1928, where there were large pools of non-voters in 1928, and in rural counties. Counterintuitively, however, the OLS estimates indicate that the joint presence of pools of non-voters and immigrants impeded shifts toward the Democrats in the Plains in 1932. Thus, precisely in those counties where we would expect particularly strong movement toward the Democrats because of the presence of two groups with weak attachments to the parties, the OLS estimates indicate that shifts to the Democrats were instead impeded.

Importantly, the OLS spatial Chow tests indicate some significant spatial heterogeneity. The OLS Chow tests are significant for the intercept, *Republican Vote*$_{1928}$, *Republican Vote*$_{1928}$ $*$ *Foreign-Born*, and *Non-Voting*$_{1928}$ $*$ *Foreign-Born*. The Chow test on the full model also indicates behavioral heterogeneity.

We next want to examine the results of the Lagrange multiplier (LM) diagnostics to see whether the OLS estimation has accounted for all spatial dependence in the data. The results of these diagnostics are reported in Table 7.2. As can be seen, each of the four LM tests is statistically significant. Using the decision rule in Section 5.3, we can see that the appropriate model is a spatial lag model. Both of the standard LM tests are significant, although the value of the LM test for spatial lag dependence is larger than the value of the LM test for spatial error dependence. Turning to the robust LM diagnostics, we can see that the robust LM lag diagnostic is again larger than the robust LM error diagnostic. As a result, we should estimate a spatial lag spatial regimes model.

7.4.1 Instrumental Variables Spatial Lag Spatial Regimes Model

I employ an instrumental variables specification for the spatial lag model. For instruments for the spatial lag term I employ lagged versions of the six covariates in the model. I again model behavioral heterogeneity in parameters via a switching regression specification. Because the Breusch–Pagan diagnostic

TABLE 7.1. *OLS Estimates for Change in Democratic Vote, 1928–1932*

Section	Covariate	Estimates	Chow
Plains	*Intercept*	−0.10** (0.03)	10.69**
South	*Intercept*	−0.24** (0.03)	
Plains	*Republican* $Vote_{1928}$	0.32** (0.05)	30.74**
South	*Republican* $Vote_{1928}$	0.69** (0.05)	
Plains	*Non-*$Voting_{1928}$	0.33** (0.06)	0.93
South	*Non-*$Voting_{1928}$	0.27** (0.03)	
Plains	*Foreign-Born*	0.60 (0.32)	0.00
South	*Foreign-Born*	0.57 (0.81)	
Plains	*Rep.*$Vote_{1928}$**Foreign-Born*	0.82 (0.53)	17.85**
South	*Rep.*$Vote_{1928}$**Foreign-Born*	−5.19** (1.32)	
Plains	*Non-*$Voting_{1928}$**Foreign-Born*	−2.25** (0.68)	23.81**
South	*Non-*$Voting_{1928}$**Foreign-Born*	3.46** (0.96)	
Plains	*Rural*	0.04** (0.01)	0.50
South	*Rural*	0.05** (0.01)	
	Model Chow		17.15**

$N = 1651$.
$R^2 = 0.57$.
* $p < 0.05$, ** $p < 0.01$.

TABLE 7.2. *Diagnostics for Spatial Dependence in OLS Model of Change in Democratic Vote, 1928–1932*

Diagnostic	Value
Lagrange multiplier (error)	660.40*
Lagrange multiplier (lag)	691.30*
Robust Lagrange multiplier (error)	35.15*
Robust Lagrange multiplier (lag)	66.05*

*$p < 0.01$.

TABLE 7.3. *OLS and IV Spatial Lag Estimates for Change in Democratic Vote, 1928–1932*

Section	Covariate	Estimator	Estimates	Estimator	Estimates	IV Chow
Plains	*Intercept*	OLS	−0.10**	IV Lag	−0.10**	11.30**
			(0.03)		(0.02)	
South	*Intercept*	OLS	−0.24**	IV Lag	−0.22**	
			(0.03)		(0.03)	
Plains	*Republican Vote*$_{1928}$	OLS	0.32**	IV Lag	0.20**	30.33**
			(0.05)		(0.04)	
South	*Republican Vote*$_{1928}$	OLS	0.69**	IV Lag	0.50**	
			(0.05)		(0.04)	
Plains	*Non-Voting*$_{1928}$	OLS	0.33**	IV Lag	0.22**	0.13
			(0.06)		(0.04)	
South	*Non-Voting*$_{1928}$	OLS	0.27**	IV Lag	0.24**	
			(0.03)		(0.03)	
Plains	*Foreign-Born*	OLS	0.60	IV Lag	0.02	0.00
			(0.32)		(0.25)	
South	*Foreign-Born*	OLS	0.57	IV Lag	0.04	
			(0.81)		(0.70)	
Plains	*Rep.Vote*$_{1928}$***Foreign-Born*	OLS	0.82	IV Lag	0.90*	7.15**
			(0.53)		(0.40)	
South	*Rep.Vote*$_{1928}$***Foreign-Born*	OLS	−5.19**	IV Lag	−2.39*	
			(1.32)		(1.17)	
Plains	*Non-Voting*$_{1928}$***Foreign-Born*	OLS	−2.25**	IV Lag	−0.84	5.75*
			(0.68)		(0.52)	
South	*Non-Voting*$_{1928}$***Foreign-Born*	OLS	3.46**	IV Lag	1.58	
			(0.96)		(0.84)	
Plains	*Rural*	OLS	0.04**	IV Lag	0.03**	0.72
			(0.01)		(0.01)	
South	*Rural*	OLS	0.05**	IV Lag	0.02**	
			(0.01)		(0.01)	
	ρ			IV Lag	0.55**	
					(0.05)	
	Model Chow					50.78**
R^2			0.57		0.64	

$N = 1651$.
* $p < 0.05$, ** $p < 0.01$.

indicates heteroskedasticity ($p < 0.01$), I estimate the instrumental variables model with a groupwise heteroskedasticity variable in which the error variances are allowed to vary across the two spatial regimes in the data. The estimates from the instrumental variables spatial regime model are reported in Table 7.3 beside the estimates for the OLS spatial regime model.

As can be seen from the estimate for the spatial autoregressive parameter, ρ, there is significant spatial lag dependence in the presence of covariates. Accounting for this spatial dependence produces some noticeable differences in the sizes of the effects of the covariates in the model. Most strikingly, the counterintuitive negative effect of the $Non\text{-}Voting_{1928} * Foreign\text{-}Born$ interaction disappears in the instrumental variables specification, failing to reach statistical significance. Thus, had we ignored the spatial dependence in the data and estimated a standard OLS model, as we typically do, we would have concluded that the joint presence of two groups with weak prior attachments to the political parties, non-voters and immigrants, impeded shifts toward the Democratic party. By modeling the spatial dependence in changes in support for the Democrats between 1928 and 1932, we can see that this negative effect is merely a methodological artifact from ignoring the spatial dependence in the OLS specification.

Modeling the spatial dependence through an instrumental variables specification also affects our understanding of the $Republican\ Vote_{1928} * Foreign\text{-}Born$ interaction. The OLS model indicates no effect of such an interaction on changes in Democratic support. The instrumental variables model, in contrast, indicates that there is an additional gain for the Democrats in the joint presence of populations particularly likely to experience conversion and mobilization during this period. Although it is impossible with aggregate data to determine the contributions of mobilization and conversion to the upsurge in Democratic support, the instrumental variables estimates are consistent with the presence of both forms of realignment dynamics. In contrast to the OLS estimates, the instrumental variables estimates give no reason to believe that past partisanship or habitual non-voting impeded the shift to the Democrats in the Plains.

Turning to the spatial Chow tests, we see that there is again evidence of spatial heterogeneity in the instrumental variables estimates. As can be seen in Table 7.3, the instrumental variables Chow tests are significant for the intercept, $Republican\ Vote_{1928}$, $Republican\ Vote_{1928} * Foreign\text{-}Born$, and $Non\text{-}Voting_{1928} * Foreign\text{-}Born$, the same covariates that exhibited spatial heterogeneity in the OLS estimates. The Chow test on the full model also indicates significant behavioral heterogeneity.

In this case, our inferences regarding heterogeneity in effects between the Plains and the South would have been the same whether we employed an OLS estimation or an instrumental variables spatial lag estimation. However, our OLS model would have been fundamentally misspecified, failing to capture the spatial lag dependence in the data. And, as a consequence, we would have drawn incorrect inferences regarding the substantive effects of some of the covariates in our model. Had we employed a standard, constant coefficients model rather than the spatial lag spatial regimes model, we would have failed to capture the spatial heterogeneity in our data. In short, employing a spatial lag spatial regimes model provides significant leverage over either an OLS

spatial regimes estimation or a standard OLS estimation in modeling spatial dependence and heterogeneity in the data.

7.5 SPATIAL EXPANSION MODELS

In contrast to the discrete spatial heterogeneity implicit in a spatial regimes approach, we may posit instead continuous spatial heterogeneity in parameters. Here, continuous parameter heterogeneity is typically conceived of as reflecting a continuous spatial drift in a parameter across spatial locations, where the parameter takes on differing values at each spatial location and there is a continuous drift in the parameter values as one moves across space. The principal approaches for modeling this continuous spatial heterogeneity are spatial expansion models and geographically weighted regression (GWR) models.

Casetti (1972) proposed a spatial expansion modeling approach for modeling spatial heterogeneity in parameters. In the spatial expansion model, the parameters of an initial model are themselves modeled as functions of a set of covariates in an expansion equation, producing a combined terminal model. As in a standard hierarchical modeling approach, lower level areal units could be conceived of as nested within higher-level areal units, with lower–level parameters modeled as a function of higher-level effects. This approach, however, will generally not prove useful in modeling continous parameter heterogeneity. Instead, we will typically model the parameters in the initial equation as functions of the *x*,*y* coordinates of the observations. Thus, the spatial expansion model for continuous parameter heterogeneity may take the form

$$y_i = \alpha_0 + X_i\beta_{1i} + \varepsilon_i \tag{7.9}$$

with

$$\beta_i = \gamma_0 + \gamma_1 z_{1i} + \gamma_2 z_{2i} + \mu_i \tag{7.10}$$

producing the combined model

$$y_i = \alpha_0 + \gamma_0 x_i + \gamma_1 z_{1i} x_i + \gamma_2 z_{2i} x_i + \mu_i x_i + \varepsilon_i, \tag{7.11}$$

where z_1 and z_2 are covariates measuring the *x*,*y* coordinates, ε_i is the error term in the initial equation, and μ_i is the error term in the expansion equation. The simple linear expansion in coordinates can be modified to reflect more realistic trend surfaces, such as a second-degree polynomial allowing for curvature of the surface or higher-degree polynomials to incorporate multiple inflection points on the surface. Clearly, the inclusion of the error term μ_i in the expansion equation induces heteroskedasticity. The error variance will include a constant variance σ_ε^2 from the initial model as well as a sum of squares of the expanded variables weighted by the error variance in the expansion equation $(\sigma_\mu^2)(x^2)$ (Anselin 1992b, 341). This heteroskedasticity is modeled via FGLS.

7.5.1 Heteroskedasticity in the Spatial Expansion Model

In an important analysis, Anselin (1992b) examined the presence of heteroskedasticity and of spatial dependence in a spatial expansion specification. Anselin considered two alternative spatial expansion models. The first is a simple random expansion model, where the initial model takes the form

$$y_i = \alpha_0 + \beta_1 x_i + \varepsilon_i \tag{7.12}$$

and the expansion equation takes the form

$$\beta_1 = \beta_0 + \gamma_1 z_1 + \gamma_2 z_2 + \mu \tag{7.13}$$

where the error term, μ, has a zero mean. The second model, a misspecified random expansion model, differs from the simple random expansion model in that an essential expansion variable or variables have been ignored. As a consequence, the error term no longer has a zero mean expectation. This misspecified random expansion model has the initial model of (7.12) combined with the following expansion equation:

$$\begin{aligned} \beta_1 &= \beta_0 + \gamma_1 z_1 + \nu \\ \nu &= \gamma_2 z_2 + \xi \end{aligned} \tag{7.14}$$

where ξ is a random error term with a mean of zero and ν is the overall error term, which only has a mean of zero when the expected value of z_2 is equal to 0 (Anselin 1992b, 338). As Anselin notes, any time that the spatial expansion model is not deterministic (i.e., any time there is an error term, as in either the random expansion model or the misspecified random expansion model), the errors will be heteroskedastic. The form of the heteroskedasticity differs between the random and misspecified expansion models, however. Consider, first, the simple random expansion model in its terminal form:

$$y = \alpha_0 + \gamma_0 x + \gamma_1 (z_1 x) + \gamma_2 (z_2 x) + \mu x + \varepsilon \tag{7.15}$$

or,

$$\begin{aligned} y &= \alpha_0 + \gamma_0 x + \gamma_1 (z_1 x) + \gamma_2 (z_2 x) + \omega \\ \omega &= \mu x + \varepsilon \end{aligned} \tag{7.16}$$

with ω as a heteroskedastic error term, with $E[\omega] = 0$ and for $E[\mu\varepsilon] = 0$, $\text{var}(\omega) = \sigma_\mu^2(x^2) + \sigma_\varepsilon^2$ (Anselin 1992b, 340–341). As is well known, heteroskedasticity does not produce bias in the parameter estimates, but does bias standard errors, resulting in the possibility of type I errors in inference. As a consequence, inference proceeds via an estimated generalized least squares (EGLS) approach.

In contrast to the random expansion model, the misspecified expansion model produces a more complex form of heteroskedasticity, as the error

term now also includes relevant unmodeled expansion variables. Presumably these relevant expansion variables have not been included in the expansion model because the researcher is unaware that they are relevant or could not collect data on them. Given the lack of knowledge of the true data generating process, the researcher is advised to instead employ any of three alternative approaches to modeling heteroskedasticity that are based on OLS estimation: White's heteroskedasticity-consistent covariance matrix estimator, Davidson and MacKinnon's heteroskedasticity-robust tests, and a nonparametric jackknife approach to conducting pseudo-significance tests for the parameters in the expansion model.

Importantly, whether the spatial expansion model includes misspecification or not, unless it is deterministic, heteroskedasticity will be induced in the errors. As a consequence, researchers employing spatial expansion models will wish to account for the nonconstant error variance that typically occurs with these models. Heterogeneity, in short, cannot be taken as merely limited to the effects of substantive covariates, but will also often extend to error variance as well.

7.5.2 Spatial Dependence in the Spatial Expansion Model

Although the spatial expansion model is designed to capture univariate spatial autocorrelation that is produced by behavioral heterogeneity across the spatial plane, this spatial heterogeneity and spatial dependence may actually exist side by side. In other words, spatial heterogeneity alone may not be the source of the univariate dependence that is diagnosed; instead behavioral diffusion and/or attributional dependence may also be present in addition to behavioral heterogeneity. As a consequence, spatial dependence may continue to exist even after heterogeneity has been modeled via an expansion of parameters.

Anselin proposes diagnostics for spatial autoregressive error dependence in the presence of heteroskedasticity in either a random expansion model or a misspecified random expansion model. Consider first, the former. Incorporating autoregressive error dependence into the heteroskedastic random expansion model produces the following specification:

$$y = \alpha_0 + \gamma_0 x + \gamma_1(z_1 x) + \gamma_2(z_2 x) + \omega$$
$$\omega = \mu x + (I - \lambda W)^{-1}\varepsilon. \qquad (7.17)$$

If the errors μ and ε are independent, the error variance matrix then takes the form

$$\mathrm{E}[\omega\omega'] = H + \sigma^2(B'B)^{-1} \qquad (7.18)$$

with $B = (I - \lambda W)$, $\sigma^2 =$ the variance of ε, and H a diagonal matrix (Anselin 1992b, 346–347). As Anselin shows, the resulting LM diagnostic for spatial

error dependence in a random expansion model with heteroskedasticity is

$$\mathrm{LM}_{\text{Expansion Error|Het}} = \frac{(e'V^{-1}WV^{-1}e)^2}{2\mathrm{tr}(V^{-1}WV^{-1}W)} \tag{7.19}$$

where, as Anselin (1992b, 347) notes, "V is the estimated error variance matrix from an EGLS procedure, and e is the associated residual ($= y - Xb_{\text{EGLS}}$)." The $\mathrm{LM}_{\text{Expansion Error|Het}}$ test is distributed as a χ^2 statistic with one degree of freedom.

The $\mathrm{LM}_{\text{Expansion Error|Het}}$ diagnostic is possible for the random expansion model because the heteroskedasticity in this model is assumed to follow a known form. This is not the case in the misspecified random expansion model. As a consequence, a testing strategy for spatial dependence in the presence of an unknown form of heteroskedasticity must be employed. Anselin (1992b) suggests a diagnostic based upon Davidson and MacKinnon's (1985) research on heteroskedastic-robust tests. This diagnostic takes the form

$$\begin{aligned}\mathrm{DM}_{\text{Expansion Error|Het}} = {} & (y-f)'MPF(\lambda)[F(\lambda)'PM\Omega(e)MPF(\lambda)]^{-1} \\ & \times F(\lambda)'PM(y-f)\end{aligned} \tag{7.20}$$

where, as Anselin (1992b, 348) notes, "$y - f$ are the OLS residuals, $\Omega(e)$ is a diagonal matrix of squared OLS residuals, $M = I - PF(\beta)[F(\beta)'PF(\beta)]^{-1}F(\beta)'P$, a projection matrix, $P = Q(Q'Q)^{-1}Q'$, with Q as a matrix of instruments, and $F(\lambda)$ and $F(\beta)$ are partial derivatives, evaluated under the null hypothesis of $\lambda = 0$." As Anselin (1992b, 348) showed, the partial derivatives simplify to $F(\beta) = X$ and $F(\lambda) = Wy - WXb$, where b is the OLS parameter estimate and $Wy - WXb = We$.

7.6 GEOGRAPHICALLY WEIGHTED REGRESSION MODELS

Geographically weighted regression (GWR) presents an alternative strategy for modeling continuous spatial heterogeneity in parameters. Where the spatial expansion method directly models the parameters as functions of the observations' coordinates, GWR employs distance weights to give more spatially proximate observations greater weight in the calculation of the spatially varying parameters (see, e.g., Darmofal 2008; Cho and Gimpel 2010). The concept is straightforward. An unweighted OLS model gives each observation equal weight in calculation of the common parameter, β. In a GWR, this approach is modified to weight observations' influences on the spatially varying parameter, β_i, by their proximity to unit i (see Fotheringham, Charlton, and Brunsdon 1998).

The GWR model takes the form

$$y_i = \beta_0(u_i, v_i) + \Sigma_k \beta_k(u_i, v_i)x_{ik} + \varepsilon_i \tag{7.21}$$

where, as Fotheringham, Brunsdon, and Charlton (2002, 52) note, "u_i, v_i denotes the coordinates of the ith point in space and $\beta_k(u_i, v_i)$ is a realization of

the continuous function $\beta_k(u,v)$ at point i." The continuous plane of parameter estimates is then sampled at particular locations. A common choice is the x,y centroids of the areal objects.

Locations near unit i are given greater weight in influencing $\beta_k(u_i, v_i)$ through the spatial weights matrix. Several alternative weights matrices have been proposed, with a Gaussian weighting function often employed. The Gaussian weighting function takes the form

$$w_{ij} = \exp[-1/2(d_{ij}/b)^2] \qquad (7.22)$$

where d_{ij} is the distance between points i and j and b refers to the bandwidth, which reflects the distance-decay of the weighting function. The bandwidth affects the spatial smoothing of the estimates, as smaller bandwidths produce a less spatially smoothed plane of estimates while larger bandwidths produce a more spatially smoothed plane (Fotheringham et al. 2002, 45).

7.7 APPLICATION: GWR MODEL OF SPATIAL HETEROGENEITY IN VOTING DURING THE NEW DEAL REALIGNMENT

We can see how GWR works in practice by examining an application to voting behavior during the New Deal realignment. In contrast to the application in Section 7.4, in which discrete heterogeneity in the sources of voting behavior during this realignment was modeled via a spatial regimes model, here I model continuous parameter heterogeneity via a GWR model. As a consequence, we can examine how our inferences regarding spatial heterogeneity in behavioral effects differ depending on the type of geographic heterogeneity we model.

Localized political geography has long played a prominent role in conceptions of political realignments.[1] Locations such as industrial cities (Andersen 1979), immigrant towns (Key 1955), urban counties (Burnham 1970), and rural antislavery locales (Sundquist 1983) have figured prominently in realignment studies, as scholars have sought to determine where changes in voting behavior have been located. Political realignments do not occur in all local electorates in a given election. Instead, they are localized, subnational phenomena, with changes in voting behavior concentrated in particular geographic locations (e.g., Key 1955; Nardulli 1995; Darmofal and Nardulli 2010). The localized nature of political realignments argues that political and demographic factors producing realignments may have disparate effects on voting behavior in different geographic locations. This spatial heterogeneity is well suited to an analysis employing GWRs.

1 Portions of this discussion of GWR models appeared previously in Darmofal (2008), which provides a more substantively focused analysis of voting during the New Deal realignment. Please also see Darmofal (2012), which provides a detailed discussion of the steps in estimating GWR models in the R package spgwr.

The focus of this application is on changes in county-level voting behavior between the 1928 presidential election and the 1932 presidential election that ushered in the New Deal realignment. The dependent variable is the county-level change in the proportion of the population voting for the Democratic Party between these two elections. I model the changes in Democratic support in the GWRs as a function of political and demographic factors. The first set of political influences involves the preexisting partisan and non-voting populations that were available to produce changes in aggregate voter support. Large previous Democratic, Republican, and non-voting populations provided ready raw pools for increases and decreases in party support. For example, where large prior Republican voting populations existed, this afforded the possibility of conversion of these Republicans into Democrats. Where large prior non-voting populations existed, this afforded the possibility of a realignment through mobilization of these non-voters.

I capture these political effects with three variables. The variable *Proportion* $Democratic_{t-1}$ measures the proportion of the county-level voting age population that voted for Al Smith in the 1928 presidential election. Because I expect the main effect of *Proportion* $Democratic_{t-1}$ to be negative (larger pools of prior Democratic voters, on their own, provide less opportunity for increases in Democratic support), I employ a one-tailed test for this variable. Two-tailed tests are employed for all other variables. The variable *Proportion* $Republican_{t-1}$ measures the proportion of the county-level voting age population that voted for Herbert Hoover in 1928. The variable *Proportion* $Non\text{-}Voting_{t-1}$ measures the proportion of the county-level voting age population that didn't vote in the 1928 election.

In addition to these main effects, it is also important to examine how social interactions between citizens and how local partisan contexts may have shaped changes in party support (Brown 1988, 1991). For example, it may be that the movement of non-voters into the Democratic camp was made more likely by the existence of a large population of preexisting Democratic voters in the county. To examine the effects of social interactions and context on voting, I included three interaction terms in the model: *Proportion* $Democratic_{t-1}$ × *Proportion* $Republican_{t-1}$, *Proportion* $Democratic_{t-1}$ × *Proportion* $Non\text{-}Voting_{t-1}$, and *Proportion* $Republican_{t-1}$ × *Proportion* $Non - Voting_{t-1}$. In addition to these interaction terms, I also included a final political variable, *Unemployment Rate*, which captures the county-level unemployment rate in 1930, as measured by U.S. Census data.

In addition to political factors, demographic factors may also have conditioned voting changes. Immigrant and Catholic populations figure prominently in accounts of the New Deal realignment, with scholars arguing that these groups were mobilized into the New Deal coalition (Key 1955; Andersen 1979). The sizes of the immigrant and Catholic populations are measured by two variables at the county level, *Proportion Foreign Born* and *Proportion Roman Catholic*. The final demographic variable is *Population Change*,

which measures the county-level population change between elections (in ten thousands).

Table 7.4 presents the GWR results for changes in Democratic support between 1928 and 1932. The first five columns in the table report, respectively, the minimum coefficient for the variable, the coefficient at the 25th percentile of the distribution, the median coefficient, the coefficient at the 75th percentile, and the maximum coefficient. The sixth column reports the coefficient for a standard model with global, nonvarying coefficients, with the standard error below in parentheses. The seventh column reports the percentage of observations with significant positive coefficients at a $p < 0.05$ level for all variables other than *Proportion Democratic*$_{t-1}$ (which had a one-tailed test). The eighth column reports, for all variables, the percentage of observations with significant negative coefficients at a $p < 0.05$ level. Reported below each model are the number of observations and the mean R^2 for the counties in the data. The GWRs are weighted by county-level voting age population.

Table 7.4 demonstrates the extensive geographic variation in the effects of the political and demographic variables. The minimum and maximum coefficients have different signs for each variable. For some variables, this is also the case for the interquartile range of coefficient values. Given this extensive geographic variation, standard global parameter estimates do not accurately capture the local effects of the political and demographic variables. This is reflected in the significance tests reported in the final two columns of the table. There are large percentages of both significant positive and negative effects for most variables.

Figure 7.1 shows how prior Democratic and Republican support, and the interaction of this support, influenced the political geography of aggregate changes in Democratic support in 1932. The upper left map in Figure 7.1 plots the GWR coefficients for *Proportion Democratic*$_{t-1}$; the upper right map plots the GWR coefficients for *Proportion Republican*$_{t-1}$; and the lower left map plots the GWR coefficients for the interaction term, *Proportion Democratic*$_{t-1}$ × *Proportion Republican*$_{t-1}$. In each map, counties with significant GWR coefficients (at a $p < 0.05$ level) are displayed in four shades of gray, with the effects of the variables on *Democratic Change* becoming less negative as the shades of gray become darker. In each map, counties with insignificant GWR coefficients are plotted in white.

As can be seen, there was significant geographic variation in both the main effects of *Proportion Democratic*$_{t-1}$ and *Proportion Republican*$_{t-1}$ and the interaction effect of the two variables on *Democratic Change* in 1932. This spatial nonstationarity would be missed by a standard model specification that assumes that parameters do not vary spatially. It is important to examine the possibility of such spatial heterogeneity rather than assuming that global parameters accurately reflect effects across the observed data.

TABLE 7.4. *GWR Estimates for Change in the Democratic Vote, 1928–1932*

	Min.	1st Qu.	Median	3rd Qu.	Max.	Global	% Sig. +	% Sig. −
1928–1932:								
Proportion Democratic$_{t-1}$	−4.892	−1.811	−0.759	−0.127	1.814	−0.162 (0.164)		72.0
Proportion Republican$_{t-1}$	−5.085	−1.746	−0.742	−0.195	1.434	−0.347 (0.153)	18.7	72.5
Proportion Non-Voting$_{t-1}$	−4.840	−1.890	−0.903	−0.309	1.370	−0.440 (0.144)	16.8	76.8
Proportion Democratic$_{t-1}$ × *Proportion Republican*$_{t-1}$	−2.130	−0.654	−0.151	0.431	1.830	−0.393 (0.152)	29.4	43.1
Proportion Democratic$_{t-1}$ × *Proportion Non-Voting*$_{t-1}$	−1.613	−0.372	0.026	0.298	2.166	−0.025 (0.110)	33.9	34.1
Proportion Republican$_{t-1}$ × *Proportion Non-Voting*$_{t-1}$	−0.777	0.134	0.351	0.619	1.423	0.706 (0.054)	80.6	9.4
Proportion Foreign Born	−1.159	−0.232	0.023	0.100	1.262	−0.232 (0.018)	41.2	38.1
Proportion Roman Catholic	−0.397	−0.278	−0.200	−0.073	0.108	−0.181 (0.011)	2.1	93.3
Population Change	−0.056	−0.004	−0.001	0.000	0.005	0.002 (0.000)	18.0	64.9
Unemployment Rate	−0.890	−0.459	−0.319	−0.217	1.183	−0.429 (0.044)	1.0	91.2
Intercept	−1.313	0.377	0.984	1.903	4.895	0.463 (0.144)	78.4	16.0
$N = 3090$, Mean $R^2 = 0.67$								

Coefficients with standard errors reported in parentheses for global model. One-tailed tests for *Proportion Democratic*$_{t-1}$, two-tailed tests for all other variables. Regressions weighted by county-level voting age population.

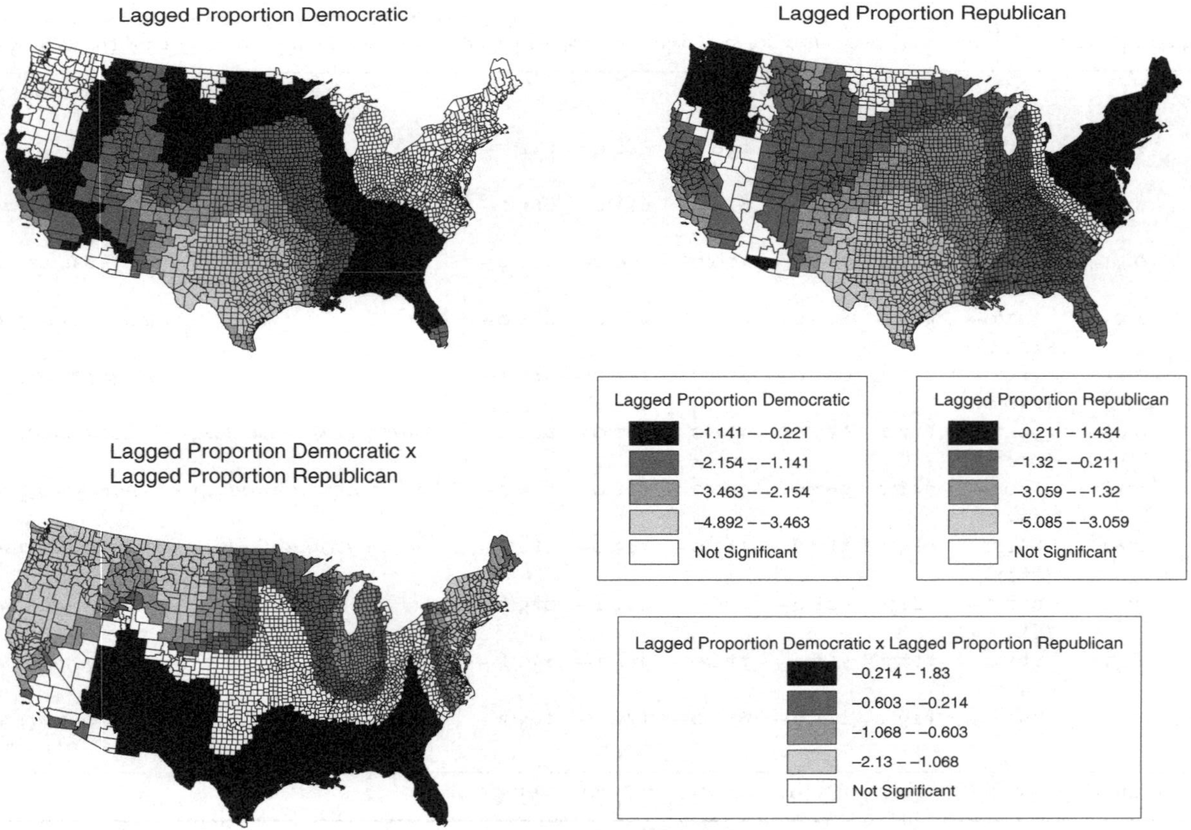

FIGURE 7.1. GWR coefficients for model of changes in the Democratic vote, 1928–1932.

7.8 CONCLUSION

Spatial heterogeneity is an often overlooked issue even among researchers who employ spatial models. Yet often in the social sciences we will have reason to expect that behavioral parameters vary across the spatial plane we are examining. The extent to which spatial heterogeneity is an issue will, of course, depend on the researcher's application. Many times, however, there is sufficient behavioral diversity among the units observed by the researcher to point toward the strong possibility of spatial heterogeneity. It has, for example, often been remarked that the United States is such a socially, politically, and culturally heterogeneous nation that we should expect significant heterogeneity in behaviors across the country (see, e.g., Gimpel and Shuknecht 2003; Chinni and Gimpel 2010).

Regardless of their particular research question, scholars should always examine whether spatial heterogeneity exists in their application. Unmodeled behavioral heterogeneity represents a serious form of model misspecification. In addition, not modeling spatial heterogeneity can lead to the unnecessary estimation of spatial econometric models to account for spatial dependence that is, in fact, the product of behavioral heterogeneity.

An attractive feature of some of the modeling approaches that have been developed for spatial heterogeneity is that they allow for much greater verisimilitude in modeling behavioral heterogeneity than is typically incorporated in models in the social sciences. Consider, for example, our standard approaches for modeling heterogeneity in the social sciences. On the one hand, scholars often use a simple dummy variable approach, allowing intercepts to vary across the categories on the dummy variable, but not the coefficients associated with the substantive covariates in the model. Sometimes the dummy variable approach is extended to $n - 1$ dummy variables via a fixed effects framework in which separate intercepts are calculated for each unit in the analysis. The coefficients for the various dummy variables, however, are rarely explored for their substantive implications. As indicators of our ignorance of what makes units different from each other (see, e.g., Przeworski and Teune 1970; Stimson 1985), fixed effects dummy variables are simply used to account for heterogeneity across the units of analysis. Likewise, random effects treat heterogeneity across units as a nuisance rather than as a substantive concern.

In comparison to this brute force approach, however, modeling approaches such as spatial switching regression models and GWR provide much greater nuance in modeling behavioral heterogeneity. The switching regressions approach allows researchers to diagnose whether substantive covariates vary in their effects across discrete spatial regimes of the data via spatial Chow tests. Heterogeneity is not limited to intercept shifts, but instead, behavioral heterogeneity in covariate effects can be diagnosed systematically across regimes. The GWR approach provides much greater flexibility in determining which units vary in these effects than do even spatial switching regressions.

The regimes chosen for switching regression models are typically determined a priori on the basis of substantive theory. However, these regimes may not accurately capture where covariates vary in their effects. The GWR modeling approach allows social scientists to identify behavioral regimes in their data that a priori expectations would not have been likely to point toward.

In summary, spatial heterogeneity is often an important substantive feature of the phenomena that social scientists seek to explain. It is rarely merely a nuisance to be accounted for. Given the substantive consequences of spatial heterogeneity for drawing accurate inferences, researchers should always examine whether spatial heterogeneity is present in their data.

PART II

ADVANCED TOPICS

8

Time-Series Cross-Sectional and Panel Data Models

Thus far this book has examined diffusion processes from a cross-sectional perspective. Diffusion processes, however, are inherently temporal: behavior diffuses across spatial locations over time. As a consequence, cross-sectional evidence can only be said to be consistent with a diffusion process; it cannot definitively demonstrate that diffusion has occurred. To gain greater leverage in the diagnosis of spatial diffusion we ideally would wish to have observations arrayed over both space and time (see also Franzese and Hays 2007).

Social scientists are increasingly employing such space–time data in which multiple observations are available for each unit over several time periods. Examples include demographic datasets where researchers have data on the population makeup of the same countries for many different time periods or political science datasets where researchers have data on voter turnout for the same counties in many different elections.

As Beck (2001) notes, there is a critical distinction between two forms of space–time data, time-series cross-sectional (TSCS) data and panel data, even though the latter term is frequently used to refer to both types of data in econometrics. In the former, the units are fixed and of interest in themselves, and appeals to asymptotics involve the time dimension (T) (since the number of units in any given time period is fixed). In contrast, in panel data, the cross-sectional observations (N) strongly outnumber the number of time periods, which often are only two or three. True panel data in this sense typically take the form of survey sample data (and thus asymptotics can be based on N). Given this distinction, most spatial models of interest involve TSCS data as the spatial locations of survey respondents are typically not publicly provided due to confidentiality concerns in survey sample panel data. The focus of this chapter therefore is largely on TSCS data rather than on panel data.

8.1 SPACE–TIME MODELS

The standard, nonspatial, TSCS or panel data model takes the form

$$Y_{it} = \alpha + \beta X_{it} + \varepsilon_{it} \tag{8.1}$$

where, in contrast to the cross-sectional models that have been considered thus far in the book, observations are indexed by both unit (i) and by time (t). Thus, rather than modeling observations measured for a single period or point in time, the TSCS model or panel data specification models repeated observations for the same units for multiple periods or points in time.

One potential limitation of the basic space–time specification in (8.1) is that this specification assumes that the intercept is the same for all units and for all points in time. Scholars recognize, however, that this assumption is often unduly restrictive and behaviorally unrealistic. As a consequence, recognizing this heterogeneity, scholars often allow the intercept to vary, typically by unit rather than by time. This variable intercept model takes the form

$$Y_{it} = \alpha_i + \beta X_{it} + \varepsilon_{it} \tag{8.2}$$

where the intercept, α, is now indexed by i, reflecting that it is allowed to vary by unit.

There are two principal approaches to modeling this heterogeneity in space–time data, the fixed effects model and the random effects model. In the fixed effects model, separate dummy variables are included for each unit (save one) in the data, and thus separate intercepts are modeled for each unit. In the random effects model, the variable intercepts are not treated as fixed, but rather as random draws from an underlying distribution.

Beyond the modeling differences in these two approaches, and the differing assumptions that they make regarding the correlation between the intercept and the covariates, they also differ in their applicability to TSCS data and panel data, with fixed effects generally viewed as applicable for the former and random effects as applicable for the latter. The reason for this differing applicability of fixed and random effects models for TSCS and panel data derives from the nature of the units being modeled. In TSCS data, the units are fixed and of interest in themselves and thus the use of fixed effect dummy variables to model a separate intercept for each unit (also of substantive interest in themselves) makes sense. Alternatively, in the panel data case, the observations are not fixed or of interest in themselves, but instead are sample data and thus the treatment of heterogeneity as a random draw from an underlying distribution makes sense for this type of data.

Whether employing a fixed effects or random effects approach to modeling heterogeneity across units, social scientists employing space–time models have also been cognizant that space–time data often exhibit either cross-sectional or temporal dependence. Explicitly spatial dependence, however, typically goes unmodeled. Instead, cross-sectional dependence is accounted for via the error

structure (e.g., through panel corrected standard errors [PCSEs] [Beck and Katz 1995]). Temporal dependence, conversely, is accounted for either through the model structure via a temporally lagged dependent variable, or via the error structure, by accounting for serial correlation in the errors.

Again, however, whether employing TSCS or panel data, the great majority of space–time models in the social sciences do not account for explicitly spatial dependence in space–time data, either through a spatially lagged dependent variable (with or without a temporal lag) or through a spatial error model. These are critical limitations in the existing space–time literature in the social sciences. The limited use of spatially lagged dependent variable models means that most social scientists do not model spatial diffusion across units in their TSCS or panel data models. The limited use of spatial error specifications in the social sciences means that most TSCS or panel data models accounting for error dependence do not take spatial proximity into account when modeling autocorrelation in the errors and thus do not employ specifications that reflect Tobler's First Law of Geography.

In the next sections, I examine a variety of models for spatial lag and spatial error dependence in space–time data. The next section examines fixed effects spatial models, considering both spatial lag and spatial error forms of these models. The succeeding section examines random effects spatial models, again examining both spatial lag and spatial error forms of these models. Next I examine spatial error components models and models with a temporal lag in their spatial lag. I conclude by considering a variety of Lagrange multiplier (LM) tests recently developed for models in which observations are available in both space and time.

8.2 FIXED EFFECTS SPATIAL MODELS

The variable intercept model in (8.2) can be written more simply in stacked form as

$$Y_t = \alpha + \beta X_t + \varepsilon_t \tag{8.3}$$

where $Y_t = (Y_{1t}, \ldots, Y_{nt})'$, $\alpha = (\alpha_1, \ldots, \alpha_n)'$, $X_t = (X'_{1t}, \ldots, X'_{nt})'$, and $\varepsilon = (\varepsilon_{1t}, \ldots, \varepsilon_{nt})'$ (Elhorst 2003, 247).[1] The fixed effects spatial lag model then takes the form

$$Y_t = \alpha + \beta X_t + \rho W Y_t + \varepsilon_t, \tag{8.4}$$

where $E(\varepsilon_t) = 0$ and $E(\varepsilon_t \varepsilon_t') = \sigma^2 I_n$ (Elhorst 2003, 249). As in standard fixed effects models, estimation proceeds by demeaning both the dependent variable and the independent variables. In other words, the observations on these variables as a consequence of demeaning become the differences between the

[1] This chapter draws on the notation and presentation in Elhorst (2003).

original values on the variable (i.e., for observation i,t) and the mean on the variable (i.e., for unit i). As a consequence of demeaning, the intercepts are absorbed and thus are not estimated but can be subsequently recovered. Generally the intercepts will be constrained to sum to zero so as to avoid perfect multicollinearity (Baltagi 2001, 13). Although ordinary least squares (OLS) is often used to estimate the demeaned fixed effects model, maximum likelihood (ML) estimation can also be employed. The log-likelihood function for the demeaned equation then is

$$
\begin{aligned}
&-\frac{NT}{2}\ln(2\pi\sigma^2) + T\sum_{i=1}^{N}\ln(1-\rho\omega_i) - \frac{1}{2\sigma^2}\sum_{t=1}^{T} e_t' e_t, e_t \\
&= (I-\rho W)(Y_t - \bar{Y}) - (X_t - \bar{X})\beta, \qquad (8.5)
\end{aligned}
$$

where $\bar{Y} = (\bar{Y}_1, \ldots, \bar{Y}_N)'$ and $\bar{X} = (\bar{X}_1, \ldots, \bar{X}_N)'$ and ω_i are the eigenvalues of the spatial weights matrix (Elhorst 2003, 250).

Instead of the fixed effects spatial lag model, scholars may instead wish to employ a fixed effects spatial error model. Such a model for stacked data takes the form

$$
\begin{aligned}
&Y_t = \alpha + \beta X_t + \varepsilon_t \\
&\varepsilon_t = \lambda W \varepsilon_t + \xi, \qquad (8.6)
\end{aligned}
$$

where, as in the spatial lag model, $E(\varepsilon_t) = 0$ and $E(\varepsilon_t \varepsilon_t') = \sigma^2 I_n$ (Elhorst 2003, 249). Once again, estimation proceeds by first demeaning both the dependent variable and the covariates. If ML estimation is then employed for the demeaned equation, the log-likelihood function for the spatial error model is

$$
\begin{aligned}
&-\frac{NT}{2}\ln(2\pi\sigma^2) + T\sum_{i=1}^{N}\ln(1-\lambda\omega_i) - \frac{1}{2\sigma^2}\sum_{t=1}^{T} e_t' e_t, e_t \\
&= (I-\lambda W)[Y_t - \bar{Y} - (X_t - \bar{X})\beta]. \qquad (8.7)
\end{aligned}
$$

As Elhorst (2003, 251) notes, space–time models with large N suffer from the same computational difficulties that cross-sectional models with large N suffer from. The estimation procedures discussed in Chapter 6 for large numbers of observations can also be employed for TSCS models or panel data models with large numbers of observations.

8.3 RANDOM EFFECTS SPATIAL MODELS

One of the criticisms of the fixed effects model is the degrees of freedom that are lost through the estimation of the many different fixed effects. The random effects model is an alternative approach for modeling heterogeneity that does

not result in this loss of degrees of freedom. The random effects model takes the following form:

$$Y_{it} = \beta X_{it} + \varepsilon_{it} \tag{8.8}$$

where, in this formulation, the error term, ε_{it}, comprises three different components:

$$\varepsilon_{it} = \alpha_i + \nu_t + \eta_{it} \tag{8.9}$$

where α_i varies across units, ν_t varies across time, and η_{it} varies across both. In this specification, $E(\alpha_i) = E(\nu_t) = E(\eta_{it}) = 0$, $E(\alpha_i\nu_t) = E(\alpha_i\eta_{it}) = E(\nu_t\eta_{it}) = 0$, $E(\alpha_i\alpha_j) = \sigma_\alpha^2$ if $i = j$ and equals 0 otherwise, $E(\nu_t\nu_s) = \sigma_\nu^2$ if $t = s$ and equals 0 otherwise, and $E(\eta_{it}\eta_{js}) = \sigma_\eta^2$ if $i = j, t = s$ and equals 0 otherwise, and $E(\alpha_i X_{it}) = E(\nu_t X_{it}) = E(\eta_{it} X_{it}) = 0$. When these conditions all hold, the variance of Y_{it} conditional on X_{it} is $\sigma_\alpha^2 + \sigma_\nu^2 + \sigma_\eta^2$ (Hsiao 1986, 33).

The random effects specification saves considerable degrees of freedom in comparison to the fixed effects specification. Rather than estimating separate intercepts for each unit, the variable intercept α_i is instead treated as a random draw from an underlying parametric distribution. Again, this assumes the particular applicability of random effects models for panel data, which, in the spatial case, may be particularly rare, as is discussed later. Note also that beyond this question of the applicability of the random effects model for spatial data, the random effects model also makes the critical assumption that the variable intercepts are independent of the covariates, an assumption that is not shared by the fixed effects model and that may not be appropriate in all cases.

Although random effects models have seen considerable use in the social sciences, these models nearly always ignore potential spatial dependence in the data. Standard random effects models can be easily extended, however, to incorporate spatial autocorrelation. The log-likelihood for the random effects spatial lag model for space–time data is

$$-\frac{NT}{2}\log(2\pi\sigma^2) + \frac{N}{2}\log\theta^2 + T\sum_{i=1}^{N}\log(1 - \rho\omega_i) - \frac{1}{2\sigma^2}\sum_{t=1}^{T} e_t' e_t, \tag{8.10}$$

where $e_t = Y_t^* - X_t^*\beta$, $Y_t^* = BY_t - (1-\theta)\bar{Y} = (I_N - \rho W)Y_t - (1-\theta)\bar{Y}$, and $X_t^* = (I_N - \rho W)X_t - (1-\theta)\bar{X}$ and ω_i are again the eigenvalues of the weights matrix (Elhorst 2003, 254). The concentrated log-likelihood function of ρ and θ^2 then is

$$C - \frac{NT}{2}\log\left(\sum_{t=1}^{T} e_t^{*\prime} e_t\right) + \frac{N}{2}\log\theta^2 + T\sum_{i=1}^{N}\log(1 - \rho\omega_i), \tag{8.11}$$

where $C = \frac{NT}{2}\log(2\pi) - \frac{NT}{2} + \frac{NT}{2}\log(NT)$ (Elhorst 2003, 255).

If, alternatively, a diffusion process does not exist in the data but spatial error dependence does, the researcher may wish to employ a spatial error random

effects model for space–time data. This takes the form

$$-\frac{NT}{2}\log(2\pi\sigma^2)-\frac{1}{2}\sum_{i=1}^{N}\log(1+T\theta^2(1-\lambda\omega_i)^2)$$

$$+T\sum_{i=1}^{N}\log(1-\lambda\omega_i)-\frac{1}{2\sigma^2}\sum_{t=1}^{T}e_t'e_t \qquad (8.12)$$

where $e_t = Y_t^* - X_t^*\beta$, $Y_t^* = P\bar{Y} + B(Y_t - \bar{Y})$, which is equivalent to $BY_t + (P - B)\bar{Y}$, which is equal to $(I_N - \lambda W)Y_t - (P - (I_N - \lambda W))\bar{Y}$; $X_t^* = (I_N - \lambda W)X_t - (P - (I_N - \lambda W))\bar{X}$; and $P'P = (T\theta^2 I_N + (B'B)^{-1})^{-1}$ (Elhorst 2003, 253). The concentrated log-likelihood function of λ and θ^2 then is

$$C-\frac{NT}{2}\log\left(\sum_{t=1}^{T}e_t'e_t\right)-\frac{1}{2}\sum_{i=1}^{N}\log(1+\theta^2(1-\lambda\omega_i)^2)+T\sum_{i=1}^{N}\log(1-\lambda\omega_i), \qquad (8.13)$$

where, again, $C = \frac{NT}{2}\log(2\pi) - \frac{NT}{2} + \frac{NT}{2}\log(NT)$ (Elhorst 2003, 253).

8.4 SPATIAL ERROR COMPONENT MODEL WITH SPATIAL AND TEMPORAL AUTOCORRELATION

In an influential recent article, Kapoor, Kelejian, and Prucha (2007) proposed a spatial random effects panel data model with both spatial and temporal autocorrelation in its error components, allowing for heteroskedasticity. Their model takes the stacked form:

$$y_N = X_N\beta + u_N,$$

with a spatial autoregressive error process pertaining to u:

$$u_N = \lambda(I_T \otimes W_N)u_N + \varepsilon_N, \qquad (8.14)$$

and an error component structure for ε that allows for temporal autocorrelation:

$$\varepsilon_N = (e_T \otimes I_N)\mu_N + \nu_N, \qquad (8.15)$$

where μ_N are the unit-specific error components, $\nu_N = [\nu_N'(1), \ldots, \nu_N'(T)]'$ are the error components that vary both cross-sectionally and temporally, and the remaining terms are as defined previously (Kapoor et al. 2007, 100). As Kapoor et al. (2007, 100) note, ε_N represents a one-way error component model, though one differing from the standard one-way error component model in that the data are grouped by T rather than N to model the spatial error dependence.

Kapoor et al. (2007) proposed three alternative generalized moments (GM) estimators for the spatial autoregressive parameter, λ, and the variance

components, σ_μ^2 and σ_ν^2 that generalize Kelejian and Prucha's (1999) GM estimator that was developed for cross-sectional applications. Like Kelejian and Prucha's GM estimator, and unlike ML estimators, Kapoor and colleagues' GM estimators do not make restrictive parametric assumptions and are computationally feasible for applications involving large numbers of observations. The first of the three GM estimators is based on a subset of three moment conditions while the second is based on these and three additional moment conditions. The third GM estimator employs a simplified weights matrix to make computation easier in large samples.

Kapoor et al. examine the small sample performance of their GM estimators as well as the ML estimator via a Monte Carlo analysis. They find that the second and third of their GM estimators perform quite well in comparison to the ML estimator in small samples. Specifically, the root mean squared errors (RMSEs) of these estimators for both λ and the variance components are only slightly larger than the RMSEs of the ML estimator. Little loss in efficiency occurs when these much more computationally feasible estimators are used in place of the ML estimator (Kapoor et al. 2007, 115).

A caveat regarding the GM estimators, is that, unlike the ML estimator, it is possible to produce estimates of λ larger than $|1|$ using these GM estimators. Kapoor et al. (2007, 117) noted that such estimates were rare in their Monte Carlos (< 0.01 of all estimates) (Kapoor et al. 2007, 117). Still, the possibility of explosive spatial autoregressive estimates is present with the generalized method of moments (GMM) estimator where it is not with the ML estimator. As a consequence, scholars may well prefer the more familiar ML estimation approach over the GMM estimation approach.

8.5 TSCS SPATIAL LAG MODEL WITH A TEMPORAL LAG

The models examined thus far have employed a simultaneous spatial autoregressive structure to model spatial dependence. An advantage of space–time data over purely cross-sectional data is that repeated observations are available for units over multiple time periods. As a consequence, unlike the case for a purely cross-sectional analysis, researchers can relax the assumption of simultaneous spatial dependence and allow this dependence to operate with a temporal lag, such as a one-period lag.

It is common for social scientists to incorporate dynamics into their TSCS or panel data models in the form of a temporally lagged dependent variable. Beck et al. (2006) proposed a TSCS model that extends the TSCS model with a temporally lagged dependent variable to include also a temporally lagged spatially lagged dependent variable. In other words, the model implies a conditional autoregressive process in which the spatial dependence is not simultaneous, but instead occurs with a one period lag, just as with the temporally lagged dependent variable. In this specification, therefore, unit *i*'s

neighbors' values on the dependent variable in the preceding period affect unit *i*'s value in the current period. This specification takes the form

$$Y_{it} = \phi y_{it-1} + \beta X_{it} + \rho W y_{it-1} + \varepsilon_{it}, \tag{8.16}$$

where ϕ is the autoregressive parameter for the temporally lagged dependent variable. A particularly attractive feature of this specification, as Beck et al. (2006, 40) note, is that it can be estimated via OLS assuming that there is no serial correlation in the errors. Of course, a critical assumption of this model is that the spatial lag occurs only with a temporal lag and is not instantaneous. If this assumption of a temporal lag is not valid, then the ease of estimation via OLS does not hold. The assumption of a temporal lag is more easily justified when the data are temporally disaggregated. Data for which observations are taken only at common but rare temporal intervals (such as decennial census data) are more likely to exhibit simultaneity in spatial dependence than are data for which daily observations, for example, are available.

8.6 APPROPRIATENESS OF RANDOM EFFECTS MODELS FOR SPATIAL AREAL DATA

The appropriateness of either a spatial lag or spatial error random effects model for most spatial areal objects has been challenged. As discussed earlier, Beck (2001) argues against the use of random effects models for TSCS data because the units in TSCS data are fixed rather than being a random sample drawn from an underlying population (as would be the case, for example, for a panel survey). The units examined by most TSCS analysts in the social sciences are irregular areal objects, even though most TSCS analysts in the social sciences likely do not conceive of their units in this spatial terminology. The notion of fixed units is thus particularly applicable for these spatial data given the irregular areal objects employed by these scholars. Irregular areal objects are, as Elhorst (2003, 255) notes, unique and exhibit features that set them apart from all other units. Typically, areal objects (such as countries) are examined because they are of interest in themselves. Spain is of interest to social scientists not because it is a random draw from an underlying population, such as a survey respondent would be, but instead because it has unique, identifiable characteristics that make it of interest as a particular areal object. From this perspective, scholars generally argue that a random effects model that would treat Spain as a randomly drawn representative of an underlying population is inappropriate.

8.7 SPATIAL HAUSMAN TEST

In addition to the differing underlying conceptions of the measured units, the fixed effects and random effects models differ in their assumption of the correlation of the unit-specific effects with the observed covariates. Specifically,

the random effects model rests on the assumption that the random effects are uncorrelated with the covariates in the model (i.e., $\mathrm{Cov}(\alpha_i, X_{it}) = 0$). When this assumption does not hold, the random effects estimator is inconsistent. The fixed effects estimator, in contrast, does not rest on the assumption that unit-specific factors are uncorrelated with substantive covariates and is consistent whether or not the covariance is zero. When the covariance is zero, however, the fixed effects estimator will be less efficient than the random effects estimator, and the (now consistent) random effects estimator will often be preferred instead. Alternatively, when there is a nonzero covariance between unit-specific factors affecting the dependent variable and substantive covariates (as is often the case), the fixed effects estimator is preferred over the random effects estimator as only the former is a consistent estimator in this case.

The Hausman test is the principal test for whether the assumption of zero correlation between the random effects and the covariates is appropriate and thus, whether the random effects model is appropriate. This test is based on the recognition that the asymptotically efficient random effects estimator will be asymptotically uncorrelated with its difference from the asymptotically inefficient fixed effects estimator when there is no correlation between the random effects and the substantive covariates (Hausman 1978, 1251).

Recently, Mutl and Pfaffermayr have applied the Hausman test to fixed effects and random effects panel data models incorporating spatial dependence. The random effects panel data model in Mutl and Pfaffermayr's spatial Hausman test builds off of Kapoor and colleagues' model with both spatial and temporal error dependence. Specifically, Mutl and Pfafferymayr extend Kapoor and colleagues' one-way error component specification incorporating spatial error dependence to also include a spatially lagged dependent variable.

Mutl and Pfaffermayr (2011, 58–59) present a four-step process for conducting the spatial Hausman test. The first step is to estimate the fixed effects model via instrumental variables while ignoring spatial error dependence by employing the standard within transformation that eliminates the individual fixed effects. Next, the estimated errors of the fixed effects transformed model are employed in a spatial GM approach to provide a consistent estimator of the autoregressive error parameter and variance components $\hat{\vartheta}_N = (\hat{\lambda}_N, \hat{\sigma}^2_{\nu,N}, \hat{\sigma}^2_{1,N})'$. Next, a spatial Cochrane–Orcutt transformation is applied and either GLS or the within transformation for the fixed effects model is used to obtain the feasible spatial GLS (random effects) and spatial fixed effects estimators, $\hat{\theta}_{\mathrm{FGLS},N}$ and $\hat{\theta}_{\mathrm{FW},N}$. Finally, the Hausman test statistic is calculated to determine whether a random effects model or a fixed effects model should be employed.

Mutl and Pfaffermayr examined the performance of their spatial Hausman test via a set of Monte Carlo experiments. They found that the spatial Hausman test is properly sized for most values of ρ or λ. Only for very large values of ρ is the test oversized. The power of the test is also strong, although it is lower for very large positive or negative values of ρ or λ. The size and power of the test improve further as either N or T grows in size, although the increase in power

is strongest for increases in N. As a consequence, the test is well suited even for applications in which only a small number of time periods are observed.

Two slight limitations of the spatial Hausman test are observed, however, when either serial correlation is present and is not modeled or the explanatory variables bear little relation to the dependent variable (Mutl and Pfaffermayr 2011, 61). If high levels of serial correlation are present in the errors and this serial correlation is not modeled, the spatial Hausman test is likely to have low power. When either ρ or λ is large and the substantive covariates have little effect on the dependent variable, the power of the spatial Hausman test is compromised. In all, however, Mutl and Pfaffermayr conclude that the spatial Hausman test generally performs well in detecting correlations between the random effects and the substantive covariates, even in small samples (Mutl and Pfaffermayr 2011, 66).

8.8 NONPARAMETRIC COVARIANCE MATRIX ESTIMATION FOR SPACE–TIME MODELS

Driscoll and Kraay (1998) proposed a GMM approach to estimation of space–time models as an extension of nonparametric covariance matrix estimation techniques developed in Newey and West (1987). As Driscoll and Kraay note, the advantage of a nonparametric approach to account for spatial error dependence is that one does not need to impose strong constraints on this autocorrelation via the estimation of (typically) a single autoregressive parameter for all observations. However, the standard nonparametric approach to correcting for serial dependence in time series is not directly applicable to the spatial case both because of the multidimensionality of spatial as opposed to temporal dependence and the fact that spatial dependence often does not exhibit the near-zero correlation for distant observations that standard time-series nonparametric approaches rely upon in the time domain (Driscoll and Kraay 1998, 549).

Another practical drawback of standard nonparametric approaches is that the cross-sectional dimension N is often much larger than the temporal dimension T. As Driscoll and Kraay (1998, 550) note, when N is large relative to T, it is impossible to estimate the many separate elements of the covariance matrix using the standard GMM approach.

Driscoll and Kraay proposed a GMM estimation approach that is applicable for the case of multidimensional spatial autocorrelation even when N is large relative to T, assuming that T is sufficiently large. (Nonparametric error covariance matrix estimation is not applicable, as Driscoll and Kraay [1998, 559] note, when only a single cross section of data is available.) Moreover, their approach relaxes the standard assumption of fixed N and is thus applicable even in the limiting case of N approaching infinity (Driscoll and Kraay 1998, 550). Driscoll and Kraay's approach is to employ a transformation of the standard orthogonality conditions for GMM estimation of the covariance

matrix. Specifically, Driscoll and Kraay (1998, 551) "define an $R \times 1$ vector of cross-sectional averages, $h_t(\theta) = (1/N)\sum_{i=1}^{N} h_{it}(\theta)\ldots$[and then] identify the model using only the $R \times 1$ vector of cross-sectional averages of the moment conditions, that is, $E[h_t(\theta)] = 0$," where R is the number of orthogonality conditions required for identification. Employing this transformation, the consistent estimator of the $R \times R$ matrix has only $R(R = 1)/2$ distinct elements, as opposed to the standard approach containing $NR(NR + 1)/2$ distinct elements, and thus the size of the cross-sectional dimension is no longer an issue in the estimation of the matrix (Driscoll and Kraay 1998, 551). Driscoll and Kraay show that their GMM estimator is consistent. In addition, it is asymptotically normally distributed when the mixing random field is asymptotically covariance stationary (Driscoll and Kraay 1998, 552–553).

Driscoll and Kraay employed Monte Carlo experiments to examine the performance of the standard nonparametric covariance matrix estimator that requires the estimation of all of the elements of the $NR \times NR$ matrix of spatial correlations, their alternative GMM estimator, the OLS estimator, and Zellner's (1962) seemingly unrelated regressions (SUR) estimator. First, they found that the standard nonparametric estimator performs poorly when N and T are similar in size, producing standard error estimates that are biased downward. As a consequence, the standard nonparametric approach to estimation of the covariance matrix should not be employed unless T is considerably larger than N.

Second, they found that the OLS estimator produces standard errors that are biased downward considerably even for only moderate levels of spatial dependence. The SUR estimator exhibits similar bias even in the absence of spatial dependence. In contrast to this, Driscoll and Kraay's GMM estimator exhibits little bias whether or not temporal dependence is present in the data generating process. Their estimator generally outperforms the OLS estimator, with one exception. When there is no spatial dependence and the number of time periods examined is small, the OLS estimator outperforms Driscoll and Kraay's nonparametric covariance matrix estimator, with the latter producing downward bias in its standard error estimates. This problem becomes less severe when the time dimension is expanded. An important limitation of Driscoll and Kraay's estimator is that it is applicable only for balanced panel data, that is, for data on which there are no missing observations for some of the units. Hoechle (2007) has recently revised Driscoll and Kraay's estimator so that it is applicable to unbalanced data and demonstrates via Monte Carlos that this revised estimator outperforms alternative estimators in the presence of spatial dependence.

8.9 LAGRANGE MULTIPLIER TESTS FOR SPACE–TIME MODELS

One of the most active areas of research on space–time models is in the development of LM tests for these models. Baltagi and his coauthors have

been particularly active in developing a variety of LM tests for space–time models (see Baltagi, Song, and Koh 2003; Baltagi et al. 2007; Baltagi and Liu 2008; Baltagi, Song, and Kwon 2009). Among these are tests for the absence of spatial lag dependence, spatial error dependence, random effects, serial correlation, and heteroskedasticity as well as joint tests for the absence of more than one feature of these data and conditional tests for a feature in the possible presence of another feature (e.g., Baltagi and colleagues' [2003] conditional LM test for the absence of spatial error dependence in the possible presence of random effects). This section examines a few of these LM tests, with additional tests discussed in the additional topics section (Section 8.11) of this chapter.

Consider, for example, Baltagi and colleagues' (2003, 128) LM test for the absence of spatial error dependence, assuming that there are no random effects. This statistic is

$$\mathrm{LM_{SE}} = \sqrt{\frac{N^2T}{b}}H, \tag{8.17}$$

where $b = \mathrm{tr}(W + W')^2/2$, $H = \tilde{u}'(I_T \otimes (W + W')/2)\tilde{u}/\tilde{u}'\tilde{u}$ and I_T is an identity matrix of dimension T. A standardization is employed to center the statistic at zero and scale its variance to one. This standardized test takes the form

$$\mathrm{SLM_{SE}} = \frac{\mathrm{LM_{SE}} - E(\mathrm{LM_{SE}})}{\sqrt{\mathrm{var}(\mathrm{LM_{SE}})}} = \frac{d_{SE} - E(d_{SE})}{\sqrt{\mathrm{var}(d_{SE})}}, \tag{8.18}$$

where $d_{\mathrm{SE}} = \tilde{u}'D_{\mathrm{SE}}\tilde{u}/\tilde{u}'\tilde{u}$ and $D_{\mathrm{SE}} = (I_T \otimes W)$. The $\mathrm{SLM_{SE}}$ test should be asymptotically normally distributed with a mean of zero and a variance of one (Baltagi et al. 2003, 128).

This baseline LM test assumes the absence of random effects. This assumption may not always be tenable in practice, and thus researchers may wish to relax the assumption. Researchers can do so via Baltagi and colleagues' conditional LM tests for the absence of spatial error dependence in the possible presence of random effects (i.e., assuming that $\sigma_\mu^2 \geq 0$). The first of these is a two-sided test, which takes the form

$$\text{Conditional } \mathrm{LM_{SE}} = \frac{\hat{D}(\lambda)^2}{[(T-1) + \hat{\sigma}_v^4/\hat{\sigma}_{\mathrm{RE}}^4]b} \tag{8.19}$$

where:

$$\hat{D}(\lambda) = \frac{1}{2}\hat{u}'\left[\frac{\hat{\sigma}_v^2}{\hat{\sigma}_{\mathrm{RE}}^4}(\bar{J}_T \otimes (W' + W)) + \frac{1}{\hat{\sigma}_v^2}(E_T \otimes (W' + W))\right]\hat{u} \tag{8.20}$$

and where $\hat{\sigma}_v^2 = \hat{u}'(E_T \otimes I_N)\hat{u}/N(T-1)$ is the ML estimate of σ_v^2 under the null, $\hat{\sigma}_{\mathrm{RE}}^2 = \hat{u}'(\bar{J}_T \otimes I_N)\hat{u}/N$ is the ML estimate of $\hat{\sigma}_{\mathrm{RE}}^2$ under the null, $\bar{J}_T = J_T/T$, $E_T = I_T - \bar{J}_T$, and $\hat{u}$ are the ML residuals under the null (Baltagi et al. 2003,

126, 130). The one-sided version of this test (e.g., against an alternative of $\lambda > 0$) is

$$\text{Conditional LM}^*_{\text{SE}} = \frac{\hat{D}(\lambda)}{\sqrt{[(T-1)+\hat{\sigma}_v^4/\hat{\sigma}_{\text{RE}}^4]b}}. \tag{8.21}$$

This one-sided test is asymptotically normally distributed with a mean of zero and a variance of one under the null for a fixed T as N approaches infinity (Baltagi et al. 2003, 130).

Alternatively, researchers may wish to employ Baltagi and colleagues' (2003) joint LM test for the absence of spatial error dependence and random effects (with the alternative hypothesis being the presence of either spatial error dependence or random effects). This test takes the form

$$\text{LM}_J = \frac{NT}{2(T-1)}G^2 + \frac{N^2T}{b}H^2, \tag{8.22}$$

where the terms are as defined previously.[2]

This is a two-sided test, which is not actually a correct test, given that the variance components cannot be negative. As a consequence, Baltagi et al. (2003, 128) propose a one-sided joint LM test for the absence of either spatial error dependence or random effects. This test takes the form

$$\chi^2_m = \begin{cases} \text{LM}^2_{\text{RE}} + \text{LM}^2_{\text{SE}} & \text{if } \text{LM}_{\text{RE}} > 0, \text{LM}_{\text{SE}} > 0 \\ \text{LM}^2_{\text{RE}} & \text{if } \text{LM}_{\text{RE}} > 0, \text{LM}_{\text{SE}} \leq 0 \\ \text{LM}^2_{\text{SE}} & \text{if } \text{LM}_{\text{RE}} \leq 0, \text{LM}_{\text{SE}} > 0 \\ 0 & \text{if } \text{LM}_{\text{RE}} \leq 0, \text{LM}_{\text{SE}} \leq 0. \end{cases} \tag{8.23}$$

Baltagi and colleagues' one-sided joint LM test has a mixed χ^2 distribution under the null

$$\chi^2_m \sim \frac{1}{4}\chi^2(0) + \frac{1}{2}\chi^2(1) + \frac{1}{4}\chi^2(2), \tag{8.24}$$

where the probability that $\chi^2(0)$ equals 0 is 1 (Baltagi et al. 2003, 129).[3]

Baltagi et al. examined the performance of the LM tests via a set of Monte Carlo experiments. They found that the test for no spatial error dependence that assumes that random effects are absent has misleading size when ϑ is .5, where $\vartheta = \sigma^2_\mu/(\sigma^2_\mu + \sigma^2_v)$ (Baltagi et al. 2003, 131). This test also has lower power than the corresponding test that allows for possible random effects for

[2] Baltagi et al. (2003, 129) also derive a likelihood ratio test for the joint absence of spatial error dependence and random effects. The LR test, of course, requires ML estimation of the spatial error model. Readers interested in this LR test are referred to Baltagi et al. (2003).

[3] An alternative one-sided joint LM test building on the work of Honda (1985) takes the form $\text{LM}^H = \frac{(\text{LM}_{\text{RE}}+\text{LM}_{\text{SE}})}{\sqrt{2}}$, which is asymptotically normally distributed with a mean of zero and a variance of 1 under the null hypothesis.

even marginal values of ϑ (i.e., $\vartheta > 0.2$) and for moderate values of λ. The difference in power becomes particularly large when ϑ and λ are large, even with large N or T (Baltagi et al. 2003, 132).

8.10 APPLICATION: GOVERNMENT IDEOLOGY AND REPRESENTATION

We can examine spatial space–time models in practice with an application to government ideology and representation. Political representation is a central concern within political science. Do elected officials represent the preferences of their constituents? Or do they act in ways that are not consistent with their constituents' preferences? Such questions carry with them critical normative implications for representative democracy. If elected officials' actions are reflective of their constituents' preferences, a delegate conception of representation is alive and well as citizens' preferences are faithfully transformed into public policies. If, alternatively, constituents' preferences exert no influence on elected officials' behavior, popular sovereignty may be compromised. At best, elected officials are pursuing their own conception of the public good even though it is at odds with their constituents' preferences; at worst, they may be engaging in rent-seeking behavior, reflecting their own interests in contrast to their constituents'. Whether citizens' preferences are reflected in the behavior of their government speaks, in short, to the influence of citizens in a representative democracy.

Scholars in a variety of disciplines are interested in the behavior of subnational governmental units. States in a federal system often provide useful variation on behaviors of interest that would be examinable over time only in a unitary system of government. By incorporating both cross-sectional and temporal variation in these behaviors in a TSCS analysis, we can gain significant leverage on the behaviors of interest to us. This is true no less for political representation. An analysis of the relationship between state-level citizen preferences in the United States and subsequent government ideology can shed considerable light on how representation operates in the United States. Because state-level government ideology is likely to be spatially clustered (e.g., conservative southern state governments and more liberal northeastern state governments), it is important to take spatial dependence into account in an analysis of the relationship between citizen preferences and subsequent government behavior.

For this analysis, I use Berry and colleagues' (2010) *State NOMINATE* scores that were utilized in Chapter 6's application to higher education spending as the measure of the ideology of state governments. The *State NOMINATE* measure actually uses Poole's (1998) first-dimension common-space NOMINATE scores for the state's members of Congress as a proxy measure for the mean ideology of the state government, under the logic that the state government should reflect the same ideological profile as the state's

congressional delegation (see Berry et al., 2010). I employ two measures to gauge citizens' preferences in the state, both from Enns and Koch (2013). The first, *Lagged Democrat*, is a measure of the percentage of Democratic Party identifiers in the state in the preceding year, and is thus a measure of lagged aggregate partisanship, or macropartisanship. The second, *Lagged Policy Mood*, is a measure of the state's citizenry's policy mood for more or less government in the preceding year, building off of Stimson's (1999) work on policy mood. For both measures, I utilize lagged versions of these variables under the assumption that responsiveness is likely to occur with a time lag as legislators gain information on the public's policy preferences. In the interests of parsimony, I include a single control variable, *Per Capita Income*, Klarner's measure of real per capita income in the state, converted to thousands of dollars. I conducted spatial TSCS analyses with state-years as the units of analysis for all 48 of the continental United States for all years from 1961 to 2010.

Before examining the results of the TSCS model, it is useful first to consider diagnostics for spatial dependence in the absence of covariates. There is reason to expect a significant spatial effect in the TSCS models. Separate year-by-year analysis of global spatial dependence in *State NOMINATE* scores utilizing the global Moran's I diagnostic and a queen contiguity definition diagnoses some significant spatial dependence. Specifically, in twenty of the fifty years examined, there was significant spatial dependence, always in a positive direction, utilizing 999 random permutations in each of these years and a pseudo-significance level of < 0.05.

I employed ML estimation for the TSCS spatial lag model using the `splm` package in R. For the fixed effects I utilized an absorbing regression, the within model, and thus there is no intercept in this model. The results for this spatial lag model are reported in Table 8.1.

As the estimates show, it is important to model spatial dependence in TSCS data. The results show significant positive spatial dependence in *State NOMINATE* scores. Neighboring states, defined by the queen contiguity definition, exhibited similar government ideologies. This spatial lag dependence would typically go unaddressed in a standard TSCS model. Substantively, in addition to the significant spatial effect, we can see that state government ideology responds to lagged macropartisanship, but not lagged policy mood. This suggests, perhaps, that responsiveness and representation work through the selection of partisan elected officials in elections rather than through elite reading of public opinion polls, though additional work is needed to determine the precise causal mechanism. Like lagged policy mood, per capita income has no effect on government ideology once partisanship and spatial effects are included in the model.[4]

4 I also estimated this model specification utilizing a GMM estimator. The substantive results were nearly identical to the ML estimates, with *Lagged Democrat* the lone statistically significant covariate, again at a $p < 0.001$ level. However, the spatial lag parameter, ρ, was only significant

TABLE 8.1. *ML Spatial Lag Estimates for State Government Ideology, 1961–2010*

Covariate	Estimates
Lagged Democrat	0.379***
	(0.025)
Lagged Mood	0.016
	(0.063)
Per Capita Income	−0.015
	(0.085)
ρ	0.219***
	(0.025)

N = 2400.
* $p < 0.05$; ** $p < 0.01$; *** $p < 0.001$.

8.11 ADDITIONAL TOPICS

The section on diagnostics in this chapter considers only a few of the LM tests developed by Baltagi and his coauthors. Researchers working with space–time data may be interested in exploring additional LM diagnostics for spatial lag dependence, serial correlation, and heteroskedasticity, and joint and conditional tests for combinations of these features of space–time data as well as spatial error dependence and random effects. Scholars interested in exploring random effects will be interested in Baltagi and colleagues' (2003) LM test for the absence of random effects (assuming no spatial error dependence) and their conditional LM test for random effects in the possible presence of spatial error dependence. They will also be interested in Baltagi and Liu's (2008) LM test for the absence of random effects in the possible presence of spatial lag dependence as well as their joint LM test for the absence of random effects and lag dependence. Scholars interested in spatial lag dependence in space–time models will also be interested in Baltagi and Liu's conditional LM test for the absence of spatial lag dependence in the possible presence of random effects.

Serial correlation in errors is often a concern in space–time data. Scholars interested in exploring this temporal error dependence will be interested in Baltagi and colleagues' (2007) conditional LM test for the absence of serial correlation in the possible presence of spatial error dependence and random

at a $p < 0.05$ level using the GMM estimator. No computational difficulties were encountered with either the ML or GMM estimation. An explosive spatial error parameter was estimated, however, utilizing the GMM spatial error specification, consistent with the cautionary note provided by Kapoor et al. (2007). Given this, the ML estimator is preferred over the GMM estimator.

effects as well as their two-dimensional conditional LM test for the absence of spatial error dependence and serial correlation in the possible presence of random effects. Scholars interested in heteroskedasticity in space–time data will be interested in Baltagi and colleagues' (2009) conditional LM test for the absence of heteroskedasticity allowing for spatial error dependence in a random effects model as well as their joint LM test for the absence of spatial error dependence and heteroskedasticity in a random effects model.

The LM tests discussed here only touch on the combinations of these features of space–time data. Scholars interested in exploring further the LM, joint LM, and conditional LM tests developed by Baltagi and his co-authors are encouraged to read further in Baltagi et al. (2003, 2007, 2009) and Baltagi and Liu (2008).

8.12 CONCLUSION

Social scientists often employ data in which observations are available both in space and time. The variation across these two dimensions allows researchers to answer research questions that would not be possible if data were simply limited to a single cross-section. For example, questions about treatment effects are questions that are inherently suited for TSCS data.

This chapter examined spatial models for TSCS and panel data. Often, scholars ignore spatial lag and spatial error dependence when employing these data. However, they should not. Just as spatial dependence affects cross-sectional data, so also does it affect data arrayed in both space and time. Scholars will thus often wish to adapt standard fixed effects and random effects models to incorporate spatial dependence in space–time data. The recent advances in LM tests for spatial dependence developed by Baltagi and co-authors provide scholars with a variety of new tests for spatial dependence in these data.

The models discussed in this chapter are appropriate when the dependent variable is continuous. Often in applied research, social scientists are interested in modeling applications in which the dependent variable is not continuous. The next chapter, on advanced spatial models, examines the application of spatial analysis to models for binary dependent variables, multinomial dependent variables, count data, and survival data.

9

Advanced Spatial Models

Thus far, this book has examined models that are appropriate when the phenomenon of interest is measured as a continuous dependent variable. Often, however, social scientists are interested in explaining phenomena that do not lend themselves to linear models for continuous dependent variables. Spatial autocorrelation also affects phenomena typically studied through these more advanced models, such as limited dependent variable models, count models, or survival models. However, although spatial dependence is likely to be present in many of these more complex phenomena, it is rarely modeled even by applied researchers employing these advanced modeling strategies. Instead, for example, event counts at one location are often assumed to be spatially independent of counts at neighboring locations. Clearly, such an assumption is untenable. This chapter examines how social scientists can incorporate spatial dependence in more advanced modeling approaches beyond the linear model. It examines several types of advanced models familiar to applied researchers in the social sciences: binary dependent variable models, multinomial models, ordinal models, count models, and survival models.

9.1 SPATIAL BINARY DEPENDENT VARIABLE MODELS

Many phenomena of interest to social scientists such as interstate conflict, marital status, recividism, and the like take the form of binary variables. As is well known, estimators for continuous dependent variables such as ordinary least squares (OLS) are not applicable for these dichotomous dependent variables. Estimators such as OLS suffer from heteroskedasticity and non-normality, assume incorrect functional form, and can produce nonsensical predictions when the dependent variable is binary (see, e.g., Long 1997, 38–40). As a consequence, scholars utilize maximum likelihood (ML) estimators such as probit or logit. However, although these estimators are widely applied in the social sciences, rarely do social scientists model spatial dependence in the binary

dependent variables of interest to them. This is problematic given the propensity of social science data toward spatial dependence. Interestingly, while spatial binary dependent variable models have been largely absent in the social science literature, these models represent a critical area of interest among current spatial analysis scholars, with many new estimators being developed in the past two decades. In this section, I examine these advances in modeling spatial dependence in dichotomous dependent variables.

The standard approach to motivating a binary dependent variable model is through the use of a latent variable framework. The observed dichotomous variable, y, is a binary indicator for the value of the underlying, unobserved latent variable y^*, where

$$y_i^* = X_i\beta + \varepsilon_i \tag{9.1}$$

$$y_i = 1 \text{ if } y_i^* > 0$$

$$y_i = 0 \text{ if } y_i^* \leq 0. \tag{9.2}$$

Thus, y_i takes on a value of 1 only if the value of the underlying latent variable y_i^* is positive, and takes on a value of 0 otherwise. In the standard binary dependent variable framework, ε_i is assumed to be an i.i.d. error term.

When the errors, ε, follow a normal distribution, the result is the probit model, with a cumulative distribution function:

$$\Phi(\varepsilon) = \int_{-\infty}^{\varepsilon} \frac{1}{\sqrt{2\pi}} \exp\left(-\frac{t^2}{2}\right) dt. \tag{9.3}$$

If, alternatively, the errors follow a logistic distribution, the result is the logit model with cumulative distribution function:

$$\Lambda(\varepsilon) = \frac{\exp(\varepsilon)}{1 + \exp(\varepsilon)}. \tag{9.4}$$

As is well known, probit and logit estimates of quantities of interest such as predicted probabilities typically are quite similar to each other.

Both the standard probit and logit estimators assume that observations are independent of each other, conditional on the covariates in the model specification. In other words, they assume no remaining spatial dependence in the data once covariates have been included in the model specification. This assumption, of course, is unlikely to hold in many applications.

Progress on spatial models for continuous dependent variables predates progress on spatial models for binary dependent variables. The latter present unique challenges to estimation. First is the particularly problematic effect of heteroskedasticity on parameter estimates in binary dependent variable models. When the dependent variable is continuous, coefficient estimates remain unbiased and consistent but are inefficient when the errors are heteroskedastic. However, when the dependent variable is dichotomous, coefficient estimates are also inconsistent (Alvarez and Brehm 1995). Because errors are typically

heteroskedastic when spatial dependence is present (see, e.g., McMillen 1992), scholars must be particularly attentive to heteroskedasticity as well as spatial autocorrelation when estimating models for binary dependent variables.

The second complication posed by spatial dependence is the fact that ML estimation of spatial models with binary dependent variables requires n-dimensional integration, where n again refers to sample size. Clearly, this is intractable in most ordinary sized samples of interest to social scientists. As a consequence, scholars have sought to overcome this difficulty through either of two approaches. The first involves an artificial restriction of spatial dependence via a restrictive neighbors definition followed by subsequent ML estimation (Case 1992). The second, more common approach, involves more realistic neighbor definitions employing estimation strategies other than ML.

9.1.1 Simplifying Estimation via the Neighbor Definition

Case (1992) seeks to overcome the difficulty of ML estimation involving n integrals, but does so through a quite artificial dependence structure. Case assumes that units are strictly nested within blocks. Within each block, units exhibit equal dependence with all other members of the block (i.e., all are treated as neighbors with a weight of 1). Units exhibit no dependence across blocks. Such a restrictive neighbor definition with equal weighting within blocks and absence of dependence across blocks eases ML estimation considerably. Case accounts for the heteroskedasticity implied by the spatial dependence and estimates her spatial error model via a ML approach. Although this approach does simplify ML estimation, the neighbor definition in such an approach is quite restrictive and does not correspond to how spatial dependence is conceived to operate in most applications. For example, it does not, except under the most restrictive definitions of distance between blocks, correspond to Tobler's First Law of Geography. Given the highly restrictive and unrealistic nature of this block diagonal approach to neighbor definition, it is unlikely to be appropriate for most applications. As a consequence, scholars will typically prefer other approaches to estimation of spatial binary dependent variable models.

9.1.2 Auto-Logistic Model

Besag (1972, 1974) provides one of the initial approaches to estimating a binary dependent variable model with spatial dependence. Unlike the models considered thus far in the book, Besag's auto-logistic model is a conditional model, where $x_{i,j}$, the observed value of the random variable, $X_{i,j}$, at the location (i,j), is estimated conditional on the values at other locations. This auto-logistic

model then takes the form

$$P(x_{i,j}|\text{all other values}) = \frac{\exp[(\alpha + \beta y_{i,j})x_{i,j}]}{1 + \exp(\alpha + \beta y_{i,j})} \tag{9.5}$$

where $y_{i,j} = x_{i-1,j} + x_{i+1,j} + x_{i,j-1} + x_{i,j+1}$ (Besag 1974, 215). Unlike a joint (simultaneous) model, the values at locations other than $x_{i,j}$ are treated as exogenous and are not explained by the model. This conditional modeling approach has seen its most extensive use in Bayesian estimation, in the form of a conditionally autoregressive (CAR) prior, which is examined within the context of spatial survival models later in this chapter.

A critical limitation of Besag's auto-logistic model is that it assumes that the errors are homoskedastic even though heteroskedasticity is typically present when spatial dependence is present. It is also of note that Besag's auto-logistic model differs from other spatial models for binary dependent variables in its use of the logistic function. Spatial probits have been employed much more frequently within spatial analysis than spatial logits because $(I - \rho W)^{-1}\varepsilon$ is not well defined when the errors follow a logistic distribution (Anselin 2002, 252).

9.1.3 The Expectation Maximization Algorithm

McMillen (1992) provides an extension of Dempster, Laird, and Rubin's (1977) expectation maximization (EM) algorithm to spatial probit models for either spatial lag or spatial error dependence. Unlike Besag's auto-logistic model, McMillen's EM spatial probit models account for the heteroskedasticity associated with spatial autocorrelation.

The EM algorithm involves a two-step process. In the first step, the expectation step, the binary dependent variable is replaced with the expectation of the underlying continuous latent variable (i.e., the expectation of y_i^* in the notation of (9.1)) given a starting value for the vector of parameters to be estimated. In the second step, the maximization step, the expectation of the log-likelihood function is maximized. The process is then repeated, with the expectation of the latent variable calculated given the estimated parameter vector and the expectation of the log-likelihood maximized again. The process is repeated until the parameter estimates converge. The resulting estimated parameters are the ML estimates.

Importantly, rather than limiting the extension to either the spatial lag or spatial error model, McMillen applies the EM algorithm to both spatial lag probit models and spatial error probit models. As Fleming (2004, 152) shows, the expected values for the spatial lag model are

$$\begin{aligned} E[y_i^*|y_i = 1] &= x_i^*\beta + E[\varepsilon_i|\varepsilon_i > -x_i^*\beta] = x_i^*\beta + \sigma_i \frac{\phi(x_i^*\beta/\sigma_i)}{\Phi(x_i^*\beta/\sigma_i)} \\ E[y_i^*|y_i = 0] &= x_i^*\beta + E[\varepsilon_i|\varepsilon_i < -x_i^*\beta] = x_i^*\beta - \sigma_i \frac{\phi(x_i^*\beta/\sigma_i)}{1 - \Phi(x_i^*\beta/\sigma_i)} \end{aligned} \tag{9.6}$$

while the expected values for the spatial error model are

$$E[y_i^*|y_i = 1] = x_i\beta + E[\varepsilon_i|\varepsilon_i > -x_i\beta] = x_i\beta + \sigma_i\frac{\phi(x_i\beta/\sigma_i)}{\Phi(x_i\beta/\sigma_i)}$$

$$E[y_i^*|y_i = 0] = x_i\beta + E[\varepsilon_i|\varepsilon_i < -x_i\beta] = x_i\beta - \sigma_i\frac{\phi(x_i\beta/\sigma_i)}{\Phi(x_i\beta/\sigma_i)}. \qquad (9.7)$$

The likelihood function used in the EM algorithm is

$$\ln L = \left(\frac{-n}{2}\right)\ln\pi - \left(\frac{1}{2}\right)\ln|\Omega| - \left(\frac{1}{2}\right)\mu'\mu, \qquad (9.8)$$

with $\mu = (I - \rho W)\hat{y}^* - X\beta$ in the spatial lag model and $\mu = (I - \lambda W)(\hat{y}^* - X\beta)$ in the spatial error model (see Fleming 2004, 152).

The final step of the process involves calculating uncertainty estimates for the estimated parameters. This is a problematic feature of the EM algorithm approach and a critical limitation of its use in practice. As McMillen (1992, 342) notes, "The n integrals of the likelihood function makes calculating the information matrix [in order to produce standard error estimates] intractable ..." McMillen offers instead a nonlinear weighted least squares approach to estimation of these standard errors. However, this approach is problematic because the resulting standard errors are calculated based on the conditional nonlinear weighted least squares approach that assumes that the spatial parameter, ρ or λ, is fixed rather than being allowed to covary with the other parameters as would be the case in an n-dimensional simultaneous ML estimation process (McMillen 1992, 343). As a consequence, the model cannot account for the covariance between ρ or λ and the other parameters (Fleming 2004, 153). The result, as McMillen (1992, 343) notes, is standard errors that are likely to be biased downward producing type I errors in inference. This is quite problematic and will lead social scientists to often prefer alternative estimation approaches for binary dependent variable models that do not lead to type I errors.

9.1.4 Spatial Expansion Model for Binary Dependent Variables

Given the computational difficulties associated with the EM algorithm and the tendency toward type I errors, McMillen (1992) also offers an alternative estimation approached based upon the spatial expansion model that was discussed in Chapter 7. Unlike the model discussed in the preceding section, this spatial expansion-based model can employ ML estimation rather than resorting to the EM algorithm.

Consider the spatial expansion model in (7.11) applied to a binary dependent variable. As McMillen (1992, 340) shows, in the probit case with $I_i = 1$ if $Y_i > 0$, the log-likelihood function for the spatial expansion model for a binary

dependent variable with no residual spatial autocorrelation is

$$\ln L = I_i \ln\left[\Phi[X_i\beta/g(Z_i\gamma)]\right] + (1 - I_i)\ln\left[1 - \Phi[X_i\beta/g(Z_i\gamma)]\right]. \quad (9.9)$$

An important feature of the spatial expansion modeling approach is that a functional form must be specified for the heteroskedasticity. If the functional form of the heteroskedasticity is properly specified, the estimates from the spatial expansion model are both consistent and efficient when there is no spatial autocorrelation in the errors (McMillen 1992, 336). Even when the errors are autocorrelated, the estimates remain consistent, though they are not efficient. As McMillen (1992, 341) notes, an attractive feature of the spatial expansion model is that it typically suggests a form for the heteroskedasticity. Unlike the EM approach, ML estimates for the spatial expansion probit model are derived through easily implemented iterated weighted least squares.

9.1.5 Recursive Importance Sampling Estimator

An alternative approach to spatial probit estimation is the computational approach developed by Vijverberg (1997) (see also Beron, Murdoch, and Vijverberg 2003). Vijverberg proposes a recursive importance sampling (RIS) estimator to evaluate the *n*-dimensional probit likelihood.

As Fleming (2004, 153) notes, the basic idea for the RIS simulation approach follows from McFadden's (1989) insight that computing the likelihood function is primarily a problem of estimating a mean. While terms in the likelihood may differ from the mean, building a probability distribution for these positive and negative errors from the mean can produce estimates for the likelihood function that closely approximate the actual value. The RIS estimator, a more general form of the widely used GHK estimator developed independently by Geweke (1989), Hajivassiliou (1993), and Keane (1994), employs an importance sampling approach that reduces the variation of these simulated probabilities (Vijverberg 1997, 283).

Beron and Vijverberg (2004) conduct a Monte Carlo analyis to examine the performance of the RIS estimators for spatial lag and for spatial error dependence. They find that the RIS estimator only very slightly overrejects the null in the absence of spatial error or lag dependence and that its performance is therefore acceptable when spatial dependence is absent. However, both the RIS simulator for lag dependence and the RIS simulator for error dependence exhibit low power when small to mild spatial dependence is present. Moreover, when these estimators do detect spatial dependence this is also not without problems as the RIS estimator for lag dependence picks up spatial autocorrelation when only spatial error dependence is present and

the RIS estimator for error dependence detects spatial autocorrelation when only lag dependence is present. Given the absence of robust LM diagnostics for lag and error dependence in binary dependent variables, Beron and Vijverberg (2004) instead proposed a decision rule focused on the likelihood ratio tests employed by the RIS estimators. If the likelihood ratio test for spatial lag (error) dependence is larger than the likelihood ratio test for spatial error (lag) dependence, the spatial lag (error) specification should be employed (Beron and Vivjerberg 2004, 182).

Importantly, Beron and Vijverberg demonstrated that both the RIS spatial lag and RIS spatial error estimators exhibit a positive bias for the estimates of the nonspatial parameter, β, in their Monte Carlo analysis. Moreover, this bias is larger for the spatial models than for a standard probit model, even when the proper form of spatial dependence is specified and modeled. Because the RIS estimator involves simulating a multidimensional integral of order n, the estimator also proves problematic for large sample sizes (see Bhat and Sener 2009, 246). As a consequence, researchers may have reasons to prefer an estimator other than the RIS simulator if their principal interest is in nonspatial model parameters.

9.1.6 GMM Estimators

Pinkse and Slade proposed (1998) a generalized method of moments (GMM) estimator for spatial error dependence. (Klier and McMillen [2008] demonstrated how Pinkse and Slade's estimator can be extended to a spatial lag model in a probit context if this form of dependence is diagnosed via their Lagrange multiplier [LM] diagnostic). Pinkse and Slade (1998, 132–34) established the conditions under which their GMM estimator achieves consistency and asymptotic normality. The estimator also accounts for heteroskedasticity in addition to spatial error dependence. The estimator proves problematic, however, in large samples because of the need for the inversion of n by n matrices (this provides the motivation for an extension of this GMM approach by Klier and McMillen in the form of a linearized logit model that avoids the problem of n by n matrix inversion). Another limitation of Pinkse and Slade's estimator is its inefficiency in comparison to other estimators.

Pinkse and Slade (1998, 132) motivated their GMM estimator within the context of a binary choice model that accounts for the heteroskedasticity produced by spatial error dependence. As Fleming (2004, 149) shows, the resulting log-likelihood function for Pinkse and Slade's model is

$$\ln L = \sum_{i=1}^{n} \left\{ y_i \ln \Phi\left(\frac{x_i\beta}{\sigma_i}\right) + (1 - y_i) \ln\left[1 - \Phi\left(\frac{x_i\beta}{\sigma_i}\right)\right]\right\}. \qquad (9.10)$$

The moments for the GMM estimator then take the form

$$\bar{m}(\beta,\lambda) = \frac{1}{n}\sum_{i=1}^{n} h_i' \left[\frac{(y_i - \Phi)\phi}{\Phi(1-\Phi)}\right], \tag{9.11}$$

with:

$$\Phi = \Phi\left(\frac{x_i\beta}{\sigma_i}\right), \tag{9.12}$$

$$\phi = \phi\left(\frac{x_i\beta}{\sigma_i}\right), \tag{9.13}$$

and h_i a row in the matrix of instrumental variables, H. The GMM model must estimate all the parameters together because the variances are not known but instead are functions of the weights matrix and λ. This involves the difficult optimization problem involving inverses of n by n matrices that are dependent on the spatial parameter (Fleming 2004, 150).

Fleming (2004) proposed two GMM estimators for binary dependent variables that avoid the complication of calculating n by n determinants. One is a spatial lag GMM estimator that is based on Kelejian and Prucha's (1998) two-stage least squares estimator for continuous dependent variables. The second is a spatial error GMM estimator that is based upon Kelejian and Prucha's (1999) spatial error GMM estimator for continuous dependent variables.

A critical limitation of Fleming's spatial error GMM estimator, in comparison to Pinkse's and Slade's GMM error estimator, is that Fleming's approach does not provide standard error estimates for the spatial error parameter, λ. As a consequence, one cannot diagnose the presence of spatial error dependence utilizing Fleming's GMM estimator. Fleming argues that this drawback may not be as severe as it first seems, as the spatial error parameter is often treated as a nuisance parameter. Still, if one is interested in diagnosing the continued presence of spatial error dependence in the presence of covariates in a binary dependent variable model, one may prefer Pinkse and Slade's estimator. Clearly, this will be applicable only in small samples because of the need to calculate n by n determinants using their estimator. In short then, a reasonable decision rule for a spatial error binary dependent variable model would suggest employing Pinkse and Slade's estimator in small sample sizes, particularly when the presence of spatial error dependence is a substantive concern of the researcher. Alternatively, in large samples, particularly when the researcher wishes to treat error dependence as a nuisance parameter, Fleming's GMM error estimator is preferred.

9.1.7 Linearized Logit and Probit Estimators

One of the problems of estimation of spatial binary dependent variable models is the need for the inversion of the $(I - \rho W)$ matrix of size $n \times n$ at each iteration (Klier and McMillen 2008, 462). Klier and McMillen (2008) proposed alternative linearized logit and probit estimators that do not require these matrix inversions and thus are applicable for large sample sizes. For researchers interested in employing a logistic specification, the linearized logit estimator also has an advantage over Besag's auto-logistic estimator in not employing a conditional specification. Both the probit and logit forms of the linearized estimator are now implemented in McMillen's **McSpatial** package for R.

Klier and McMillen's spatial lag estimator is a linearized extension of Pinkse and Slade's (1998) spatial error GMM estimator. Klier and McMillen's approach is premised on the recognition that the nonlinear model can be linearized with ρ set to zero. When $\rho = 0$, standard logit or probit can be employed and matrix inversion is unnecessary. In the initial step of Klier and McMillen's two-step estimation procedure, a standard logit or probit without spatial dependence is estimated. The probability estimates produced by this first-stage regression are $p = \Phi X\hat{\beta}$ and the generalized error, e, is $\frac{(y-p)\phi(X\hat{\beta})}{p(1-p)}$. The second stage involves a standard two-stage least squares estimation of $u = e + gX\hat{\beta}$ on gX and $gWX\hat{\beta}$ using instruments, Z, where g is the gradient vector. The final estimates minimize $e'Z(Z'Z)^{-1}Z'e$ with e linearized around $\hat{\beta}$ and $p = 0$ (see Klier and McMillen 2008, 462; McMillen 2013, 108). It is common to use X and WX as the instruments.

Klier and McMillen employed Monte Carlos to examine the performance of their linearized logit estimator. For small values of $\rho \leq 0.5$, the two-step approach produces accurate estimates. The linearized logit estimator does, however, overstate ρ at larger values of ρ.

9.1.8 Partial Maximum Likelihood Estimation

Recently, Wang, Iglesias, and Wooldridge (2010) have proposed a partial ML estimator for probit models with spatial error dependence. Wang and colleagues' approach involves dividing the spatial data into small groups or clusters in which adjacent observations are all members of a shared group. The partial ML approach provides for consistent estimates and more efficient estimates than a GMM approach. However, the division of observations into groups comes at a price of biased variance–covariance matrix estimates because of the spatial correlation between groups. As a consequence, Wang et al. employed the Newey–West approach also applied by Conley (1999) in Section 6.7. As Wang et al. note, the partial ML estimation approach occupies a middle ground between GMM estimators and full information ML estimators. As a consequence, it can provide a more efficient estimator than the GMM

approach without the computational difficulties of a full ML approach (Wang et al. 2010, 21).

9.1.9 Bayesian Estimation

LeSage (2000) proposed a Bayesian approach to estimating spatial models for binary dependent variables.[1] In the frequentist approach employed thus far in this book, the true population parameter of interest (say, θ) is fixed and the sample estimates ($\hat{\theta}$) used to draw inferences to this parameter are random. In contrast, in a Bayesian analysis, θ is random and the estimates $\hat{\theta}$ are treated as fixed, conditional on the observed data (Jackman 2000, 376–77). The quantity of interest in a Bayesian analysis is the posterior distribution of the parameter or parameters, conditional on the data. This posterior distribution is proportional to (i.e., the relative probabilities are preserved) the product of a prior distribution (which represents the researcher's beliefs about the value of θ prior to the analysis) and the likelihood (i.e., the likelihood of observing the parameter vector, given the data):

$$p(\theta|y) \propto p(\theta)L(\theta|y), \tag{9.14}$$

where θ again is the parameter vector of interest, y is the observed data, $p(\theta)$ is the prior on θ and $L(\theta|y)$ is the likelihood (Jackman 2000, 377).

LeSage (2000) employed this Bayesian approach to estimate the posterior distributions of parameters both in a probit model and in a Tobit model. (Tobit models are employed when observations on the dependent variable are censored beyond a certain value.) LeSage (2000, 33–34) notes that the Bayesian approach provides several advantages over alternative estimation approaches for binary dependent variable models. First, a Bayesian approach avoids the problems posed by multidimensional integration. Instead, a Markov Chain Monte Carlo (MCMC) simulation approach is employed. Moreover, unlike McMillen's EM algorithm approach, which provides biased estimates of dispersion, the Bayesian approach gives accurate measures of the dispersion in the posterior distributions. Also unlike the EM approach, the researcher does not need to specify a functional form (which, of course, may be incorrect) for the heteroskedasticity. Also, assuming that the researcher has prior knowledge of the parameter values, this can be incorporated in the Bayesian approach.

LeSage applied his approach both to homoskedastic models without outliers and to models that can accommodate heteroskedasticity and outliers. LeSage presents both spatial lag and spatial error versions of these models. An important distinction between LeSage's approach and the simultaneous autoregressive approaches to estimation discussed thus far is that he allows for the estimation of the autoregressive parameter for either the lag or error model conditional on the values of β and σ. LeSage employed Metropolis sampling to

1 For thorough introductions to Bayesian analysis, see Gill (2002) and Gelman et al. (2004).

sample from the posterior distributions of interest. LeSage demonstrates that the Bayesian estimation approach is computationally feasible even for large samples of 3107 (equal to the number of counties in the United States). (See http://www.spatial-econometrics.com for information on LeSage's econometrics toolboox of MATLAB® functions for Bayesian estimation.) Thus, in large sample sizes, where the researcher is faced with the computational difficulties of dealing with n-dimensional integration, the Bayesian Markov Chain Monte Carlo (MCMC) approach provides an attractive alternative.

9.1.10 Farlie–Gumbel–Morgenstern Copula Approach

Bhat and Sener (2009) have recently proposed a copula-based approach to estimating a binary dependent variable model that can be employed even for large samples. Their approach, which employs the Farlie–Gumbel–Morgenstern (FGM) copula, produces a spatial error logit model that controls for heteroskedasticity, which they label the spatially correlated heteroscedastic binary logit model (SCHBL). The copula-based approach employs knowledge of the marginal distributions of correlated random variables to derive the joint multivariate distribution of these variables. Specifically, as Bhat and Sener (2009, 248) explain, "[A] copula is a device or function that generates a stochastic dependence relationship among random variables with pre-specified marginal distributions. In essence, the copula approach separates the marginal distributions from the dependence structure, so that the dependence structure is entirely unaffected by the marginal distributions assumed. This provides substantial flexibility in correlating random variables, which may not even have the same marginal distributions."

Bhat and Sener (2009, 250) note that the FGM copula provides advantages over other approaches for modeling spatial dependence in binary dependent variables. Its closed-form analytical solution allows for direct ML estimation rather than the use of a simulation-based approach such as the RIS simulator. Unlike Case's (1992) restrictive approach, the FGM copula approach is quite flexible in the types of spatial patterns it can model.

One limitation of the SCHBL model, however, is that it can only capture small to moderate levels of spatial error dependence. Bhat and Sener (2009, 250) argue that this is not a serious drawback as high levels of spatial error dependence are unlikely if a model is well-specified. However, spatial error dependence is often quite high in practice. Especially in disciplines favoring parsimonious models (see, e.g., Achen 2002), the inability of the SCHBL approach to capture more than small to moderate levels of error dependence may pose a serious problem for researchers.

Bhat and Sener examined the performance of their FGM copula-based model (the SCHBL model) against the performance of a nonspatial binary logit model (ABL). They found that the SCHBL model provides a better fit to the data via

a likelihood ratio test (Bhat and Sener 2009, 265). They also found that the ABL produces misleading effects for explanatory variables in the presence of heteroskedasticity and spatial correlation (269). As a consequence, they argue for the use of their SCHBL model over the nonspatial alternative.

9.2 DIAGNOSTICS FOR SPATIAL DEPENDENCE IN BINARY DEPENDENT VARIABLE MODELS

In contrast to the continuous dependent variable case, research into diagnostics for spatial dependence when the dependent variable is dichotomous has been much more limited. Chapter 4 discussed join-count statistics that can be employed when the dependent variable is dichotomous. These statistics serve as a useful first step in diagnosing spatial dependence in binary dependent variables. If the researcher wishes to examine dependence in binary dependent variables in the presence of covariates, however, her choices to date are quite limited.

One critical exception is Pinkse and Slade's (1998) LM diagnostic for spatial error dependence in a probit model.[2] Because the error for the unobserved latent variable is not observed, Pinkse and Slade instead motivate their diagnostic by utilizing generalized residuals. Specifically, Pinkse and Slade employed generalized residuals corrected for heteroskedasticity, $\tilde{\mu}_i$:

$$\tilde{\mu}_i = \frac{y_i - \Phi(X_i'\hat{\beta}^P)}{\sqrt{\Phi(x_i'\hat{\beta}^P)\left[1 - \Phi(x_i'\hat{\beta}^P)\right]}}, \tag{9.15}$$

where $\hat{\beta}^P$ is the probit estimate.

The LM diagnostic is

$$\text{LM}_{\text{ErrorProbit}} = \frac{[\tilde{\mu}_i' W \tilde{\mu}_i]^2}{\Omega}, \tag{9.16}$$

where $\Omega = \text{tr}(W^2 + W'W)$. Pinkse and Slade (1998, 131) note that the $\text{LM}_{\text{ErrorProbit}}$ diagnostic does not have a limiting χ^2 distribution but instead a limiting distribution that depends on the weights matrix W. As a consequence, they proposed that a general replication-based approach be employed to determine pseudo-significance rather than employing a distributional approach to inference that will vary depending on the particular weights matrix that is chosen.

[2] In another study examining the application of diagnostics to binary dependent variable models, Kelejian and Prucha (2001) established the asymptotic normality of the Moran's I diagnostic for probit models.

9.3 APPLICATION: SPATIAL PROBIT MODEL OF IMMIGRANT DEMOGRAPHICS

We can examine how spatial binary dependent variable models can be applied by employing Klier and McMillen's (2008) linearized probit GMM estimator to an analysis of immigrant demographics in the United States. Specifically, this application focuses on the factors that promote counties having larger than average immigrant populations. The data for this application are for the year 2000. The dependent variable is coded 1 if the county had a larger immigrant population than the national county-level average in 2000 and 0 if the county had a smaller immigrant population than the national county-level average.

I model this binary dependent variable as a function of five substantive covariates. *South* is a dummy variable for whether the state had been one of the states of the Confederacy.[3] *West Coast* is a dummy variable, with states on the West Coast (Washington, California, and Oregon) given values of 1 and all of the remaining continental United States given a value of 0. *African American Proportion* is a measure of the proportion of the county's population that was African American in 2000. *Population Density* is a measure of the county's population density. *Rural* is a measure of whether the county was a rural county in 2000.

In addition to these five substantive covariates, I utilized a set of instruments, Z, for the spatially lagged dependent variable. The set of instruments I employed are the covariates in the model, X, and their spatially weighted versions, WX, where W in this case refers to a queen contiguity weights matrix.

The results of the GMM spatial linearized probit estimation are reported in Table 9.1 alongside those from a standard probit estimation without a spatial term in it. As we can see from the estimate for the spatial autoregressive coefficient, ρ, there is strong evidence of positive spatial dependence in this linearized probit model. In fact, the ρ estimate is unusually large at 0.989. Recall from the discussion in Section 9.1.7 that Klier and McMillen's (2008) Monte Carlos for the linearized logit estimator showed a tendency for this estimator to overstate spatial dependence as spatial dependence increases. As a consequence, we should be cautious about interpreting too much into this quite high point estimate for the autoregressive parameter.

Accounting for spatial dependence in the data, we can see that two covariates exhibit significant effects on the probability of a county having a larger than average immigrant population. Counties with larger African American proportions of their population had a decreased probability of having a larger than average immigrant population. Rural counties also had a decreased probability of having larger than average immigrant populations than other

[3] Alabama, Arkansas, Florida, Georgia, Louisiana, Mississippi, North Carolina, South Carolina, Texas, and Virginia are given values of 1 on this variable; each of the remaining continental states in the United States is given a value of 0.

TABLE 9.1. *ML Probit and GMM Spatial Linearized Probit Estimates for Models of Immigrant Demographics*

Covariate	(1)	(2)
South	1.194***	0.292
	(0.068)	(0.153)
West Coast	0.978***	0.013
	(0.122)	(0.167)
African American Proportion	−2.958***	−1.252**
	(0.272)	(0.444)
Population Density	0.000***	0.000
	(0.000)	(0.000)
Rural	−1.076***	−0.661***
	(0.062)	(0.074)
Intercept	−0.199***	0.424*
	(0.058)	(0.173)
ρ		0.989***
		(0.119)

$N = 3107$.
* $p < 0.05$; ** $p < 0.01$; *** $p < 0.001$.
(1) = Standard ML probit estimates.
(2) = GMM spatial linearized probit estimates.

counties in 2000. The remaining covariates had insignificant effects in this model.

Comparing the spatial probit estimates in column 2 to the nonspatial probit estimates in column 1, we can further see the importance of modeling spatial dependence. All of the covariates have statistically significant effects in the nonspatial probit model that ignores the spatial dependence in the data. The statistical significance of the *South*, *West Coast*, and *Population Density* variables vanishes in the spatial probit estimates. We would erroneously infer statistical significance for these three covariates if we had ignored the spatial dependence in the data, as we typically do in binary dependent variable models.

9.4 SPATIAL MULTINOMIAL MODELS

Spatial binary dependent variable models are applicable when the dependent variable can take either of two values. At times, however, social scientists are interested in dependent variables that may take any of more than two values. Such dependent variables are often called polychotomous (as they can take more than the two values that a dichotomous variable can take) and when the categories are unordered are examined via multinomial models. Alternatively, when the values of the polychotomous dependent variable can be ordered, such ordinal dependent variables are studied via ordered probit or ordered logit

models. Multinomial models are applicable across many social sciences. For example, political scientists often study voting behavior in multiparty elections. Demographers study migration to various destination choices. Sociologists study transitions into new occupations. Clearly, many of these multinomial choices involve a strong spatial component.

Two principal multinomial models are the multinomial logit and multinomial probit models. In addition to the differing link functions, the two models differ in how they treat alternatives other than the comparison being modeled. The multinomial logit model makes the quite restrictive independence of irrelevant alternatives (IIA) assumption while the multinomial probit model does not. The IIA assumption presumes that the odds of choosing alternative A versus alternative B are unaffected by addding or altering other alternative outcomes (Long 1997, 182). A classic example of a violation of the IIA assumption involves choosing between driving to work and taking a bus to work. If the probability of driving to work is 0.5 and the probability of taking a bus to work is 0.5, then the IIA assumption requires that the creation of a new bus company which differs from the current bus company only in the color of its buses does not change the odds of driving versus taking a bus (i.e., the probability of driving must then be 1/3, the probability of using the first bus company must be 1/3 and the probability of using the new bus company must be 1/3). However, from a behavioral perspective, it is much more likely that the probability of driving a car will remain 0.5 with the remaining 0.5 probability split equally between using either bus company (since they differ only in the color of their buses) (Long 1997, 182–183).

This IIA assumption is, of course, an unrealistic behavioral assumption that will often not hold in many social science applications. As a consequence, social scientists may wish to relax the IIA assumption when modeling multinomial outcomes. The multinomial probit model does not make the IIA assumption. The multinomial probit model allows for error correlation across choices because these correlations can be easily incorporated in the multivariate normal distribution (Long 1997, 185). However, the behavioral verisimilitude offered by the multinomial probit model comes at a high computational price. The multinomial probit requires the calculation of multidimensional integrals making the model computationally intensive. As a consquence, in practice, scholars often estimate the simpler multinomial logit model.

Bolduc, Fortin, and Fournier (1996) present a multinomial probit model with spatial autoregressive error dependence to account for spatial dependence in physicians' choices of the locations of their initial practices, where these location choices are measured as a polychotomous dependent variable. To ease estimation, these authors employ a method of maximum simulated likelihood estimation rather than ML estimation. In their model, physicians choose a location for their practice from a choice set of $j = 1,\ldots,J$ regions. Physicians are assumed to seek to maximize an indirect utility function V_j conditional on practicing medicine in region j, where V_j is a function of substantive covariates

in their model. The spatial multinomial model then takes the form

$$y_{ij} = \begin{cases} 1 & \text{if} \quad V_{ij} \geq V_{ik} \quad \text{for} \quad k = 1, \ldots, J, \\ 0 & \text{otherwise} \end{cases} \tag{9.17}$$

with

$$V_{ij} = X_{ij}\beta + \epsilon_{ij}, \tag{9.18}$$

with y_{ij} the physician's choice, V_{ij} the conditional indirect utility of establishing a practice in region j for physician i, and X_{ij} the K by 1 vector of covariates that produces this utility.

In Bolduc and colleagues' specification, the error term is assumed to reflect two independent components:

$$\epsilon_{ij} = \sigma_j \xi_{ij} + \nu_{ij}, \tag{9.19}$$

with σ_j reflecting a region-specific standard deviation and

$$\xi_{ij} = \lambda \sum_{k \neq j}^{J} w_{jk} \xi_{ik} + \zeta_{ij}, \quad \zeta_{ij} \sim \text{i.i.d. } N(0, 1). \tag{9.20}$$

Thus, one of the two components of the error process incorporates autoregressive dependence.

As Bolduc et al. note, these equations can be rewritten as

$$V_i = X_i \beta + \epsilon, \quad i = 1, \ldots, I, \tag{9.21}$$

where

$$\epsilon_i = T\xi_i + \nu_i, \tag{9.22}$$

with $\xi_i = \lambda W \xi_i + \zeta_i, \quad \zeta_i \sim N(0, I_J)$, and T a $(J \times J)$ diagonal matrix with standard deviations $\sigma_j, j = 2, \ldots, J$, on the diagonal of the matrix (Bolduc et al. 1996, 728–729). With $L = (I_J - \lambda W)$, (9.21) can be rewritten as

$$V_i = X_i \beta + TL^{-1} \zeta_i + \nu_i. \tag{9.23}$$

Bolduc et al. (1996, 729) demonstrated how response probabilities are calculated in their spatial autoregressive multinomial probit model. With $\delta = [\beta', \sigma', \lambda]'$, where σ is the vector of standard deviations and λ is the spatial autoregressive error parameter, "Define $P_i(j|\delta)$ as the probability of drawing a latent vector V_i with $V_{ij} > V_{ik}$ for $k \neq j \ldots$" The conditional response probability of choosing alternative j, given the vector ζ_i is, then

$$\Lambda_i(j|\delta, \zeta_i) = \frac{\exp\{x_{ij}\beta + T_j L^{-1} \zeta_i\}}{\sum_{k=1}^{J} \exp\{x_{ik}\beta + T_k L^{-1} \zeta_i\}} \tag{9.24}$$

with T_j denoting row j in matrix T (Bolduc et al. 1996, 729). The unconditional choice probability is then

$$P_i(j|\delta) = \int_{\zeta} \Lambda_i(j|\delta,\zeta)n(\zeta,I_j)d\zeta, \tag{9.25}$$

where, as Bolduc et al. (1996, 729) note, "$n(\zeta,I_J)$ is a multivariate normal density with mean 0 and covariance matrix I_J. A natural simulator based on R replications for $P_i(j|\delta)$ is therefore"

$$f_i(j|\delta) = \frac{1}{R}\sum_{r=1}^{R} \Lambda_i(j|\delta,\zeta_r), \tag{9.26}$$

which is a continuous function such that the sum of the $f_i(j|\delta)$ is 1.

Bolduc and colleagues' (1996, 730) maximum simulated likelihood estimator substitutes $f_i(j|\delta)$ for the probability $P_i(j|\delta)$. The maximum simulated likelihood estimator of δ, $\tilde{\delta}$, is consistent and asymptotically normally distributed. Equally important, as Bolduc et al. (1996, 730) note, "When the number of replications increases to infinity, the asymptotic distribution of the MSL [maximum simulated likelihood] estimator $\tilde{\delta}$ coincides with that of the ML estimator."

As Bolduc, Fortin, and Gordon (1997, 78) note, a criticism of Bolduc and colleagues' estimation approach is the specification error that could be induced by assuming that the error process is a mixture of a normally distributed component and an i.i.d. component. As a consequence, Bolduc et al. (1997) examine two alternative estimation approaches, a GHK simulator approach and a Bayesian approach, for estimating a multinomial probit model driven by a single error process reflecting a joint normal distribution.

Consider again a spatial multinomial model with the following notation:

$$y_{ij} = \begin{cases} 1 & \text{if } V_{ij} \geq V_{ik} \text{ for } k = 1,\ldots,J, \\ 0 & \text{otherwise} \end{cases} \tag{9.27}$$

Here, however, employ the following notation for the conditional indirect utility, V_{ij}, of establishing a practice in region j for physician i:

$$V_{ij} = Z_{ij}\beta + \varepsilon_{ij} \tag{9.28}$$

where Z_{ij} is the 1 by K vector of covariates for physician i and region j and the remaining notation is as in Bolduc and colleagues' (1996) specification. Equation (9.28) can be rewritten in vector form as

$$V_i = Z_i\beta + \varepsilon_i, \quad \varepsilon_i \sim N(0,\Sigma). \tag{9.29}$$

As Bolduc et al. (1997, 84) note, "the only identifiable parameters in the original model...[9.29]...are those that can be retrieved uniquely from the parameters of a scaled model differenced with respect to the utility of an

arbitrary alternative. Below, the first alternative is used as the base and the scaling is performed by setting the variance of the first error term in the differenced model equal to one. The *estimable* form of the model can be written as"

$$U_i = X_i\beta + \eta_i, \quad \eta_i \sim N(0, \Omega) \tag{9.30}$$

where (9.30) is (9.29) written as deviations from the utility of the first alternative choice, V_{i1} and Ω includes $h(h-1)/2-1$ independent terms, $\omega_{21}, \omega_{31}, \ldots, \omega_{h1}, \omega_{22}, \omega_{32}, \ldots, \omega_{hh}$. As a consequence, $U_{ij} = V_{ij} - V_{i1}, i = 2, \ldots, J$. The variance of the η terms is set such that $\text{var}(\eta_{i1}) = \text{var}(\varepsilon_{i2} - \varepsilon_{i1}) = 1$ (Bolduc et al. 1997, 84–85).

The spatial component of the multinomial model arises from the fact that the utilities, and thus the alternative choices of neighboring regions exhibit spatial autocorrelation. Bolduc et al. (1997) incorporate this attributional dependence via a spatial autoregressive error process, resulting in the following notation for the spatial multinomial model:

$$V_i = Z_i\beta + L^{-1}T\zeta_i, \quad \zeta_i \sim N(0, I_J), \tag{9.31}$$

where T is a J-diagonal matrix containing the standard deviations and $L = I_J - \lambda W$ captures the covariance effects (Bolduc et al. 1997, 85).

When employing the GHK simulator, the probability that individual n will choose multinomial alternative i, $P_n(i)$, is not directly computed but instead is replaced by an expectation computed from R independent draws as

$$f_n(i) = \frac{1}{R}\sum_{r=1}^{R} f_{nr}(i), \tag{9.32}$$

where, as Bolduc et al. (1997, 86) note, "$f_{nr}(i) = \Pi_{l=1}^{h}\Phi(a_{nrl})$, is a product of $h = J - 1$ univariate normal CDF evaluated at a_{nrl}." The maximum simulated likelihood then involves maximizing $L = \sum_{n=1}^{N} \ln f_n(i_n)$, where i_n denotes the choice that is made by individual n (Bolduc et al. 1997, 86).

The Bayesian approach to spatial multinomial probit estimation involves Gibbs sampling in the following sequence:

$$\begin{aligned} &(1)\quad U \sim p(U|\beta, T, \lambda, X, y) \\ &(2)\quad \beta \sim p(\beta|T, \lambda, U, X, y) \\ &(3)\quad T \sim p(T|\beta, \lambda, U, X, y) \\ &(4)\quad \lambda \sim p(\lambda|\beta, T, U, X, y), \end{aligned} \tag{9.33}$$

where the notation is as defined previously. When priors about T_j follow the inverse-gamma prior $p(T_j^{-2}) \sim G(\hat{a}, \hat{b})$, the conditional posterior distribution

for T_j^2 is

$$p(T_j^{-2}|\beta,\lambda,U,X,y) = G[\hat{a}+N/2,\hat{b}+(1/2)\sum_{n=1}^{N}\tilde{\eta}_{jn}^2]. \tag{9.34}$$

Bolduc et al. (1997, 99) examined the performance of both the GHK simulator and the Bayesian estimation approach. Both perform well and are found to be superior to a standard nonspatial multinomial probit model in identifying choice of practice location (as is Bolduc, Fortin, and Fournier's estimator). The Bayesian approach, however, has advantages over the GHK simulator in computational ease as it does not require the calculation of multinomial choice probabilities.[4]

9.5 SPATIAL COUNT MODELS

As stated earlier, interest in spatial clustering in events dates at least back to John Snow's pioneering epidemiological work on the spread of cholera from the Broad Street pump in London. Modern social scientists retain this interest in the spatial locations of events and are often interested in phenomena that take the form of event counts: non-negative, integer counts of the number of times that a particular event has occurred. Event count data are found in criminology (the number of crimes per neighborhood), demography (the number of live births per region), political science (the number of regime transitions), and other social sciences. Count data present problems for the linear regression model developed for continuous dependent variables. Linear models can produce biased, inconsistent, and inefficient estimates when applied to count data. As a result, scholars have developed several alternative event count models for count data.

The Poisson regression model is the most basic event count model. This model assumes that the count data are produced by a Poisson process, with a conditional mean that is captured by the covariates in the model:

$$\Pr(y_i|x_i) = \frac{\exp(-\mu_i)\mu_i^{y_i}}{y_i!} \tag{9.35}$$

where $\mu_i = \exp(x_i\beta)$. Because the Poisson model is a log-linear model, the expected count changes by a factor of $\exp(\beta_k)$ for a unit change in x_k. One of the restrictive assumptions of the Poisson model is that events are independent of

4 Recently, Carrion-Flores, Flores-Lagunes, and Guci (2009) have extended Klier and McMillen's (2008) linearized logit estimator to the case of a spatial lag model with a multinomial dependent variable. As with Klier and McMillen's approach, the advantage of the linearization in the multinomial setting is that it avoids the inversion of large matrices. The approach consists of two steps. First a nonspatial multinomial logit model is estimated. Next, the linearized model accounting for the spatial dependence is estimated via two-stage least squares (Carrion-Flores et al. 2009, 6).

each other. When this assumption is not met, the conditional variance exceeds the conditional mean and overdispersion is present. Typically, most researchers conceive of non-independence of events as a form of contagion that occurs over time within units. That is, the occurrence of an event for unit i increases the probability of unit i experiencing the same type of event in the future. Contagion, however, may also take a spatial form in which non-independence occurs across units. This spatial contagion is less frequently examined in event count models in the social sciences, but is a critical concern given the propensity of social science data toward spatial dependence.

Besag (1974) proposed one of the initial models to account for spatial dependence in event counts. Besag's (1974, 202) auto-Poisson model assumes "that X_i has a conditional Poisson distribution with mean μ_i dependent upon the [neighboring] site values" and with μ_i taking the form

$$\mu_i = \exp(\alpha_i + \Sigma\beta_{i,j}x_j). \tag{9.36}$$

Besag's auto-Poisson model (part of his broader class of auto-models, which also includes the auto-logistic model presented in Section 9.1.2), however, carries a critical assumption that limits its use in practice. Specifically, because the range of X_i is assumed to be infinite, the spatial autocorrelation between the values at any two locations must be assumed to be ≤ 0 for the model to be summable over x. In other words, the auto-Poisson model is only applicable in spatial analysis for cases of negative spatial autocorrelation. This is highly problematic, as positive spatial autocorrelation is much more common in the social sciences than negative spatial autocorrelation, as discussed in Chapter 3.

Spatial analysts, therefore, require modeling approaches that allow for positive spatial autocorrelation in event counts. Two principal approaches have been proposed. I discuss these approaches, the Winsorized Poisson model and the spatial filter model, in the next subsections.

9.5.1 Winsorized Poisson Model

One strategy for avoiding the infinite sum problem in the Poisson probability model (and thus the need to constrain spatial dependence to negative dependence) is to replace high counts with an accepted cutoff value that then assumes the highest possible count value in the dataset. This process is known as Winsoring the event counts (Griffith 2006, 165). As Griffith notes, Kaiser and Cressie (1997) propose that this maximum count value be three times the expected value of the non-Winsorized Poisson variable ($3\hat{\mu}$). As Griffith notes, the Winsorizing approach has some intuitive appeal as in practice the sum of the event counts will not approach infinity in any application. However, Griffith (2006, 176–178) also notes the computational complexity involved in estimating a Winsorized Poisson model and also found that the Winsorized model accounts for less of the variation in event counts than an

alternative spatial filter approach and that it also suffers in comparison to this latter estimation approach in exhibiting prediction bias in a cross-validation analysis. The next section explores this alternative spatial filter modeling approach.

9.5.2 Spatial Filter Model

The spatial filter model favored in Griffith's (2006) analysis is an ML approach that involves estimating distinct spatial patterns in the data as parameters based upon the eigenfunctions of the matrix $(I - \frac{11'}{n})C(I - \frac{11'}{n})$, with I the identity matrix and 1 an n by 1 vector of ones (Griffith 2006, 166). Through this process, then, distinct spatial parameters are estimated to capture independent spatial patterns in the data where these patterns are reflected in the independent eigenvectors. As Griffith (2003) (quoted in Griffith 2006, 166) notes, the first eigenvector is the set of numerical values with the largest Moran's I for the spatial weights matrix W defined by the researcher to reflect the expected neighbor definitions in the data. The next eigenvector then is the set of numerical values that has the largest Moran's I for any set of numerical values uncorrelated with the first eigenvector. The process proceeds by defining additional orthogonal eigenvectors until the final eigenvector, which is the set of numerical values with the largest negative Moran's I coefficient that is uncorrelated with the previous eigenvectors.

A critical feature of this spatial filtering approach is the recognition of the possibility of multiple spatial patterns in the data that are estimable via separate parameters. As discussed previously, scholars typically seek to estimate a single autoregressive lag or error parameter to capture spatial dependence. The spatial filter event count approach differs from this standard modeling framework. At the same time, if multiple spatial patterns are present in the data, they should be modeled via multiple parameters to produce spatial independence in the residuals. The stronger predictive value of the spatial filtering approach versus the Winsorizing approach also argues in favor of the former over the latter.

9.6 SPATIAL SURVIVAL MODELS

Often social scientists are interested in explaining the timing of events. Criminologists, for example, study recividism and time to subsequent offenses (Visher, Lattimore, and Linster 1991). Political scientists study the timing of government failures (Warwick 1992). Sociologists study the timing of the formation of interpersonal ties in social networks (de Nooy 2011). Many social science theories recognize that the timing of these events is not independent across units, but instead often incorporates a spatial dimension in which the occurrence of an event in one location is associated with similar events in neighboring locations. Within political science, for example, concepts such as the domino effect, waves of democratization, and policy diffusion highlight the

spatial dimension in many political event processes (Huntington 1991; Berry and Berry 1992).[5]

Although concepts of spatial interaction and diffusion are central to many of our theories of event processes in the social sciences, our approach to modeling this spatial dimension in survival models has often been quite limited. Generally, spatial dependence in survival data has been modeled via simple indicators such as the number or proportion of neighboring units that previously experienced the event of interest (Berry and Berry 1990; but see Berry and Baybeck 2005; see also Starr 1991).

As is well known, standard econometric approaches developed for continuous dependent variables are not applicable for survival data. Right-censoring of time-to-event data produces observational equivalence between units experiencing the event at the end of the observation period and those censored and yet to experience the event. As a consequence, survival or event history models incorporating a censoring indicator are employed to model event processes (Box-Steffensmeier and Jones 2004). (The term survival model derives from the study of patient mortality in biostatistics, an important field in the development of these models. Social scientists also refer to these models as survival models. Within the social sciences, however, the interest is not in physical mortality, but instead in the survival of units until they experience an event of interest. Thus, for example, political scientists speak of government or cabinet survival [Warwick 1992], conflict survival [Regan 2002], and survival in office [Jones 1994]. Survival models are also known as event history and duration models.)

Recently, the nonspatial survival modeling literature has seen an increased interest in the use of random effects models to account for unobserved heterogeneity in units' risk propensity (Hill, Axinn, and Thornton 1993; Klein and Moeschberger 1997; Hougaard 2000). Here, scholars account for unmeasured sources of variation in risk propensity via either unit-specific (individual) or hierarchical (shared) random effects, or frailty terms. By incorporating such random effects, scholars can account for the fact that some units are more frail than others – and thus have a higher propensity to experience the event of interest – and avoid biased parameter estimates and violations of the proportional hazards assumption that are induced by a false assumption of homogeneity (see, e.g., Box-Steffensmeier and Jones 2004, 147–148). Testing for unobserved heterogeneity then simply involves estimating the variance term, θ, of the random effects. A significant positive value of θ indicates unmodeled heterogeneity in risk propensity while a value of θ that is indistinguishable from zero indicates that sources of variation in risk propensity are accounted for via the covariates in the model.

[5] Much of this discussion of survival models and spatial survival models appeared previously in "Bayesian Spatial Survival Models in Political Event Processes." *American Journal of Political Science* 53(1): 241–257.

Recent years have seen considerable progress in the use of frailty models within the social sciences (Carpenter 2002; Gordon 2002; Chiozza and Goemans 2004; Colaresi 2004; Box-Steffensmeier and De Boef 2006). These studies demonstrate the importance of accounting for unobserved or unmeasured sources of heterogeneity in event occurrence. But although some of these studies examine dependence across competing risks (Gordon 2002) or repeated events (Box-Steffensmeier and De Boef 2006), typical applications of frailty models in the social sciences assume that the random effects are spatially independent. Given the theoretical predictions of spatial dependence in event processes in the social sciences, researchers will, I argue, often wish to allow for spatial dependence across random effects in their survival models. In this chapter, I present an approach to modeling spatially autocorrelated random effects in survival data.

Specifically, I apply a Bayesian approach in which random effects at neighboring locations are allowed to exhibit spatial dependence (Banerjee and Carlin 2003; Banerjee, Wall, and Carlin 2003; Banerjee, Carlin, and Gelfand 2004). This spatial dependence is incorporated by specifying a CAR prior. I employ the CAR prior to allow for spatially autocorrelated random effects in time-to-event data across neighboring units, with the neighbors defined via an adjacency matrix.

9.7 APPLICATION: SPATIAL SURVIVAL MODELS OF NAFTA POSITION ANNOUNCEMENTS

A critical distinction in survival analysis is how the baseline hazard (the hazard of the event in the absence of any covariate effects, i.e., the time dependency in the event process) is parameterized. In the semiparametric Cox model, no parametric distribution is specified for the baseline hazard. As a consequence, rather than employing a specific distribution for the intervals between event occurrences, the Cox model incorporates information only for the observed event times. In contrast, in parametric survival models such as the Weibull or Gompertz, a specific parametric form is assumed for the underlying baseline hazard. In choosing between the Cox model and its parametric alternatives, one faces a tradeoff between the Cox model's flexibility (to various shapes of the baseline hazard) versus the parametric models' more precise estimates of duration dependency (if the correct parametric distribution is chosen) and capacity for out-of-sample prediction. In this spatial analysis, I examine both the semiparametric Cox model and a frequently used parametric alternative, the Weibull model.

As Banerjee et al. (2004) and Box-Steffensmeier and Jones (2004) show, the hazard rate in the Cox model takes the form

$$h(t_i;x_i) = h_0(t_i)\exp(\beta' x_i), \tag{9.37}$$

where t_i is the time to event or censoring for unit i, h_o is the baseline hazard, x_i is a vector of covariates, and β is a vector of parameters. The Cox model, unlike parametric survival models, includes no intercept because the baseline hazard is not parameterized (Box-Steffensmeier and Jones 2004, 49; see also Banerjee and Carlin 2003). In the Weibull model, the hazard rate is

$$h(t_i;x_i) = \rho t_i^{\rho-1}\exp(\beta' x_i), \tag{9.38}$$

where ρ is a shape parameter for the baseline hazard, β now includes an intercept term (as the baseline hazard is modeled using the Weibull distribution), and the remaining notation is as in (9.37). The shape parameter, ρ, reflects the shape of the monotonic hazard in the Weibull model, with $\rho > 1$ reflecting a monotonically rising hazard rate, $\rho < 1$ reflecting a monotonically declining hazard, and $\rho = 1$ reflecting a flat hazard (Box-Steffensmeier and Jones 2004, 25).

9.7.1 Standard Frailty Models

The Cox and Weibull models in (9.37) and (9.38) assume that factors affecting the hazard of event occurrence are included in the covariate vector, x_i. What is the effect of omitting factors that affect the hazard? As Box-Steffensmeier and Jones (2004, 147) note, omitting such factors reduces the effect of covariates in the model that increase the hazard and increases the effect of covariates that reduce the hazard. Thus, scholars will wish to have a way to account for covariates excluded from the model that affect the hazard rate.

One strategy for accounting for such omitted covariates is the inclusion of random effect, or frailty terms. The frailty terms account for the fact that some units are at greater risk of experiencing the event of interest, that is, are more frail, due to factors not incorporated in the model. Either of two standard frailty approaches are adopted, depending on the researcher's prior beliefs about the nature of the unobserved heterogeneity in risk propensity. If the researcher believes that units exhibit their own unique frailties, she will incorporate unit-specific, or individual frailty terms for each unit in her data. Alternatively, if she believes that units are clustered such that units within the same cluster share the same frailty while frailties are independent across clusters, she will incorporate hierarchical, or shared frailty terms for each cluster in her data.

9.7.2 Individual and Shared Frailty Models with Independent Random Effects

The hazard rate in the Cox model with standard independent individual frailties takes the form

$$h(t_i;x_i) = h_o(t_i)\exp(\beta' x_i + W_i), \tag{9.39}$$

while the hazard rate in the Weibull model with standard independent individual frailties takes the form

$$h(t_i;x_i) = \rho t_i^{\rho-1}\exp(\beta' x_i + W_i), \tag{9.40}$$

where $W_i \equiv \log\omega_i$ is the individual frailty term, the remaining notation in (9.39) is as in (9.37), and in (9.40) as in (9.38) (Banerjee, Carlin, and Gelfand 2004; Box-Steffensmeier and Jones 2004). As can be seen from the equations, the hazard in the frailty model is a function not only of the covariate vector, x_i, but also of the random effect, W_i.

If unmodeled factors produce significant heterogeneity in risk propensity, the variance of the frailties will be distinguishable from zero. Thus, estimating whether random effects should be included in the model involves specifying a probability distribution for the frailties and estimating the variance, θ, of the frailties. The gamma and inverse Gaussian are often chosen for the random effects distribution (Therneau and Grambsch 2000, 232–234).

The individual frailty modeling approach is appropriate only if the researcher believes that each unit has a unique unmodeled frailty. If, however, the researcher believes that units are clustered in a hierarchical structure, such that units within the same cluster share a common frailty, a hierarchical, shared frailty modeling approach is appropriate instead. Here the Cox and Weibull shared frailty models take the form

$$h(t_{ij};x_{ij}) = h_0(t_{ij})\exp(\beta' x_{ij} + W_j), \tag{9.41}$$

and

$$h(t_{ij};x_{ij}) = \rho t_{ij}^{\rho-1}\exp(\beta' x_{ij} + W_j), \tag{9.42}$$

where unit i is now nested in cluster or stratum j, and the individual frailty, W_i, is now replaced by a shared frailty, $W_j \equiv \log\omega_j$, for units nested in stratum j (Banerjee and Carlin 2003; Banerjee et al. 2003; Box-Steffensmeier and Jones 2004). Inference regarding the appropriateness of the shared frailty model proceeds analogously to the individual frailty case. A probability distribution is specified for the shared frailty terms, and a variance, θ, that is distinguishable from zero indicates that there are unmodeled shared risk factors.

Both the individual and shared frailty approaches make a critical assumption. In both approaches, the random effects are assumed to be independent. In the individual frailty model, each unit has a unique frailty that is independent of other individual random effects. In the shared frailty model, units within the same cluster share a common frailty, but the frailties are assumed independent across these higher-level units.

This assumption of independent random effects will often be unrealistic in social science data. Theories of event processes in the social sciences often predict spatial dependence in event occurrence. If we are unable to model fully this spatial dependence via substantive covariates, this will produce spatially autocorrelated random effects.

It is important to note that the modeling approach I examine here also provides a more realistic and flexible approach to modeling dependent data than standard hierarchical models. The standard approach makes a knife-edge assumption: units in the same strata are assumed to exhibit dependence, but the strata themselves, even neighboring strata, are assumed to be independent. Thus, for example, in a shared frailty model of legislative behavior with state-level strata (a commonly employed choice for clustering social science data), Democratic Representatives Jerrold Nadler of New York's 8th Congressional District and Robert Menendez of New Jersey's neighboring 13th Congressional District would be treated as spatially independent in the 103rd Congress. This is not consistent with our understanding of how spatial proximity promotes legislative interaction (see Caldeira and Patterson 1987). More generally, because event processes are inherently social and interdependent, spatial dependence often does not stop at the stratum's edge. Instead, neighboring strata often exhibit spatial dependence. As a consequence, scholars will often wish to incorporate spatial dependence between strata rather than making the knife-edge assumption of spatial independence across strata.

9.7.3 Bayesian Spatial Survival Modeling

The critical step that distinguishes spatial modeling of event processes from standard modeling approaches for event processes is the use of spatial weights matrices incorporating neighbor definitions for the observations and the parameterization of spatial dependence across neighboring polygons.[6] From a Bayesian perspective, this involves incorporating a prior to account for the spatial dependence in the hazards. Typically, a CAR prior incorporating adjacency information is employed to model this spatial dependence.

Neighbors are defined via the weights matrix, A. In an unnormalized weights matrix such as that employed in this chapter's NAFTA application, each neighbor of a unit is given a weight of 1, while each non-neighbor of a unit is given a weight of 0. (Thus, $a_{ii'} = 1$ if units i and i' are neighbors and $a_{ii'} = 0$ if units i and i' are non-neighbors.) This spatial weights approach differs from the standard i.i.d. perspective on random effects, which, in a Bayesian framework, implies an exchangeable prior with a (nonspatial) weights matrix. In the exchangeable prior, all nondiagonal elements of the nonspatial weights matrix are given a common value, such as 1. In such an approach, the random effects are exchangeable under any geographic permutation of the data (Bernardinelli and Montomoli 1992, 988).

6 This discussion draws on the presentation and notation in Bernardinelli and Montomoli (1992), Banerjee and Carlin (2003), and Banerjee et al. (2003, 2004).

9.7.4 The CAR Prior

The standard, nonspatial frailty models presented above all assume that the random effects or frailty terms are independent. From a Bayesian perspective, this is consistent with a specification in which the random effects distribution is conditional on a hyperparameter, λ, with an exchangeable prior, where λ refers to the precision (the inverse variance, i.e., the inverse of θ) of the random effects distribution. As in the case of the CAR prior, the λ prior is a unidimensional precision prior for the joint distribution of the random effects vector. The single dimensional prior for the random effects distribution is employed in survival modeling research by, for example, Banerjee et al. (2003, 2004), and Lawson (2008). As stated earlier, the exchangeable prior is induced by not distinguishing between neighboring and non-neighboring units in the weights matrix, but instead treating both neighbors and non-neighbors as exchangeable.

The exchangeable prior, however, is likely to be problematic for many survival modeling applications. As Galton's problem recognizes, neighboring units are likely to share similar risk propensities, due either to behavioral diffusion or to shared risk factors. If we are unable to model fully the sources of risk propensity, neighboring units will share spatially autocorrelated frailties. As a consequence, we will often wish to relax the assumption of exchangeability. This is accomplished by allowing the precision parameter, λ, to reflect a CAR prior that incorporates neighbor definitions via the spatial weights matrix.

In the spatial individual frailty model, this CAR(λ) prior has a joint distribution proportional to

$$\lambda^{(I-G)/2}\exp\left[-\frac{\lambda}{2}\sum_{i \text{ adj } i'}(W_i - W_{i'})^2\right]$$
$$\propto \lambda^{(I-G)/2}\exp\left[-\frac{\lambda}{2}\sum_{i=1}^{I} m_i W_i(W_i - \overline{W}_i)\right], \tag{9.43}$$

where I is the number of units in the data, G is the number of unconnected (island) units, i adj i' indicates that units i and i' are adjacent, $\overline{W}_i$ is the average of the $W_{i' \neq i}$ neighboring W_i, and m_i is the number of adjacencies (Bernardinelli and Montomoli 1992; Banerjee et al. 2003, 126).

The conditional distribution of the spatial random effects that results from the CAR prior is then

$$W_i | W_{i' \neq i} \sim N(\overline{W}_i, 1/(\lambda m_i)). \tag{9.44}$$

By incorporating the spatial locations of units, the CAR prior thus produces a conditional distribution for the random effects that is normally distributed with a conditional mean equal to the average of the random effects for neighbors of i, and a conditional variance that is inversely proportional to the number

of units neighboring i (Thomas et al. 2004). Thus, where the exchangeable prior displaces the random effect estimates toward a global mean by not distinguishing between neighbors and non-neighbors, the spatial CAR prior displaces these estimates toward a local mean (Bernardinelli and Montomoli 1992, 989).

The CAR prior for the spatial shared frailty model follows accordingly. In the spatial shared frailty model, the individual unit i is now nested in a higher-level cluster or stratum j, and the random effect refers to this higher-level stratum, W_j. The CAR(λ) prior for the spatial shared frailty model has a joint distribution proportional to

$$\lambda^{(J-H)/2}\exp\left[-\frac{\lambda}{2}\sum_{j \text{ adj } j'}(W_j - W_{j'})^2\right]$$

$$\propto \lambda^{(J-H)/2}\exp\left[-\frac{\lambda}{2}\sum_{j=1}^{J} m_j W_j(W_j - \overline{W}_j)\right], \tag{9.45}$$

where J is the number of higher-level strata in the data, H is the number of unconnected (island) strata, j adj j' indicates that strata j and j' are adjacent, $\overline{W}_j$ is the average of the $W_{j' \neq j}$ neighboring W_j, and m_j is the number of higher-level adjacencies (Bernardinelli and Montomoli 1992; Banerjee et al. 2003, 126).

The resulting conditional distribution for the strata-level spatial random effects is then

$$W_j | W_{j' \neq j} \sim N(\overline{W}_j, 1/(\lambda m_j)). \tag{9.46}$$

Analogous to the individual frailty case, the CAR prior thus produces a conditional distribution for the spatial shared frailties that is normally distributed with a conditional mean equal to the average of the random effects for strata neighboring stratum j, and a conditional variance that is inversely proportional to the number of strata neighboring j (Thomas et al. 2004). The individual and shared spatial frailty models also require that a hyperprior, $p(\lambda)$, be assigned to λ. Generally, a Gamma(a,b) hyperprior is chosen (Banerjee et al. 2004). A reference prior should also be employed to gauge the effect of the Gamma hyperprior (see, e.g., Gelman et al. 2004; Gelman 2006).

The CAR prior is an improper prior, with the mean of the distribution of the spatial random effects undefined. Any constant can be added to the random effects and the prior remains unchanged (Banerjee et al. 2004, 80). As a consequence of its impropriety, the CAR model can only be used as a prior and not as a likelihood (Banerjee et al. 2004, 80). Because the CAR prior, as a pairwise-difference prior, is identified only up to an additive constant, a constraint must be imposed on the frailties to identify an intercept term (Besag et al. 1995; Banerjee et al. 2003, 126). To identify an intercept in the Weibull models, I thus impose the constraint that the frailties sum to zero.

9.7.5 Semiparametric Cox Models with Spatial Frailties

For the Bayesian semiparametric Cox model, the joint posterior distribution is

$$p(\beta, W, \lambda | t, x, y) \propto L(\beta, W; t, x, y) p(W|\lambda) p(\beta) p(\lambda), \tag{9.47}$$

where t is the collection of event times, y is the collection of event indicators, and the remaining notation is as in previous equations. The first term on the right in (9.47) is the Cox likelihood and the remaining terms are the CAR distribution of the frailties, the priors on β, and the hyperprior on λ. The likelihood for the Bayesian Cox model with spatial individual frailties is then[7]

$$L(\beta, W; t, x, y) \propto \prod_{i=1}^{I} \{h_0(t_i; x_i)\}^{y_i} \exp\{-H_0(t_i) \exp(\beta' x_i + W_i)\}, \tag{9.48}$$

while, as Banerjee and Carlin (2003) show, the likelihood for the Bayesian Cox model with spatial shared frailties is

$$L(\beta, W; t, x, y) \propto \prod_{j=1}^{J} \prod_{i=1}^{n_j} \{h_0(t_{ij}; x_{ij})\}^{y_{ij}} \exp\{-H_0(t_{ij}) \exp(\beta' x_{ij} + W_j)\}. \tag{9.49}$$

In contrast to standard Cox frailty models, the inclusion of the CAR prior in the Cox spatial frailty models incorporates the potential spatial dependence among frailties at neighboring locations. The individual and shared frailty Cox models are completed by assigning appropriate priors for β and λ.

9.7.6 Parametric Weibull Models with Spatial Frailties

The joint posterior distribution for the Bayesian parametric Weibull model is

$$p(\beta, W, \rho, \lambda | t, x, y) \propto L(\beta, W, \rho; t, x, y) p(W|\lambda) p(\beta) p(\rho) p(\lambda), \tag{9.50}$$

where the notation is as in (9.47), except that ρ, the shape parameter for the baseline hazard in the Weibull, is now included (Banerjee et al. 2003). The first term on the right is now the Weibull likelihood, the second is again the CAR distribution of the random effects, and the remaining terms are the remaining prior distributions.

The likelihood for the Weibull model with spatial individual frailties is proportional to

$$\prod_{i=1}^{I} \{\rho t_i^{\rho-1} \exp(\beta' x_i + W_i)\}^{y_i} \exp\{-t_i^{\rho} \exp(\beta' x_i + W_i)\}, \tag{9.51}$$

7 The Cox model with spatial individual frailties, like its nonspatial counterpart, is identified only in the presence of time-varying covariates. My NAFTA application does not include time-varying covariates and thus I do not estimate Cox models with individual frailties.

while the likelihood for the Weibull model with spatial shared frailties is proportional to

$$\prod_{j=1}^{J}\prod_{i=1}^{n_j}\{\rho t_{ij}^{\rho-1}\exp(\beta' x_{ij}+W_j)\}^{\gamma_{ij}}\exp\{-t_{ij}^{\rho}\exp(\beta' x_{ij}+W_j)\}. \tag{9.52}$$

As in the Cox spatial frailty specification, the Weibull spatial frailty model differs from the standard Weibull model in its inclusion of the CAR prior. The individual and shared spatial Weibull specifications are then completed by assigning appropriate priors for β, ρ, and λ. Generally, a Gamma(α,1/α) prior is chosen for ρ and, as in the Cox model, a Gamma(a,b) prior is chosen for λ (Banerjee et al. 2004, 304).

I apply Bayesian spatial frailty modeling to the timing of position announcements by members of the U.S. House of Representatives on the North American Free Trade Agreement (NAFTA). In their analysis of position timing on NAFTA, Box-Steffensmeier, Arnold, and Zorn (1997) incorporated spatial influences via a dummy variable indicating whether the member's district shared a land border with Mexico. Spatial effects in position announcements, however, were unlikely to be limited to the border's edge. I posit, instead, that members from neighboring locations were likely to announce positions at similar times, and thus exhibit spatial dependence in position timing. Consistent with Galton's problem, two sets of factors were likely to produce this spatial autocorrelation.

On the one hand, spatial dependence in position timing may have occurred as a result of behavioral diffusion. Caldeira and Patterson (1987) demonstrate that members from neighboring legislative districts are more likely to develop friendships with each other than are members from more spatially distant districts. Accordingly, I expect more frequent – and more effective – interpersonal interaction among members from neighboring districts than among members from more distant districts, and greater similarity in the timing of legislative position announcements as a result.

Alternatively, spatially proximate members may announce positions at similar times despite little or no communication between each other. Members from neighboring locations are more likely to share similar constituencies, and similar constituent concerns, than more spatially distant members. Thus, similar factors that lead to cue-taking and cue-giving among same-state senators (Matthews and Stimson 1975) may also produce spatial dependence in the timing of position announcements among neighboring House members. Members from neighboring locations may also share similar partisan, ideological, or demographic characteristics, producing similarity in both policy positions and in the timing of announcements of these positions. Thus, even if members from neighboring districts rarely talk, they may still exhibit spatially dependent position timing due to common district or personal attributes.

My analysis thus contrasts with many previous analyses of legislative behavior that have focused on dependence *within* same-state delegations in

that I allow for dependence across state boundaries. In addition to potential spatial effects, I model three sets of factors likely to affect position timing. These three sets of factors are constituency, institutional, and individual (member) influences (see Box-Steffensmeier et al. 1997). (I chose the covariates for illustrative purposes, to examine the effects of unmodeled and modeled spatial dependence on frailty and substantive covariate estimates and model choice statistics.)

I model constituency factors with two covariates. NAFTA carried different policy effects for constituents with different economic profiles. Specifically, NAFTA was expected to pose significant dislocation effects on union members and low-income citizens, with the high-paying jobs of the former and the low-skill jobs of the latter particularly threatened by foreign competition. As a result, I include the covariates, *Union Membership*, measuring the percentage of private-sector workers in the member's district who were union members, and *Household Income*, measuring the district's median household income. As Box-Steffensmeier et al. (1997, 327) note, these covariates as coded in their analysis and mine do not present clear expectations for effects on the timing of NAFTA announcements. In each case, members with high or low values on the variable are expected to announce earlier than members with intermediate levels due to clearer signals of policy preferences from constituents. I retain Box-Steffensmeier and colleagues' operationalization of these covariates.

Institutional influences in the House of Representatives are measured with three covariates. *NAFTA Committee* is a dichotomous measure indicating whether the member was on a committee that acted on NAFTA implementing legislation. Because committee membership provides an effective stage for cue-giving to other members, NAFTA committee members are expected to announce positions earlier than non-committee members. *Republican Leadership* and *Democratic Leadership* are dummy variables indicating whether the member held a position in his or her party's leadership in the House. Because Republican leaders were united in their support for NAFTA, a Republican leadership position is expected to be associated with earlier position taking. In contrast, Democratic leaders were divided on the trade agreement, cross-pressured in some cases by opposition to the agreement among constituents and support for the agreement by the Clinton administration. As a consequence, this covariate does not present clear expectations for the timing of members' announcements.

Finally, two interaction terms incorporating member ideology are included in the model to capture individual-level influences. The two covariates are *Ideology*Union Membership* and *Ideology*Household Income*. (As Box-Steffensmeier et al. [1997, 17] note, *Ideology* is not entered separately in the model because doing so would produce an intercept in the Cox model.) Box-Steffensmeier et al. (1997) measured ideology with members' Chamber of Commerce voting scores (purged of the NAFTA vote) on economic issues. Members with voting scores > 50 (indicating more pro-business voting records)

are scored 1 on the dichotomous measure, while members with scores at or below 50 are scored 0. Box-Steffensmeier et al. (1997) posit that it is the interaction of member ideology and district ideology (as proxied by union membership and household income) that is most relevant for the timing of NAFTA position announcements. I follow their specification and incorporate these two interaction terms in the model. Because of potential cross-pressures between member and district ideology, neither interaction term presents clear expectations regarding effects on position timing.

9.7.7 Neighbor Definitions and Priors

I employ distinct neighbor definitions for the individual and hierarchical frailty models. For the individual frailty model, I created an adjacency matrix with a queen contiguity definition, in which each district contiguous to member *i*'s district in the 103rd Congress is a neighbor of member *i* and each district that is not contiguous to member *i*'s district is a non-neighbor. For the hierarchical model, I nest members of Congress within states and allow for spatial dependence across the state-level random effects. Again I employ a queen contiguity neighbor definition, in which each state contiguous to state *i* is a neighbor of state *i* and each state not contiguous to state *i* is a non-neighbor of state *i*. The data thus differ in the individual and shared frailty analyses. Rep. Don Young (R-AK) is excluded from both analyses, since his district is not contiguous to any other districts. Rep. Neil Abercrombie (D-HI) and Rep. Patsy Mink (D-HI) are included in the individual frailty analysis because their districts are contiguous to each other but are excluded from the hierarchical frailty analysis because Hawaii is not contiguous to any other states.

I complete the specifications by specifying appropriate priors for the parameters in the models. Given that prior substantive research provides little information regarding the values of the spatial random effects or the values of substantive covariates in the presence of these spatial frailties, I prefer vague prior distributions, relying on the data to overwhelm the priors. I employ a vague hyperprior for λ of Gamma(0.01, 0.01), a prior of $N(0, 0.001)$ for β_0 in the Weibull model, and priors of $N(0, 0.00001)$ for the remaining β in both the Cox and Weibull models. To examine the sensitivity of the results to the gamma CAR prior, I also estimated the models using a uniform reference prior for the CAR prior, following Gelman (2006) and Gelman et al. (2004). The results are similar whether the gamma or uniform priors are used. Although the posterior means for the frailty variance parameter, θ, are somewhat smaller under the uniform prior (0.191 vs. 0.195 in the spatial Cox shared frailty models, 0.005 vs. 0.011 in the spatial Weibull individual frailty models, and 0.007 vs. 0.018 in the spatial Weibull shared frailty models), in all cases, the 95 percent Bayesian credible intervals for this parameter are distinguishable from zero. The estimates for the other parameters exhibit only marginal changes. The reference prior estimates are available from the author. I set $\alpha = 0.01$, producing

a Gamma(0.01, 100) prior for the shape parameter, ρ, in the Weibull model. I employ an Andersen-Gill counting process formulation for the Cox model. The counting process requires the specification of two additional priors for c, the researcher's degree of confidence in her belief regarding the underlying hazard function, and r, the researcher's prior regarding the failure rate per unit of time. I express weak priors regarding both the values of the hazard function and the failure rate via priors on c and r of (0.0001, 0.00001) and (0.001, 0.0001), respectively. For additional information on the counting process approach, see Andersen and Gill (1982), Clayton (1991), and Spiegelhalter et al. (2003).

I employ MCMC techniques to characterize the posterior densities of the parameters and hyperparameters of interest. Specifically, I employed Gibbs sampling for two separate Markov chains with overdispersed starting values of 0 and 1 for the intercept, β_0, in the Weibull models, $\pm$ 3 standard errors from the frequentist Cox estimates in Box-Steffensmeier et al. (1997, 331) for the remaining β, 0.01 and 0.1 for ρ, 0.001 and 1 for λ, and 0.01 and 0.1 for c and r. I employed 5,000 burn-in iterations for each Markov chain. Convergence was diagnosed via Gelman and Rubin's diagnostic (Gill 2002, 399–402), with the diagnostic indicating convergence for each parameter in each model. I retained 10,000 post burn-in iterations for each chain, providing a sample size of 20,000.

9.7.8 Spatial Dependence in the Timing of Position Taking on NAFTA

I first examine how the risk of a U.S. House member announcing a position on NAFTA varied as a function of time. I retain Box-Steffensmeier and colleagues' (1997, 330) coding and assume that members came under risk of announcing a position on August 12, 1992, the day that Rep. Peter Visclosky (D-IN) announced his opposition to NAFTA. "Undecided" and "leaning" positions are not included in this measure. Members who did not make a public announcement of their position prior to the House vote on H.R. 3450, NAFTA Implementation Act, on November 17, 1993 are recorded as announcing their position on this date. Full descriptions of the data can be found in Box-Steffensmeier et al. (1997). The empirical baseline hazard for the Cox model is nonmonotonic, but generally increasing over time. Member announcements on NAFTA were backloaded – more than 90 percent of announcements occurred more than 300 days after Rep. Peter Visclosky's (D-IN) announcement of his opposition to NAFTA on August 12, 1992. The data are, moreover, heavily clustered. More than 80 percent of members announced their positions on September 9, 1993 or later; nearly half of members announced their positions in the month leading up to the House vote.

Such heavily clustered data mitigate against finding spatial dependence. With so many members announcing their positions concurrently, it is clear that nonspatial effects played a significant role in the timing of position taking. Thus,

my particular application serves as a conservative test of spatial dependence in time-to-event data. If we find evidence of significant spatial effects even in survival data marked by large spikes in event occurrence such as those in the timing of NAFTA position announcements, we will have reason to expect even stronger spatial effects in less temporally clustered data.

9.7.9 Assessing Model Choice

I use the deviance information criterion (DIC) (Spiegelhalter et al. 2002) to assess model choice across the spatial and nonspatial Cox and Weibull survival models. The DIC, like the more familiar Akaike information criterion (AIC), combines measures both of model fit and of the effective number of parameters (the latter component penalizes models that overfit the data). The deviance statistic is central to the model fit component of the DIC. The deviance statistic takes the form

$$D(\theta) = -2 \log f(y|\theta) + 2 \log h(y), \tag{9.53}$$

where, as Banerjee and Carlin (2003, 532) note, $f(y|\theta)$ is the likelihood for the observed data given the parameter vector θ and $h(y)$ is a function of only the data.[8] The intuition behind the deviance statistic is to examine the improvement in fit produced by the estimation of the parameter vector θ. The model fit is then summarized using the posterior expectation of the deviance, $\overline{D} = \mathrm{E}_{\theta|y}[D]$.

Because the estimation of unnecessary parameters in the parameter vector θ naturally improves model fit, it is important to penalize for overfitting the model. This is done by calculating the effective number of parameters, p_D, for the model. The effective number of parameters reflects the relative role that the data play in estimating the parameters versus the priors, with larger estimates of the effective number of parameters indicating that the data play a larger role. As Gelman et al. (2004, 182) note, in calculating the effective number of parameters, a parameter receives a value of 1 if it is estimated from the data alone with no input from the prior, a value of 0 if it is estimated from the prior alone with no input from the data, and an intermediate value between 1 and 0 depending on the relative contributions of the data and the prior. The effective number of parameters is calculated as

$$p_D = E_{\theta|y}[D] - D(E_{\theta|y}[\theta]) = \overline{D} - D(\overline{\theta}) \tag{9.54}$$

where $\overline{D}$ is, again, the posterior expectation of the deviance and $D(\overline{\theta})$ is the deviance taken at the posterior expectations (Banerjee et al. 2003, 127). The effective number of parameters is thus the deviance of the posterior means subtracted from the posterior mean of the deviance (Spiegelhalter et al. 2003).

[8] This section draws on the discussion and notation in Banerjee and Carlin (2003) and Banerjee et al. (2003).

TABLE 9.2. *Model Choice Statistics for Models of the Timing of NAFTA Position Announcements*

Model	p_D	DIC
Standard Cox	77.43	5201.97
Cox with nonspatial shared frailties	98.92	5170.03
Cox with spatial shared frailties	95.45	5166.85
Standard Weibull	9.24	5204.68
Weibull with nonspatial individual frailties	12.17	5228.10
Weibull with spatial individual frailties	12.33	5219.19
Weibull with nonspatial shared frailties	12.41	5195.71
Weibull with spatial shared frailties	11.77	5192.05

Combining the measure of model fit with the penalty for overfitting, the DIC then takes the form

$$\text{DIC} = \overline{D} + p_D. \tag{9.55}$$

The DIC of models fit to the same data can be compared to determine the appropriate model choice. As with other information criteria, smaller values of the DIC are favored over larger values. As Banerjee and Carlin (2003, 532) note, this can be seen from the fact that small values of the posterior expectation of the deviance reflect a good fit while a small number of effective parameters reflects parsimony. The goal, as with any information criterion, is thus to combine model fit and parsimony.

Table 9.2 reports the effective number of parameters and DIC values for three Cox models and five Weibull models: standard Cox and Weibull models with no random effects, Cox and Weibulls with nonspatial shared (state-level) random effects, Cox and Weibulls with spatial shared (state-level) random effects, a Weibull model with nonspatial individual (district-level) random effects, and a Weibull model with spatial, individual (district-level) random effects. In each model, the specification included the covariates discussed previously.

As Table 9.2 shows, in each of the three comparisons between the spatial and nonspatial frailty models, the spatial frailty models outperform their nonspatial counterparts, as indicated by the smaller DIC values. There is, in short, spatial dependence in the timing of NAFTA announcements that is not fully captured by the substantive covariates in the model. Treating the random effects as though they were spatially independent, as we typically do, reflects model misspecification.

Importantly, the information criterion advantages are not produced by overfitting the models with additional parameters. In both the case of the Cox model and the shared frailty Weibull model, the spatial frailty model has a smaller effective number of parameters (p_D) than does the nonspatial

frailty model. These spatial frailty models thus enjoy a parsimony advantage over their nonspatial counterparts. In the third comparison, for the individual frailty Weibull models, the spatial model has only a very marginal increase in the effective number of parameters over its nonspatial counterpart (12.33 vs. 12.17).

Examining the DICs for the various models, clear patterns emerge. The models that incorporate spatial dependence in state-level frailties are the preferred model in both the semiparametric Cox and parametric Weibull cases. The Cox model with spatial shared frailties outperforms both the standard Cox model and the Cox model with nonspatial shared frailties. The Weibull with spatial shared frailties outperforms the standard Weibull, the Weibull with nonspatial shared frailties, and the two Weibull individual frailty specifications. Whether considering a semiparametric or parametric modeling approach, in this case scholars should fit a model that accounts for spatial dependence across state-level effects rather than fitting either a standard model that doesn't account for unmodeled heterogeneity in risk propensity, or a frailty model that treats this heterogeneity as spatially independent.

More broadly, scholars modeling legislative behavior have become accustomed to clustering legislators by state and treating members from different states as independent, conditional on the covariates. The DIC values in Table 9.2 question the validity of such an approach. Scholars, instead, should consider the possibility that members from neighboring states share common unmeasured characteristics that impact the behavior of interest. The results also argue that modeling heterogeneity via unit-specific random effects is not ideal either. The DICs indicate that the argument that the uniqueness of each individual actor precludes conceptual generalization is not valid for this particular case of legislative behavior. House members are not independent actors; neighboring legislators share common risk factors, whether due to direct behavioral interaction or shared attributes.

9.7.10 Cox and Weibull Results

I examine spatial dependence in the timing of NAFTA position announcements as well as its effects on substantive covariates via summaries of the posterior densities from the Bayesian Cox and Weibull analyses. (The Grambsch and Therneau global test and Harrell's rho covariate-specific tests showed no violations of the proportional hazards assumption.) Table 9.3 presents the summaries for the semiparametric Cox MCMC analysis, while Table 9.4 presents the summaries for the parametric Weibull MCMC analysis. In both tables, the first cell entry is the mean of the posterior density of the particular parameter of interest while the cell entry in parentheses below is the corresponding 95% Bayesian credible interval (formed by taking the 2.5 and 97.5 posterior percentiles). Descriptions of the models in each column are provided below the tables.

TABLE 9.3. *Posterior Summaries for Cox Models of the Timing of NAFTA Position Announcements*

Covariate	(1)	(2)	(3)
Union Membership	3.512	3.424	2.736
	(1.875, 5.154)	(1.243, 5.534)	(0.393, 5.055)
Household Income	−0.041	−0.106	−0.132
	(−0.168, 0.087)	(−0.245, 0.027)	(−0.272, 0.009)
NAFTA Committee	−0.009	−0.023	−0.040
	(−0.160, 0.142)	(−0.177, 0.130)	(−0.193, 0.114)
Republican Leadership	0.348	0.407	0.418
	(−0.008, 0.678)	(0.040, 0.758)	(0.051, 0.764)
Democratic Leadership	0.091	0.033	0.018
	(−0.244, 0.405)	(−0.312, 0.354)	(−0.328, 0.339)
*Ideology*Union Membership*	−4.174	−3.873	−3.778
	(−6.676, −1.664)	(−6.491, −1.201)	(−6.429, −1.138)
*Ideology*Household Income*	0.142	0.128	0.145
	(−0.035, 0.317)	(−0.052, 0.307)	(−0.034, 0.324)
θ		0.082	0.195
		(0.026, 0.178)	(0.056, 0.442)

Cell entries are the posterior means, with 95% credible intervals in parentheses.
(1) = Standard Cox model.
(2) = Cox model with nonspatial shared frailties.
(3) = Cox model with spatial shared frailties.

Examining the Cox summaries in Table 9.3, we can see that employing a standard nonspatial frailty model understates the frailty variance estimate in comparison to the spatial frailty model favored by the DICs. The posterior mean of the variance of the random effects, θ, is more than twice as large in the spatial model as in the nonspatial model. Spatially proximate members share common unmodeled risk factors that distinguish them from their spatially distant colleagues. Modeling these risk factors as though they were spatially independent understates the unmodeled heterogeneity in risk propensity.

By mapping the frailties from the nonspatial and spatial Cox models, we can further see the problems that are induced by modeling spatially dependent risk factors as though they were spatially independent. Figure 9.1 presents a map of the posterior means of the nonspatial state-level frailties – means estimated under the assumption of spatial independence. Figure 9.1 suggests a checkerboard pattern, with little spatial clustering in the random effects.

Figure 9.2 maps the posterior means from the spatial Cox model that takes into account the spatial dependence between the state-level frailties. As can be seen from Figure 9.2, there is, in fact, a strong spatial clustering in

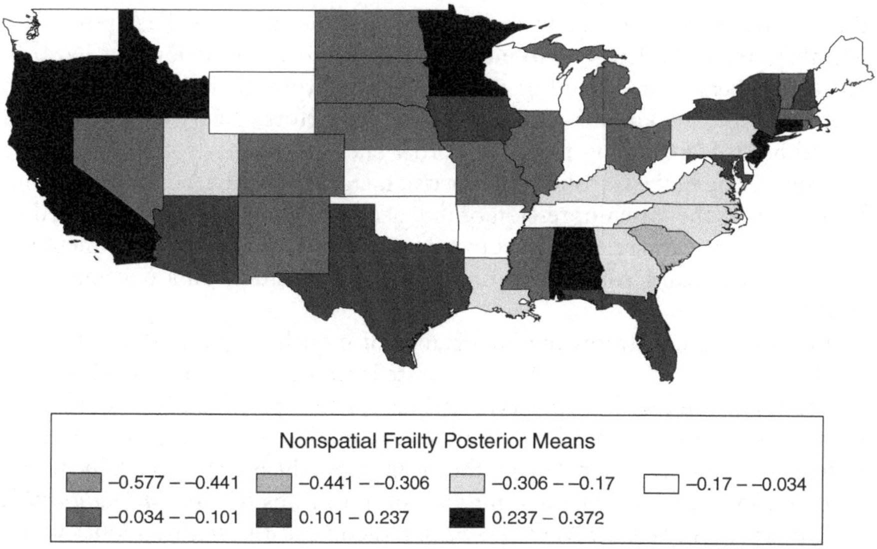

FIGURE 9.1. Nonspatial Cox state-level frailties for model of the timing of NAFTA position announcements.

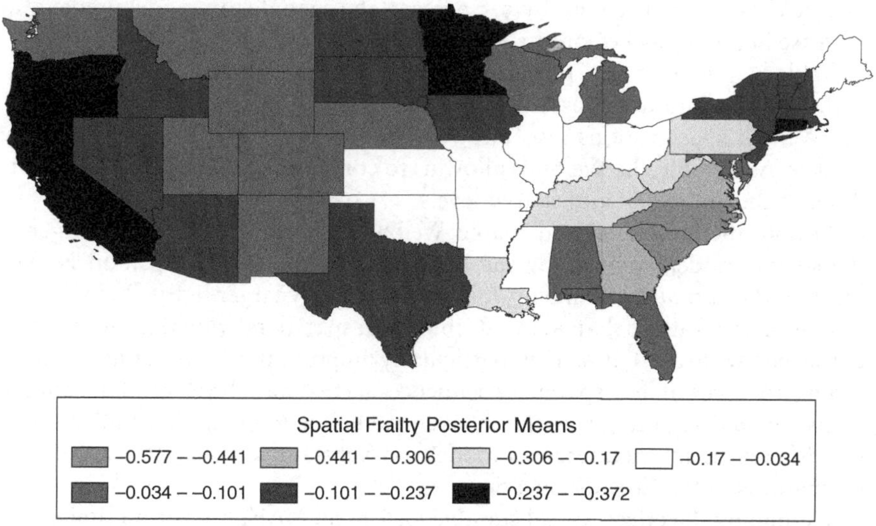

FIGURE 9.2. Spatial Cox state-level frailties for model of the timing of NAFTA position announcements.

the unobserved risk factors. There are distinct spatial bands in the random effects. Portions of the Northeast, upper Plains, and West were marked by particularly high risk propensity (and thus, all else equal, members from

these states were more likely to be early announcers of NAFTA positions). Members from the Rocky Mountain states shared the next level of hazards. Next, members from a band of states extending from the industrial Midwest, southwest into Oklahoma shared similar risk factors. Next, we see a set of shared hazards extending from the border states to Pennsylvania. Finally, we see a clustering in the Carolinas of low risk factors for NAFTA announcements. In contrast to the false impression of independent random effects suggested by Figure 9.1, we can see from Figure 9.2 that the spatial location of members played a significant role in the timing of their position announcements on NAFTA.

Table 9.3 demonstrates the importance of modeling spatial dependence in random effects if we wish to draw accurate inferences about other substantive covariates of interest. The posterior means for the spatial frailty model differ from those in the standard, nonfrailty Cox model, and in all but one case, differ more from the latter than do the means from the nonspatial frailty model. Note, for example, the changes in the posterior means for *Union Membership* and the *Ideology*Union Membership* interaction in the spatial model versus the standard Cox model. Similarly, the means for the *Democratic Leadership* effects are noticeably different across the two models. Where the standard Cox model predicts that a position in the Democratic leadership increases the hazard of a NAFTA announcement by 9.5 percent, the spatial Cox model predicts an increase in the hazard of only 1.8 percent.

Table 9.4 reports the posterior summaries for the five Weibull models. Although the parametric assumption of the Weibull makes it more restrictive, the Weibull specifications also allow for the estimation of individual frailty models. As a result, the Weibulls allow us to compare how spatial frailty effects differ at the individual and shared levels.

In both the individual and shared Weibulls, the frailty effects are larger in the spatial models favored by the DICs than in the nonspatial models. The mean of the variance parameter, θ, is also noticeably larger in the Weibull with spatial shared frailties than in the Weibull with spatial individual frailties. Thus, consistent with the DICs, it is particularly important in estimating position timing to account for spatial dependence across state-level random effects. As we would expect given the smaller values of θ in the Weibull models, the differences in effects across models on substantive covariates are not as dramatic as in the Cox specifications.

Examining the effects of substantive factors on NAFTA position timing, we can gauge the effect of constituency, institutional, and individual factors by examining the posterior summaries from the best-performing model according to the DIC, the Cox spatial shared frailty model. As we can see from Table 9.3, the main effect of large union memberships in a member's district was to increase the hazard of a NAFTA position announcement. Economically conservative members from districts with large union memberships, however, had reduced hazards of NAFTA announcements, as indicated by the negative

TABLE 9.4. *Posterior Summaries for Weibull Models of the Timing of NAFTA Position Announcements*

Covariate	(1)	(2)	(3)	(4)	(5)
Constant	−19.14	−18.59	−18.84	−18.83	−18.91
	(−21.24, −17.29)	(−20.09, −17.04)	(−20.35, −17.63)	(−20.43, −17.09)	(−20.61, −17.09)
Union Membership	1.154	1.102	0.966	1.021	1.006
	(−1.035, 3.290)	(−1.094, 3.212)	(−1.292, 3.238)	(−1.267, 3.266)	(−1.344, 3.271)
Household Income	−0.034	−0.034	−0.042	−0.041	−0.044
	(−0.203, 0.133)	(−0.207, 0.136)	(−0.210, 0.128)	(−0.213, 0.129)	(−0.216, 0.129)
NAFTA Committee	−0.011	−0.011	−0.007	−0.008	−0.008
	(−0.220, 0.196)	(−0.222, 0.194)	(−0.217, 0.199)	(−0.217, 0.200)	(−0.216, 0.197)
Republican Leadership	0.119	0.117	0.124	0.123	0.124
	(−0.392, 0.585)	(−0.397, 0.582)	(−0.386, 0.587)	(−0.391, 0.584)	(−0.386, 0.588)
Democratic Leadership	0.027	0.025	0.026	0.026	0.028
	(−0.438, 0.453)	(−0.456, 0.456)	(−0.439, 0.452)	(−0.443, 0.455)	(−0.446, 0.454)
*Ideology*Union Membership*	−1.593	−1.514	−1.350	−1.412	−1.434
	(−5.167, 1.962)	(−5.028, 2.003)	(−4.977, 2.180)	(−5.057, 2.182)	(−5.006, 2.187)
*Ideology*Household Income*	0.043	0.040	0.048	0.044	0.048
	(−0.194, 0.282)	(−0.197, 0.281)	(−0.192, 0.288)	(−0.200, 0.285)	(−0.193, 0.286)
ρ	3.173	3.081	3.123	3.121	3.134
	(2.869, 3.520)	(2.828, 3.330)	(2.925, 3.371)	(2.834, 3.383)	(2.835, 3.413)
θ		0.008	0.011	0.011	0.018
		(0.002, 0.021)	(0.002, 0.032)	(0.003, 0.030)	(0.003, 0.064)

Cell entries are the posterior means, with 95% credible intervals in parentheses.
(1) = Standard Weibull model.
(2) = Weibull model with nonspatial individual frailties.
(3) = Weibull model with spatial individual frailties.
(4) = Weibull model with nonspatial shared frailties.
(5) = Weibull model with spatial shared frailties.

value for the mean on the *Ideology*Union Membership* interaction. This suggests, then, that cross-pressures delayed announcements for some members. Also of note, members of the Republican leadership had increased hazards of NAFTA announcements; this is as we would expect given the Republican leadership's united support for the trade agreement. Overall, constituency, institutional, and individual characteristics all influenced the timing of NAFTA position announcements.

This application has presented an approach to modeling spatial dependence in event processes. The importance of modeling spatial autocorrelation in survival data is clear: many of our theories of event processes in the social sciences predict spatial dependence among neighboring units. If we are unable to model fully this spatial dependence, the result will be spatially autocorrelated unmeasured risk factors among neighboring units. Social scientists examining event processes will, therefore, often not wish to assume that frailties among neighboring observations are spatially independent. Instead, scholars will often have strong theoretical justification for modeling spatial dependence in the random effects among neighboring observations. The CAR prior allows social scientists to incorporate this spatial dependence in their survival models.

The application's results highlight the importance of modeling the spatial autocorrelation that is common to so many social science data. The DIC values favored the spatial shared frailty models (in both semiparametric and parametric forms) over both standard nonfrailty models and nonspatial frailty models. The posterior mean of the random effects variance parameter in both models also differed from the mean for the nonspatial variance parameter. Incorporating the spatial CAR prior also produced distinct changes in the posterior means for substantive covariates.

9.8 CONCLUSION

Some of the most interesting questions in the social sciences do not involve linear models for continuous dependent variables. Social scientists employing binary dependent variable, multinomial, count, and survival models rarely consider how spatial dependence may affect the substantive inferences they draw from these models. However, just as for more familiar models, it is also important for scholars employing these advanced modeling approaches to model the spatial dependence in the data generating processes they seek to explain.

This chapter has presented a variety of advanced spatial modeling approaches when the standard linear model for continuous dependent

variables is not applicable. Many of the subjects covered in this chapter, such as models for binary dependent variables, are areas in which significant advances in spatial analysis are currently being made. As a consequence, they represent some of the areas in which spatial analysis is most likely to advance in the coming years.

10

Conclusion

Much of the motivation for the research questions investigated by social scientists arises from the uniquely social and interactive nature of human beings. Social science phenomena are uniquely interesting, many social scientists argue, because of the consequences for both individuals and societies that are produced by the interactions between family members, co-workers, fellow citizens, tribes, and nation-states. These same interactions uniquely predispose social science data toward spatial dependence. Shared concerns between social actors combine with spatial proximity to promote familiarity. In turn, this familiarity between social actors breeds both contempt and conflict and interaction and interdependence. And by extension, it produces similar behaviors (even when these behaviors are shared conflict) between spatially proximate actors – in short, it produces spatial dependence. Alternatively, as Galton's problem recognizes, even in those instances in which actors do not interact with each other, their spatial locations can induce spatial dependence because of shared attributes that influence human behavior.

The time has never been better for social scientists to model the spatial dependence that is predicted by our theories of human behavior and that exists in the data we employ. The past two decades have witnessed a unique confluence of advances in four areas: (1) the geocoding of social science data, (2) the computational capabilities of computers, (3) the development of diagnostics and estimators for spatial autocorrelation, and (4) the inclusion of routines for spatial diagnosis and estimation in both general and more spatially specialized software packages. This book has sought to demonstrate how social scientists can diagnose and model spatial dependence. In the process, it has examined a variety of spatial diagnostics and estimators. It has also explored some of the concerns that pose challenges for spatial analysis such as the modifiable areal unit problem (MAUP) and the boundary value problem.

Going forward, three particular concerns are particularly important for future developments in spatial analysis. The first of these is the critical need

for additional theoretical development regarding our understanding of the two sources of spatial dependence posed by Galton's problem. The second is the need for spatial analysis methods to keep pace with the increased availability of large datasets in the social sciences. The final concern is the increased use of diagnostics for spatial models in applied research. I explore each of these three concerns in the remainder of this concluding chapter.

10.1 THEORETICAL DEVELOPMENT ON GEOGRAPHIC INFLUENCES IN THE SOCIAL SCIENCES

It is fair to say that developments in spatial empirics have outpaced developments in spatial theory in the social sciences. Although many of our theories in the social sciences have a geographic component and predict that spatial proximity affects units' behavior, these theories are much less precise in either their explanation or prediction of how distances between units shape behavior. As a consequence, we know much more about how to estimate spatial effects via maximum likelihood estimation, generalized method of moments (GMM) estimation, specialized models such as spatial probits, and the like, than we know how the two sources of spatial dependence posed by Galton's problem shape human behavior.

Consider, for example, some of the fundamental theoretical questions about spatial distance whose answers still elude social scientists. How does distance between actors affect the probability of interactions between these actors and thus their propensity for spatial dependence? How does proximity differ in its relevance for different behaviors both within and across social science disciplines? What distances are most relevant for inducing attributional dependence? In short, we need to know much more about how geography conditions the behaviors of interest to social scientists.

These theoretical concerns are most relevant for social scientists' definition of neighbors via spatial weights matrices. This book has argued that social scientists should use substantive theory to guide their construction of spatial weights matrices. Too often, however, we lack this guidance from prior substantive theory in the social sciences. As a consequence, weights matrices are often designed on an ad hoc and inductive basis. Practically, researchers rarely examine information criteria to examine the utility of alternative weights matrices and neighbor definitions. Much more frequently, researchers employ a single spatial weights matrix that seems intuitively valid for their research question.

Happily, as social scientists increasingly model the spatial dependence in their data in the coming decades, this will spur theoretical advances in our understanding of how geography influences behaviors in the social sciences. As is generally the case, these advances will result from the iterative dialogue between data, results, and theory. Most certainly, we should not expect a "one

size fits all" theory that will be applicable for both sources of spatial dependence in Galton's problem across all social sciences. The research questions that social scientists explore are far too varied for a single geographic theory to account for all of the many sociological, demographic, criminological, political, and other behaviors in which humans engage. Much work, however, remains to be done in determining the ways in which geogaphy conditions the specific behaviors of interest to social scientists.

Indeed, one particularly important and potentially fruitful avenue of future theoretical development is in the linking of spatial analysis and network analysis. Many of the questions posed in these two fields are quite similar – for example, How do routine social interactions between actors produce similarities in their behaviors? However, despite the similarities in research questions, the methods used and the answers derived by scholars in these fields are quite distinct. Indeed, the two fields have largely developed along separate parallel tracks with too little exchange between scholars in these fields. Rarely, for example, do network analysts examine how spatial proximity between network members shapes their behaviors. Rarely do spatial analysts seek to map the networks of the actors they study. The few studies that do explore the connections between these fields, such as Hays, Kachi, and Franzese (2010) and Franzese, Hays, and Kachi (2012), are both promising and welcome.

10.2 DEVELOPMENT OF SPATIAL METHODS FOR LARGE SAMPLES IN THE SOCIAL SCIENCES

As was stated earlier, one of the factors that makes spatial analysis particularly attractive for use in the social sciences today is the explosion of available geocoded datasets. In contrast to the much more limited social science data sets available in previous decades, these georeferenced datasets are often quite large (see, e.g., King 2011). As this book has discussed, large samples create considerable computational burdens for many estimation procedures. These computational burdens, moreover, are often greater in spatial analyses than in nonspatial analyses, as simultanous spatial autoregressive processes, for example, are modeled along with the behavioral parameters typically of interest to scholars. Thus, both because of the spatial dependence of interest to scholars and the large number of geocoded observations available to scholars, spatial analysis creates particular practical challenges for research in the social sciences.

Chapter 6, for example, demonstrated the many alternatives being proposed to ease maximum likelihood estimation of spatial models in large samples. Continued progress is going to be needed on this front in the coming decades. This is made all the more imperative by the rising interest in and use of Big Data in the social sciences, where the size of datasets can reach into terabytes and exabytes.

The challenge for spatial analysts going forward is to develop estimation methods for Big Data as the size of geocoded datasets continues to increase markedly. Spatial analysts' ability to outpace the growth in the size of geocoded datasets will be a critical determinant of spatial methods' continued applicability for applied researchers in the social sciences. If advances in estimation methods are able to outpace the growth of datasets, spatial methods will continue to be of considerable use for applied social scientists regardless of their research questions. If, however, the spatial questions of interest to social scientists are increasingly answerable only with increasingly large georeferenced datasets and computational processes do not keep pace with these new data sources, social scientists could find themselves forced to take shortcuts in choice of either estimation procedures or data sources that are not optimal. Happily, work continues to be done in advancing spatial analysis for large samples and thus there is every reason to believe that spatial methods will continue to be of use for researchers wishing to analyze the spatial datasets of 2020 or 2030 (see, e.g., Wieland et al. 2006; Torrens 2010).

10.3 USE OF DIAGNOSTICS FOR SPATIAL MODELS

One of the principal arguments that this book has made is that spatial diagnostics are critical for the proper specification of spatial models. The book's highly diagnostic approach stands in contrast to some of the existing research in applied spatial analysis. Often a spatial lag or spatial error model is applied without the use of prior diagnostics to determine whether this is the proper alternative. Often, for example, scholars will employ a spatial lag specification because theoretical expectations predict the existence of a diffusion process. At other times, scholars will estimate a spatial error model as a corrective for any uncaptured spatial dependence.

It is important, however, to examine whether these expectations are supported via spatial diagnostics. If a spatial lag (spatial error) model is estimated when a spatial error (spatial lag) model is more appropriate, a serious form of model misspecification will have occurred. The ready availability of spatial diagnostics such as the robust Lagrange multiplier diagnostics affords the applied researcher the opportunity to diagnose whether a spatial lag or spatial error model is more appropriate for her data. It is much better, in short, to employ the diagnostic step emphasized in this book before deciding on which model to estimate. Only the use of these diagnostics can ensure that researchers are properly modeling a spatial diffusion or spatial error process.

10.4 CONCLUSION

As Sir Francis Galton recognized more than 100 years ago, behaviors of interest to social scientists are often likely to exhibit dependence. Sir Galton would, no doubt, be quite surprised (and, one hopes, pleased) by the advances that have

been made in modeling dependence in data since his comment at the Royal Anthropological Institute. Many of these advances have, in fact, been made in just the past few decades, demonstrating what a dynamic field spatial analysis is. As a consequence of these advances, social scientists are now able to model in a quite sophisticated and precise manner the spatial dependence in their data.

In the years ahead, as geocoded spatial data become even more readily available, the premium placed on modeling spatial dependence within the social sciences will only increase. This book has sought to provide applied researchers in the social sciences with the information necessary to diagnose and model spatial dependence. Appendix A, which follows, presents a brief discussion of the steps necessary for getting one's data ready for a spatial analysis. Appendix B presents a variety of spatial software that researchers can employ for spatial analysis. Appendix C presents a variety of spatial websites that scholars will find helpful as they begin to model spatial dependence in the social sciences. By employing the software and the Web resources in combination with the spatial methods discussed in this book, social scientists have the opportunity to bring to fruition Sir Francis Galton's wish that researchers effectively model the dependence in their data.

PART III

APPENDICES ON IMPLEMENTING SPATIAL ANALYSES

Appendix A

Getting Data Ready for a Spatial Analysis

Spatial data require some minimal work at the early stages of analysis to get these data ready for a spatial analysis. This work is not onerous and can typically be completed in just a few minutes. However, the steps in this work are unique to spatial data and many researchers in the social sciences are not familiar with these steps. As a consequence, it is useful to briefly discuss them. Researchers interested in exploring the details of these steps will find additional, detailed information on them in manuals for geographic information systems (GIS) and other software.

The main issue in setting up data for a spatial analysis is that datasets in the social sciences do not include geometric information on the units the researcher is seeking to examine. To be sure, these data do typically include identifiers and use of these geographic identifiers, such as Federal Information Processing Standards (FIPS) codes, is very helpful in linking social science data up to files that contain features of the polygons examined, such as their size, boundaries, and locations. But typically, social science data do not include these latter features themselves, and thus researchers must link, or join, their datasets to a file that contains this information.

The standard such geographic file in spatial analysis is the shapefile developed by Environmental Systems Research Institute (ESRI) for use with its Arcview GIS software in the early 1990s. Today, ESRI's principal GIS product is ArcGIS, which includes a suite of component applications, including ArcMap, ArcCatalog, ArcScene, and ArcGlobe. One of the more efficient ways to join one's data is to do so in ArcMap, utilizing an identifier variable that is included in both the shapefile and in the researcher's dataset. Often this variable will be the units' FIPS codes.

Shapefiles are readily available for a variety of polygons of interest via the Internet. Many colleges and universities have GIS units on campus that can aid researchers in finding shapefiles if a search on the Web proves unsuccessful. Once the researcher has obtained a shapefile for the polygons she is interested

in, the next step is to join the data in this shapefile to her dataset. Assuming the researcher is using ArcMap to accomplish this, she will wish to bring up the shapefile as a layer in ArcMap and add a second set of data in the form of her dataset, often in a .dbf or .csv format. Once both the shapefile's geometric data and the researcher's data have been brought up in ArcMap, she simply right-clicks on the name for the shapefile, chooses the join option, and selects the identifier variables in the shapefile and her dataset. Once these two layers have been successfully joined, she can export the joined shapefile under a new file name for analysis.

The next step is to create a neighbor definition from the new, merged shapefile. I find that it is often easiest to do this in GeoDa. This software can create a variety of neighbor definitions that can subsequently be exported for analysis in other packages such as R or utilized for analysis in GeoDa itself. Appendix B discusses alternative software options that are available for scholars wishing to diagnose and model the spatial dependence in their data.

Appendix B

Spatial Software

Stata®: This software from Stata Corporation, widely used in the social sciences, does not include much spatial functionality in its standard release. However, there are some user-written functions that allow for the diagnosis and modeling of spatial dependence. Commands written by Maurizio Pisati allow for the importation and generation of spatial weights matrices, the diagnosis of spatial dependence in the absence of covariates, the diagnosis of spatial dependence for ordinary least squares (OLS) regressions, and maximum likelihood estimation of spatial lag and spatial error models (see Pisati 2001). Weights matrices can be imported from external objects or created in Stata using the `spatwmat` command. The `spatgsa` command provides three alternative global spatial diagnostics, Moran's *I*, Geary's *c*, and Ord and Getis's *G* statistic. The `spatlsa` command provides four local spatial diagnostics, the local Moran's *I*, the local Geary's *c*, and the G_i and G_i^* statistics. Five diagnostics for spatial dependence in OLS regressions can be carried out via the `spatdiag` command: the Moran's *I* diagnostic, the Lagrange multiplier (LM) diagnostic against error dependence (LM_{Error}), the robust LM diagnostic against error dependence (Robust LM_{Error}), the LM diagnostic against spatial lag dependence (LM_{Lag}), and the robust LM diagnostic against spatial lag dependence (Robust LM_{Lag}). Finally, spatial lag and spatial error models can be estimated via maximum likelihood estimation by using the `spatreg` command.

Recently, David M. Drukker, Hua Peng, Ingmar Prucha, and Rafal Raciborski have created **SPPACK**, a Stata module for the estimation of cross-sectional spatial autoregressive models (see Drukker et al. 2013; Drukker, Prucha, and Raciborski 2013a; and Drukker, Prucha, and Raciborski 2013b). The module's `spmat` command provides a variety of options involving spatial weights matrices. Researchers can create contiguity matrices and inverse distance matrices or import matrices based on variables (such as distances) that are already stored in existing Stata datasets. Features of spatial weights matrices can also be summarized using the `spmat summarize` command. **SPPACK's**

spreg command allows for either maximum likelihood or generalized spatial two-stage least-squares estimation of spatial autoregressive models with spatial autoregressive errors. Its spivreg command estimates spatial autoregressive models with spatial autoregressive errors and additional endogenous variables. Both spreg and spivreg support postestimation commands.

For researchers interested in spatial generalized method of moments (GMM) estimation, Timothy Conley provides Stata code to employ the spatial GMM approach presented in his 1999 *Journal of Econometrics* article, "GMM Estimation with Cross Sectional Dependence" on his website (http://economics.uwo.ca/people/faculty/conley.html). Stata do files, written by Jean Pierre Dube, provide code both for two-step spatial GMM estimation as well as OLS estimation with spatial standard errors. Dube's code also allows for the creation of a set of coordinates based on a distance matrix via multidimensional scaling. The code provided by Conley also includes code by Rob Vigfusson to estimate a spatial logit model in which the standard errors are corrected for spatial dependence.

Recently, Federico Belotti, Gordon Hughes, and Andrea Piano Mortari have written xsmle, a Stata command for spatial panel data analysis. This command fits models for balanced panel data and allows for a wide variety of alternative modeling approaches. Spatial lag and error models can be estimated along with spatial Durbin models. Both fixed and random effects models can be estimated. The xsmle command also can estimate direct spatial effects, indirect effects, and total effects.

Eric Neumayer and Thomas Plümper (2010a) have recently written Stata commands for generating spatial effect variables in monadic (single-unit) and dyadic (two-unit) data (see also Neumayer and Plümper 2010b). The command spmon creates a spatial contagion variable for a monadic dataset. The command spundir creates a spatial contagion variable for an undirected dyad (a dyad in which the direction of influence is unimportant) while the spdir command creates a spatial contagion variable for dyads in which the researcher is interested in the direction of influence. The command spagg is used to model spatial dependence involving aggregate source or target contagion while the command spspc is used to model spatial dependence involving specific source or target contagion (see Neumayer and Plümper [2010b] for a discussion of aggregate and specific target and source contagion).

In addition, Mark Pearce has written commands for the estimation of geographically weighted regressions (GWR) in Stata (see Pearce 1998). Researchers can estimate a GWR via the gwr command. Alternatively, researchers can speed estimation for large datasets by fitting a grid over the area for which estimates are sought and estimating the GWR via the gwrgrid command. Bandwidths can either be specified by the user (utilizing the bandwidth option) or estimated from the data (the default option).

R: A variety of spatial packages have been developed for R. As with other R packages, these spatial packages have the advantages of frequent updates

(and thus the incorporation of recently developed estimators and diagnostics) and excellent graphing capabilities. The **spdep** package is the principal package for spatial regression analysis with areal data. Written by Roger Bivand, with contributions by many spatial researchers, the **spdep** package includes a variety of functions for importing and creating weights matrices, diagnosing spatial dependence, and modeling this dependence. GAL format weights files created by GIS software can be read into R by utilizing the `read.gal` function. Once this is done, a weights object can be created for use in spatial diagnostics and spatial models via the `nb2listw` function. The global Moran's *I* can be computed using the `moran` function while the local Moran's *I* can be computed using the `localmoran` function. The standard LM lag and error diagnostics can be computed using the `lm.LMtests` function with, respectively, the `test=LMlag` and `test=LMerr` options specified. The robust versions of these diagnostics can be specified using the `lm.LMtests` function and the `test=RLMlag` and `test=RLMerror` options. Spatial lag models can be estimated using the `lagsarlm` function while spatial error models can be estimated using the `errorsarlm` function.

The **splm** package, written by Giovanni Millo and Gianfranco Piras, provides functions for estimating models for (TSCS) data. The package provides for both maximum likelihood (ML) and GMM estimation and also provides for the inclusion of either fixed or random effects. The `spml` function provides for ML estimation of spatial panel models. The within estimator is specified by employing the `model=c("within")` option while the random effects model is specified by employing the `model=c("random")`. The GMM estimator is employed by utilizing the `spgm` function, with the within and random options used as in the ML estimation.

The **spgwr** package, written by Roger Bivand and Danlin Yu, with contributions by Tomoki Nakaya, and a function based on a contribution by Miquel-Angel Garcia-Lopez, provides for the estimation of GWR models. Bandwidths can be calculated using the `gwr.sel` function. Weights can be calculated using the `gwr.bisquare`, `gwr.gauss`, and `gwr.tricube` functions. GWR models can be estimated using the `gwr` function.

Daniel McMillen's **McSpatial** package provides a variety of GMM and ML estimators for spatial binary dependent variable models. Klier and McMillen's linearized GMM logit and probit estimators can be applied utilizing the `splogit` and `spprobit` functions. ML estimation for the spatial probit model can be applied utilizing the `spprobitml` function. The **spatialprobit** package, written by Stefan Wilhelm and Miguel Godinho de Matos, provides for estimation of spatial probit models. The package employs the Bayesian approach discussed in this book and allows for estimation of both spatial lag and spatial error probit models. The former is estimated using the `sarprobit` function while the latter is estimated using the `semprobit` function.

Other spatial R packages include **spsurvey**, written by Tom Kincaid and Tony Olsen, for survey design and analysis, **DCluster**, written by Virgilio

Gómez-Rubio, Juan Ferrándiz-Ferragud, and Antonio López-Quílez, for spatial disease cluster detection, **geoRglm**, written by Ole F. Christensen and Paulo J. Ribeiro, Jr., for generalized linear spatial models, and **spBayes**, written by Andrew O. Finley, Sudipto Banerjee, and Bradley P. Carlin, for Markov Chain Monte Carlo (MCMC) estimation of univariate and multivariate spatial models.

GeoDa: This free downloadable software package for spatial analysis developed by Luc Anselin can be downloaded from the GeoDa Center for Geospatial Analysis and Computation at Arizona State University at http://geodacenter.asu.edu/software/downloads. Among other functions, GeoDa allows for spatial weights matrix creation, exploratory spatial data analysis, and a basic set of spatial regression models. Weights can be based upon rook, queen, distance-based, *k*-nearest, or higher order contiguity neighbor definitions. GeoDa has nice mapping capabilities and provides for a variety of map options, including cartograms and box maps, and also provides a map movie option in which polygons are highlighted based upon their values on a variable of interest. The software also provides global and local diagnostics for spatial dependence and ML estimation of spatial regression models. An active listserv, Openspace, exists for user queries for GeoDa and other software tools developed through the NSF-funded Center for Spatially Integrated Social Science (CSISS). Information on subscribing to Openspace can be found at http://geodacenter.asu.edu/support/community.

ArcGIS®: Produced by ESRI, based in Redlands, California, ArcGIS has long been the commercial standard for GIS software. ArcGIS includes a suite of products, including ArcInfo, ArcEditor, and ArcView. ArcGIS allows the researcher to create and edit maps, provides a wide variety of geocoded data, and allows for the estimation of GWRs.

GRASS: This is a free, open-source GIS software available at http://grass.osgeo.org/. A product of the Open Source Geospatial Foundation, GRASS contains much of the functionality of commercial GIS software while also providing more frequent updates due to its open-source nature. GRASS can be used for data management, data visualization (including 2D, 2.5D, and 3D visualization), and spatial analysis.

QGIS: QGIS is a free, open-source GIS package that can be found at http://www.qgis.org. Begun in 2002, QGIS runs on a variety of operating systems, including Windows, OS X, and UNIX. The software employs a user-friendly graphical user interface (GUI) interface and provides the capabilities that one would expect in a GIS system. A variety of data formats are supported as are a variety of projections (at this writing, 2700 coordinate reference systems are supported) (QGIS User Guide Release 2.2 2014, 55).

CrimeStat™: Distributed by the National Institute of Justice, CrimeStat is a widely employed spatial program in criminology. CrimeStat provides for several spatial diagnostics, space–time analysis, and journey-to-crime analysis

(for identifying the likely residence of criminal offenders) (see Levine 2006). A particular focus of CrimeStat is hot spot analysis for the identification of high-crime locations.

MATLAB®: Several spatial routines have been written for use in MATLAB®, a product of The MathWorks™, based in Natick, Massachusetts. One of the principal user-written contributions is James LeSage's econometrics toolbox. LeSage's toolbox includes a variety of spatial routines, including functions for estimating spatial expansion models, GWR models, spatial regression models, spatial panel data models, and spatial probit models. LeSage's econometrics toolbox can be downloaded at http://www.spatial-econometrics.com/. R. Kelley Pace's Spatial Statistics Toolbox 2.0 includes functions for estimating simultaneous autoregressive models and conditional autoregressive models and can be downloaded at http://www.spatial-statistics.com. Donald J. Lacombe has written several spatial functions for use in MATLAB. Among these are functions for a variety of LM diagnostics, including the LM_{Lag} and LM_{Error} diagnostics, their robust versions, an $LM_{Error\ Components}$ diagnostic, an LM diagnostic for the joint presence of lag and error dependence, and LeSage and Pace's spatial Hausman test. Lacombe also provides LM tests for panel data as well as code to calculate distance-based weights matrices. Lacombe's functions can be downloaded at http://www.rri.wvu.edu/lacombe/matlab.html.

PySAL: Developed by Luc Anselin and Serge Rey, PySAL is designed to unite previous work conducted separately by these two researchers, respectively, on PySpace and STARS. PySal is a cross-platform open source library of spatial procedures written in Python. PySpace, developed by Anselin, is an open-source project focused on spatial regression diagnostics and spatial lag and spatial error model estimation. STARS, Space Time Analysis for Regional Systems, developed by Rey, is an open-source program specializing in applications for data located in both time and space. Among other functions, STARS provides spatial descriptive statistics, inequality analysis, and spatial Markov analysis (Rey and Janikas 2006). Further information on PySAL can be found at http://geodacenter.asu.edu/projects/pysal.

SAS®: Produced by SAS Institute, Inc., based in Cary, North Carolina, SAS incorporates functions for spatial variograms (the `proc variogram` command) and for kriging (the `proc krige2d` command). SAS Institute also produces SAS/GIS software for visualizing and analyzing data.

SpaceStat™: This software, compiled in Gauss, was developed by Luc Anselin and first released in 1991. Since then it has been updated several times. TerraSeer, Inc. acquired the software in 2002 and continues to market it to researchers. Employing a menu structure, SpaceStat provides a variety of diagnostics and estimators developed in the literature through the 1990s. Among the diagnostics are Moran's I (both global and local versions), Geary's c, and Ord and Getis's G_i and G_i^* statistics. The software also provides for spatial error estimation (both ML and GMM estimation) and spatial lag estimation

(both ML and instrumental variables estimation). SpaceStat has particular advantages over many programs in estimating models for continuous spatial heterogeneity (trend surface models and spatial expansion models) and discrete spatial heterogeneity (spatial regimes models).

S+SpatialStats®: Produced by Insightful Corporation, S+SpatialStats builds on the company's S-PLUS software. It has the GUI and visualization advantages long associated with S-PLUS. The software contains functions for each of the three forms of spatial data, point pattern, geostatistical, and areal data. It thus includes functions for empirical variogram estimation, kriging, and Ripley's *k*-function, in addition to the more commonly available functions for areal data such as Moran's *I* and Geary's *c* diagnostics and spatial regression models.

Appendix C

Web Resources for Spatial Analysis

Several helpful websites and listservs for spatial analysis have been developed as the use of spatial techniques has increased over the past two decades. This appendix considers some of the most helpful Web resources on spatial analysis in these two categories.

WEBSITES

AI-GEOSTATS (http://www.ai-geostats.org/): This website provides a variety of resources for geostatistics and spatial analysis. Among these are links to software, papers, books, conferences, and job openings. The site also provides links to the **AI-GEOSTATS** mailing list.

Center for Spatially Integrated Social Science (CSISS) (http://www.csiss.org/): Funded in 1999 by the National Science Foundation, The Center for Spatially Integrated Social Science (CSISS) (housed at the University of California, Santa Barbara) is designed to advance the dissemination of spatial techniques and perspectives in the social sciences. The CSISS website provides a variety of resources for social scientists wishing to apply spatial analysis in their research. Among these are a searchable database of more than 17,000 references featuring spatial applications in the social sciences from 1990 to 2004. The website also includes video clips of workshops, descriptions of "classic" geographically oriented studies in the social sciences, and links to software tools.

GeoDa Center (http://geodacenter.asu.edu/): Founded by Luc Anselin, the GeoDa Center for Geospatial Analysis and Computation at Arizona State University has become a leading repository for spatial studies, the dissemination of spatial software tools, and the provision of training and support. The website provides a link for downloading GeoDa and also provides tutorials for GeoDa and for spatial packages in R. The site also provides an extensive set of e-talks,

lectures on spatial analysis, tools, and techniques. The website also provides links to recent working papers by scholars affiliated with the GeoDa Center as well as to spatial data that can be downloaded for analysis.

GISpopsci.org (http://gispopsci.org): This project is a collaboration between the Population Research Institute (The Pennsylvania State University) and the Center for Spatially Integrated Social Science (University of California, Santa Barbara). The site, whose development was funded in part by the Eunice Kennedy Shriver National Institute of Child Health and Human Development (NICHD), provides a variety of resources for research and instruction on advanced spatial analysis in the population sciences and spatial demography. The website maintains an extensive bibliography of citations applicable to research in spatial demography and the population sciences. The site also contains links to course syllabi on spatial topics.

National Center for Geographic Information and Analysis (NCGIA) (http://www.ncgia.ucsb.edu/): Founded in 1988, the National Center for Geographic Information and Analysis (NCGIA) is a consortium comprising the University of California, Santa Barbara, the University at Buffalo, and the University of Maine. The NCGIA seeks to promote research and training in geographic information science. Its website includes links to publications, education projects, research programs, and software.

spatial@ucsb (http://spatial.ucsb.edu): Sponsored by the Center for Spatial Studies at the University of California, Santa Barbara, spatial@ucsb provides a wealth of resources on spatial analysis and geographic information systems (GIS). As the website notes, the "Center [for Spatial Studies] mission is to engage in interdisciplinary research and education in how people and technology solve spatial problems." The spatial@ucsb website reflects this strong interdisciplinary orientation, providing a variety of reports as well as links to information on the Center's annual Specialist Meetings that bring together researchers from a variety of disciplines and its ThinkSpatial talks for the local community.

Spatial Econometrics Association (http://spatialeconometr.altervista.org/): As its website notes, the Spatial Econometrics Association was created, in part, "to promote the development of theoretical tools and sound applications of the discipline of spatial econometrics, including spatial statistics and spatial data analysis." Reflecting this, the Spatial Econometrics Association's website includes links to the Association's Annual World Conference, its annual Spatial Econometrics Advanced Institute, sponsored meetings and courses, as well as a list of the Association's Fellows. The website also includes a link at which researchers can join the Spatial Econometrics Association.

LISTSERVS

AI-GEOSTATS: The **AI-GEOSTATS** mailing list seeks to bring together researchers in a variety of disciplines who are interested in geostatistics and

spatial analysis. Information on subscribing to **AI-GEOSTATS** and rules for using the mailing list can be found at http://www.ai-geostats.org/.

BUGS: The **BUGS** mailing list is an active moderated list for discussing modeling issues in BUGS, including Bayesian spatial modeling. The **BUGS** mailing list can be subscribed to at jiscmail@jiscmail.ac.uk.

Openspace: The **Openspace** mailing list serves as a source of support for questions about software tools developed through CSISS. The list is particularly active on questions regarding GeoDa. The **Openspace** mailing list can be subscribed to at: openspace-list-subscribe@googlegroups.com.

R-sig-Geo: This is a very active mailing list for the discussion of spatial packages in R. **R-sig-Geo** can be subscribed to at: https://www.stat.math.ethz.ch/mailman/listinfo/r-sig-geo.

Glossary

Areal data The observed data are polygonal areal objects. Areal data may be either regular, reflecting a grid of square or rectangular objects, or irregular, differing in shape from unit to unit. Irregular areal data are more common than regular areal data.

Boundary value problem Observed areal units may be spatially autocorrelated with unobserved areal units.

Focused spatial diagnostics Diagnostics with a specific alternative hypothesis, such as spatial lag or spatial error dependence. Examples of focused diagnostics include the LM_{Lag} and LM_{Error} diagnostics and the Robust LM_{Lag} and Robust LM_{Error} diagnostics.

Galton's problem Recognition that similarities in behaviors may be produced by diffusion or common exposure to the sources of behaviors.

Geographically weighted regression (GWR) An approach for modeling continuous spatial heterogeneity in parameters. GWR differs from a standard regression model in giving more spatially proximate observations greater weight in the calculation of location-specific parameters via a spatial weights matrix.

Geostatistical data Observed data are sample data drawn from a continuous underlying surface. The researcher's principal interest in geostatistical data is inferring information about values on the variable of interest at unobserved locations from the sample data.

Global spatial autocorrelation diagnostics Diagnose whether the data as a whole exhibit spatial dependence as well as the strength and direction (positive or negative) of any global spatial dependence.

Kelejian–Robinson diagnostic An unfocused nonparametric diagnostic for spatial dependence that does not assume linearity or normality. The diagnostic

is unfocused in that it does not have a specific alternative hypothesis of lag versus error dependence.

Lagrange multiplier diagnostics Focused diagnostics for spatial lag or spatial error dependence in regression residuals. These standard Lagrange multiplier (LM) diagnostics present a specific alternative hypothesis of lag or error dependence, but unlike their robust counterparts are also sensitive to the presence of the alternative form of dependence. As a consequence, the LM diagnostic for lag dependence may diagnose this dependence when spatial error dependence is present but spatial lag dependence is absent. Similarly, the LM diagnostic for spatial error dependence may diagnose dependence when spatial lag dependence is present but spatial error dependence is absent.

LISA statistics (Local indicators of spatial association) The LISA statistic for each observation measures the extent of significant spatial clustering of values around an observation and the sum of LISAs for all observations is proportional to a corresponding global indicator of spatial association.

Modifiable Areal Unit Problem (MAUP) Spatial autocorrelation estimates are dependent upon the areal units chosen for study. MAUP comprises two distinct problems. The *scale problem* refers to the dependence of spatial autocorrelation estimates on the number of areal units into which a spatial plane is divided. The *aggregation problem* refers to the dependence of spatial autocorrelation findings on the way that the spatial plane is divided into a particular number of polygons.

Moran's *I* diagnostic Commonly used spatial diagnostic that is the spatial analogue of the Durbin–Watson statistic. The global Moran's *I* diagnoses spatial dependence in the data as a whole. The local Moran's *I* diagnoses the local spatial dependence for individual spatial units. Because the local Moran's *I* is a LISA statistic, it is proportional to the global Moran's *I* and allows for the identification of the units producing any global pattern of spatial dependence. The Moran's *I* diagnostic can be employed as a univariate spatial diagnostic or as a spatial diagnostic for the presence of spatial dependence in regression residuals.

Point pattern data The observed spatial locations mark the locations of discrete events. The researcher's interest in point pattern data often is in determining whether the observed locations of events reflect spatial clustering or dispersion in comparison to a null of complete spatial randomness.

Robust Lagrange multiplier diagnostics Focused diagnostics for spatial lag or error dependence in regression residuals. Unlike their nonrobust counterparts, the robust LM diagnostic for lag dependence is robust to the presence of spatial error dependence while the robust LM diagnostic for error dependence is robust to the presence of lag dependence.

Spatial autocorrelation A nonzero covariance between the values on a random variable for neighboring locations. Unlike temporal autocorrelation, spatial autocorrelation is simultaneous. Positive spatial autocorrelation exists when neighboring units share similar values on the random variable. Negative spatial autocorrelation exists when neighboring units have dissimilar values on the random variable.

Spatial binary dependent variable models Spatial models in which the dependent variable is dichotomous. A variety of spatial binary dependent variable estimation approaches have been proposed, including auto-logistic models, the expectation maximization (EM) algorithm, the recursive importance sampling estimator, generalized method of moments (GMM) estimators, linearized, logit estimators, partial maximum likelihood estimators, Bayesian estimators, and copula-based estimators.

Spatial Chow test A test for discrete spatial heterogeneity in parameters. The spatial Chow test is a test of the equivalence of the parameters across distinct spatial regimes in a spatial regimes model. A rejection of the null indicates that the behavioral parameter or parameters differ across the spatial regimes in the data.

Spatial count models Event count models that incorporate spatial dependence in event counts.

Spatial Durbin model A spatial autoregressive error model can be rewritten as a spatial Durbin model in which λ, the spatial autoregressive parameter from the spatial error model, is applied to a spatially lagged dependent variable and spatially lagged independent variables if a set of common factor constraints are met.

Spatial error model A model in which the spatial dependence pertains to the error terms. In the spatial autoregressive error model, the spatial dependence is parameterized in a spatial autoregressive parameter, λ, and the spatial dependence produces a nonzero covariance between the error terms at all locations. In the spatial moving average error model, the spatial dependence is parameterized in a spatial moving average parameter, γ, and the spatial dependence is more localized than in the spatial autoregressive error model, extending only to first- and second-order neighbors. In the spatial error components model, the error process is separated into two uncorrelated error components: a region-specific component incorporating a spatial spillover with neighboring error terms and a unit-specific error component. Like the spatial moving average error model, the spatial error components model implies a more localized form of spatial error dependence than the spatial autoregressive error model.

Spatial expansion model A model for continuous spatial heterogeneity in parameters. The parameters of an initial model are modeled as functions of a set

of covariates, typically the x, y coordinates of the observations, in an expansion model.

Spatial heterogeneity Often takes the form of spatial heterogeneity in parameters, in which behavioral relationships in the data are not constant across the spatial plane, but instead vary as a function of the spatial locations of units. Spatial heterogeneity in parameters may be discrete, with parameters constant within discrete spatial regimes but varying across these regimes. Alternatively, spatial heterogeneity in parameters may be continuous across the spatial plane.

Spatial lag model A model in which the spatial dependence pertains to a spatially lagged dependent variable. The spatial dependence is parameterized in an autoregressive parameter, ρ. The spatial lag model is consistent with a spatial diffusion process.

Spatial survival models Survival models that differ from standard survival models by modeling spatial dependence in time-to-event data.

Spatial TSCS models Models for data in which repeated cross-sections of data for the same units are available. Spatial time-series cross-sectional models can take the form of spatial lag or spatial error models.

Spatial weights matrix Matrix containing the neighbor information for each spatial unit.

Tobler's First Law of Geography "everything is related to everything else, but near things are more related than distant things" (Tobler 1970, 236).

Unfocused spatial diagnostics Diagnostics that simply diagnose the presence of spatial dependence without indicating the specific form (e.g., spatial lag or spatial error) that this dependence takes. Examples of unfocused spatial diagnostics include the Moran's *I* and Kelejian–Robinson diagnostics.

Bibliography

Abrams, Samuel J., and Morris P. Fiorina. 2012. 'The Big Sort' That Wasn't: A Skeptical Reexamination." *PS: Political Science & Politics* 45(2): 203–210.

Achen, Christopher H. 2000. "Why Lagged Dependent Variables Can Suppress the Explanatory Power of Other Independent Variables." Paper presented at the Annual Meeting of the Society for Political Methodology, Los Angeles, CA.

Achen, Christopher H. 2002. "Toward a New Political Methodology: Microfoundations and ART." *Annual Review of Political Science* 5: 423–450.

Aldstadt, Jared, and Arthur Getis. 2006. "Using AMOEBA to Create a Spatial Weights Matrix and Identify Spatial Clusters." *Geographical Analysis* 38: 327–343.

Alvarez, R. Michael, and John Brehm. 1995. "American Ambivalence Towards Abortion Policy: Development of a Heteroskedastic Probit Model of Competing Values." *American Journal of Political Science* 39(4): 1055–1082.

Andersen, Kristi. 1979. *The Creation of a Democratic Majority, 1928–1936*. Chicago: University of Chicago Press.

Andersen, Per Kragh, and R. D. Gill. 1982. "Cox's Regression Model for Counting Processes: A Large Sample Study." *The Annals of Statistics* 10: 1100–1120.

Anselin, Luc. 1984. "Specification Tests on the Structure of Interaction in Spatial Econometric Models." *Papers in Regional Science* 54(1): 165–182.

Anselin, Luc. 1986. "Non-Nested Tests on the Weight Structure in Spatial Autoregressive Models: Some Monte Carlo Results." *Journal of Regional Science* 26(2): 267–284.

Anselin, Luc. 1988a. "Lagrange Multiplier Test Diagnostics for Spatial Dependence and Spatial Heterogeneity." *Geographical Analysis* 20: 1–17.

Anselin, Luc. 1988b. "Model Validation in Spatial Econometrics: A Review and Evaluation of Alternative Approaches." *International Regional Science Review* 11(3): 279–316.

Anselin, Luc. 1988c. *Spatial Econometrics: Methods and Models*. Dordrecht: Kluwer.

Anselin, Luc. 1990a. "Some Robust Approaches to Testing and Estimation in Spatial Econometrics." *Regional Science and Urban Economics* 20: 141–163.

Anselin, Luc. 1990b. "Spatial Dependence and Spatial Structural Instability in Applied Regression Analysis." *Journal of Regional Science* 30(2): 185–207.

Anselin, Luc. 1992a. "SpaceStat Tutorial: A Workbook for Using SpaceStat in the Analysis of Spatial Data." Typescript. University of Illinois at Urbana-Champaign.

Anselin, Luc. 1992b. "Spatial Dependence and Spatial Heterogeneity: Model Specification Issues in the Spatial Expansion Paradigm." In *Applications of the Expansion Method*, eds. John Paul Jones, III and Emilio Casetti, pp. 334–354. London: Routledge.

Anselin, Luc. 1994. "Testing for Spatial Dependence in Linear Regression Models: A Review." Regional Research Institute Research Paper 94–16, West Virginia University.

Anselin, Luc. 1995. "Local Indicators of Spatial Association – LISA." *Geographical Analysis* 27(2): 93–115.

Anselin, Luc. 2002. "Under the Hood: Issues in the Specification and Interpretation of Spatial Regression Models." *Agricultural Economics* 27: 247–267.

Anselin, Luc. 2005. "Spatial Regression Analysis in R: A Workbook." Typescript. University of Illinois at Urbana-Champaign and Center for Spatially Integrated Social Science.

Anselin, Luc, and Anil K. Bera. 1998. "Spatial Dependence in Linear Regression Models with an Introduction to Spatial Econometrics." In *Handbook of Applied Economic Statistics*, eds. Aman Ullah and David E. A. Giles, pp. 237–290. New York: Marcel Dekker.

Anselin, Luc, Anil K. Bera, Raymond Florax, and Mann J. Yoon. 1996. "Simple Diagnostic Tests for Spatial Dependence." *Regional Science and Urban Economics* 26: 77–104.

Anselin, Luc, and Daniel A. Griffith. 1988. "Do Spatial Effects Really Matter in Regression Analysis?" *Papers of the Regional Science Association* 65: 11–34.

Anselin, Luc, and Raymond J. G. M. Florax. 1995. "Small Sample Properties of Tests for Spatial Dependence in Regression Models: Some Further Results." In *New Directions in Spatial Econometrics*, eds. Luc Anselin and Raymond J. G., pp. 21–74. Florax. Berlin: Springer-Verlag.

Anselin, Luc, and Rosina Moreno. 2003. "Properties of Tests for Spatial Error Components." *Regional Science and Urban Economics* 33: 595–618.

Anselin, Luc, and Serge Rey. 1990. "Properties of Tests for Spatial Dependence in a Linear Regression." Technical Report, National Center for Geographic Information and Analysis (NCGIA), University of California, Santa Barbara.

Anselin, Luc, and Serge Rey. 1991. "Properties of Tests for Spatial Dependence in Linear Regression Models." *Geographical Analysis* 23(2): 112–131.

Anselin, Luc, and Wendy K. Tam Cho. 2002. "Spatial Effects and Ecological Inference." *Political Analysis* 10(3): 276–297.

Ansolabehere, Stephen, James M. Snyder, Jr., and Charles Stewart III. 2001. "The Effects of Party and Preferences on Congressional Roll-Call Voting." *Legislative Studies Quarterly* 26: 533–572.

Azomahou, Théophile, Claude Diebolt, and Tapas Mishra. 2009. "Spatial Persistence of Demographic Shocks and Economic Growth." *Journal of Macroeconomics* 31(1): 98–127.

Baller, Robert D., and Kelly K. Richardson. 2002. "Social Integration, Imitation, and the Geographic Patterning of Suicide." *American Sociological Review* 67(6): 873–888.

Baltagi, Badi H. 2001. *Econometric Analysis of Panel Data*, 2nd Ed. Chichester, UK: Wiley.

Baltagi, Badi H., and Dong Li. 2001. "LM Tests for Functional Form and Spatial Error Correlation." *International Regional Science Review* 24: 194–225.

Baltagi, Badi H., and Dong Li. 2005. "Testing for Linear and Log-Linear Models against Box-Cox Alternatives with Spatial Lag Dependence." In *Advances in Econometrics*, Vol. 18: *Spatial and Spatiotemporal Econometrics*, eds. James P. LeSage and R. Kelley Pace, pp. 35–74. Oxford: Elsevier.

Baltagi, Badi H., Georges Bresson, and Alain Pirotte. 2007. "Panel Unit Root Tests and Spatial Dependence." *Journal of Applied Econometrics* 22: 339–360.

Baltagi, Badi H., and Long Liu. 2008. "Testing for Random Effects and Spatial Lag Dependence in Panel Data Models." *Statistics and Probability Letters* 78: 3304–3306.

Baltagi, Badi H., Seuck Heun Song, Byoung Cheol Jung, and Won Koh. 2007. "Testing for Serial Correlation, Spatial Autocorrelation and Random Effects Using Panel Data." *Journal of Econometrics* 140: 5–51.

Baltagi, Badi H., Seuck Heun Song, and Won Koh. 2003. "Testing Panel Data Regression Models with Spatial Error Correlation." *Journal of Econometrics* 117: 123–150.

Baltagi, Badi H., Seuck Heun Song, and Jae Hyeok Kwon. 2009. "Testing for Heteroskedasticity and Spatial Correlation in a Random Effects Panel Data Model." *Computational Statistics and Data Analysis* 53: 2897–2922.

Banerjee, Sudipto, and Bradley P. Carlin. 2003. "Semiparametric Spatio-Temporal Frailty Modeling." *Environmetrics* 14: 523–535.

Banerjee, Sudipto, Bradley P. Carlin, and Alan E. Gelfand. 2004. *Hierarchical Modeling and Analysis for Spatial Data*. Boca Raton, FL: Chapman & Hall.

Banerjee, Sudipto, Melanie M. Wall, and Bradley P. Carlin. 2003. "Frailty Modeling for Spatially Correlated Survival Data, with Application to Infant Mortality in Minnesota." *Biostatistics* 4(1): 123–142.

Bates, Charles, and Halbert White. 1985. "A Unified Theory of Consistent Estimation for Parametric Models." *Econometric Theory* 1(2): 151–178.

Baybeck, Brady, and Robert Huckfeldt. 2002. "Urban Contexts, Spatially Dispersed Networks, and the Diffusion of Political Information." *Political Geography* 21: 195–220.

Beck, Nathaniel. 2001. "Time-Series-Cross-Section Data: What Have We Learned in the Past Few Years?" *Annual Review of Political Science* 4: 271–293.

Beck, Nathaniel, Kristian Gleditsch, and Kyle Beardsley. 2006. "Space Is More than Geography: Using Spatial Econometrics in the Study of Political Economy." Vol. 50, pp. 27–44 *International Studies Quarterly*.

Beck, Nathaniel, and Jonathan N. Katz. 1995. "What to Do (and Not to Do) with Time-Series Cross-Section Data." *American Political Science Review* 89(3): 634–647.

Beck, Nathaniel, and Simon Jackman. 1998. "Beyond Linearity by Default: Generalized Additive Models." *American Journal of Political Science* 42(2): 596–627.

Beenstock, Michael, and Daniel Felsenstein. 2010. "Spatial Error Correction and Cointegration in Nonstationary Panel Data: Regional House Prices in Israel." *Journal of Geographical Systems* 12(2): 189–206.

Beenstock, Michael, and Daniel Felsenstein. 2012. "Nonparametric Estimation of the Spatial Connectivity Matrix Using Spatial Panel Data." *Geographical Analysis* 44: 386–397.

Bell, Kathleen P., and Nancy E. Bockstael. 2000. "Applying the Generalized-Moments Estimation Approach to Spatial Problems Involving Microlevel Data." *The Review of Economics and Statistics* 82(1): 72–82.

Bera, Anil K., and Mann J. Yoon. 1993. "Specification Testing with Locally Misspecified Alternatives." *Econometric Theory* 9: 649–658.

Beron, Kurt J., James C. Murdoch, and Wim P. M. Vijverberg. 2003. "Why Cooperate? Public Goods, Economic Power, and the Montreal Protocol." *The Review of Economics and Statistics* 85(2): 286–297.

Beron, Kurt J., and Wim P. M. Vijverberg. 2004. "Probit in a Spatial Context: A Monte Carlo Analysis." In *Advances in Spatial Econometrics: Methodology, Tools and Applications*, eds. L. Anselin, R. J. G. M. Florax, and S. J. Rey, pp. 169–195. Berlin: Springer Science + Business Media.

Berry, Frances Stokes, and William D. Berry. 1990. "State Lottery Adoptions as Policy Innovations: An Event History Analysis." *American Political Science Review* 84(2): 395–415.

Berry, Frances Stokes, and William D. Berry. 1992. "Tax Innovation in the States: Capitalizing on Political Opportunity." *American Journal of Political Science* 36(3): 715–742.

Berry, William D., and Brady Baybeck. 2005. "Using Geographic Information Systems to Study Interstate Competition." *American Political Science Review* 99(4): 505–519.

Berry, William D., Richard C. Fording, Evan J. Ringquist, Russell L. Hanson, and Carl E. Klarner. 2010. "Measuring Citizen and Government Ideology in the United States: A Reappraisal." *State Politics & Policy Quarterly* 10(2): 117–135.

Bernardinelli, L., and C. Montomoli. 1992. "Empirical Bayes versus Fully Bayesian Analysis of Geographical Variation in Disease Risk." *Statistics in Medicine* 11: 983–1007.

Besag, Julian. 1972. "Nearest-Neighbour Systems and the Auto-Logistic Model for Binary Data." *Journal of the Royal Statistical Society B: Methodological* 34(1): 75–83.

Besag, Julian. 1974. "Spatial Interaction and the Statistical Analysis of Areal Systems." *Journal of the Royal Statistical Society B: Methodological* 36(2): 192–236.

Besag, Julian, Jeremy York, and Annie Mollie. 1991. "Bayesian Image Restoration, with Two Applications in Spatial Statistics." *Annals of the Institute of Statistical Mathematics* 43: 1–59.

Besag, Julian, Peter Green, David Higdon, and Kerrie Mengersen. 1995. "Bayesian Computation and Stochastic Systems." *Statistical Science* 10(1): 3–41.

Bhat, Chandra R., and Ipek N. Sener. 2009. "A Copula-Based Closed-Form Binary Logit Choice Model for Accommodating Spatial Correlation Across Observational Units." *Journal of Geographical Systems* 11: 243–272.

Bishop, Bill, with Robert G. Cushing. 2008. *The Big Sort: Why the Clustering of Like-Minded America Is Tearing Us Apart*. Boston: Houghton Mifflin.

Bolduc, Denis, Bernard Fortin, and Marc-Andre Fournier. 1996. "The Effect of Incentive Policies on the Practice Location of Doctors: A Multinomial Probit Analysis." *Journal of Labor Economics* 14(4): 703–732.

Bolduc, Denis, Bernard Fortin, and Stephen Gordon. 1997. "Multinomial Probit Estimation of Spatially Interdependent Choices: An Empirical Comparison of Two New Techniques." *International Regional Science Review* 20(1 & 2): 77–101.

Box-Steffensmeier, Janet M., Laura W. Arnold, and Christopher J.W. Zorn. 1997. "The Strategic Timing of Position Taking in Congress: A Study of the North American Free Trade Agreement." *American Political Science Review* 91: 324–338.

Box-Steffensmeier, Janet M., and Bradford S. Jones. 2004. *Event History Modeling: A Guide for Social Scientists*. Cambridge: Cambridge University Press.

Box-Steffensmeier, Janet M., and Suzanna De Boef. 2006. "Repeated Events Survival Models: The Conditional Frailty Model." *Statistics in Medicine* 25(20): 3518–3533.

Brandsma, A. S., and R. H. Ketellapper. 1979. "A Biparametric Approach to Spatial Autocorrelation." *Environment and Planning A* 11: 51–58.

Brock, William A., W. Davis Dechert, and Jose A. Scheinkman. 1987. "A Test for Independence Based on the Correlation Dimension." Working Paper No. 8702, Department of Economics, University of Wisconsin.

Brooks, Sarah M. 2004. "Explaining Capital Account Liberalization in Latin America: A Transitional Cost Approach." *World Politics* 56(3): 389–430.

Brown, Courtney. 1988. "Mass Dynamics of U.S. Presidential Competitions, 1928-1936." *American Political Science Review* 82: 1153–1181.

Brown, Courtney. 1991. *Ballots of Tumult: A Portrait of Volatility in American Voting*. Ann Arbor: University of Michigan Press.

Burnham, Kenneth P., and David R. Anderson. 2002. *Model Selection and Inference: A Practical Information-Theoretic Approach*, 2nd ed. New York: Springer Science + Business Media.

Burnham, Walter Dean. 1970. *Critical Elections and the Mainsprings of American Politics*. New York: W. W. Norton.

Burridge, P. 1980. "On the Cliff-Ord Test for Spatial Correlation." *Journal of the Royal Statistical Society B: Methodological* 42(1): 107–108.

Busch, Marc L., and Eric Reinhardt. 2000. "Geography, International Trade, and Political Mobilization in U.S. Industries." *American Journal of Political Science* 44(4): 703–719.

Buse, A. 1973. "Goodness of Fit in Generalized Least Squares Estimation." *The American Statistician* 27(3): 106–108.

Caldeira, Gregory A., and Samuel C. Patterson. 1987. "Political Friendship in the Legislature." *Journal of Politics* 49(4): 953–975.

Caldeira, Gregory A., and Samuel C. Patterson. 1988. "Contours of Friendship and Respect in the Legislature." *American Politics Quarterly* 16: 466–485.

Cardoso, Fernando Henrique, and Enzo Faletto. 1979. *Dependency and Development in Latin America*. Berkeley: University of California Press.

Carpenter, Daniel P. 2002. "Groups, the Media, Agency Waiting Costs, and FDA Drug Approval." *American Journal of Political Science* 46(3): 490–505.

Carrion-Flores, Carmen E., Alfonso Flores-Lagunes, and Ledia Guci. 2009. "Land Use Change: A Spatial Multinomial Chocie Analysis." Paper presented at the Third World Conference of Spatial Econometrics, Barcelona, Spain.

Carroll, Robert Todd. 2003. *The Skeptic's Dictionary: A Collection of Strange Beliefs, Amusing Deceptions, and Dangerous Delusions*. New York: John Wiley & Sons.

Case, Anne. 1992. "Neighborhood Influence and Technological Change." *Regional Science and Urban Economics* 22: 491–508.

Casetti, Emilio. 1972. "Generating Models by the Expansion Method: Applications to Geographic Research." *Geographical Analysis* 4: 81–91.

Chen, Jarvis T., David H. Rehkopf, Pamela D. Waterman, S.V. Subramanian, Brent A. Coull, Bruce Cohen, Mary Ostrem, and Nancy Krieger. 2006. "Mapping and Measuring Social Disparities in Premature Mortality: The Impact of Census Tract

Poverty within and across Boston Neighborhoods, 1999–2001." *Journal of Urban Health: Bulletin of the New York Academy of Medicine* 83(6): 1063–1084.

Chen, Xiaoheng, and Timothy G. Conley. 2001. "A New Semiparametric Spatial Model for Panel Time Series." *Journal of Econometrics* 105(1): 59–83.

Chica-Olmo, Jorge. 2007. "Prediction of Housing Location Price by a Multivariate Spatial Method: Cokriging." *Journal of Real Estate Research* 29(1): 91–114.

Chilès, Jean-Paul, and Pierre Delfiner. 1999. *Geostatistics: Modeling Spatial Uncertainty*. New York: John Wiley & Sons.

Chinni, Dante, and James Gimpel. 2010. *Our Patchwork Nation: The Surprising Truth about the "Real" America*. New York: Gotham Books.

Chiozza, Giacomo, and H.E. Goemans. 2004. "International Conflict and the Tenure of Leaders: Is War Still 'Ex Post' Inefficient?" *American Journal of Political Science* 48(3): 604–619.

Cho, Wendy K. Tam. 2003. "Contagion Effects and Ethnic Contribution Networks." *American Journal of Political Science* 47(2): 368–387.

Cho, Wendy K. Tam, and James G. Gimpel. 2007. "Prospecting for (Campaign) Gold." *American Journal of Political Science* 51(2): 255–268.

Cho, Wendy K. Tam, and James G. Gimpel. 2010. "Rough Terrain: Spatial Variation in Campaign Contributing and Volunteerism." *American Journal of Political Science* 54(1): 74–89.

Clapp, John M., and Yazhen Wang. 2006. "Defining Neighborhood Boundaries: Are Census Tracts Obsolete?" *Journal of Urban Economics* 59: 259–284.

Clayton, David G. 1991. "A Monte Carlo Method for Bayesian Inference in Frailty Models." *Biometrics* 47(2): 467–485.

Cliff, A. D., and J. K. Ord. 1972. "Testing for Spatial Autocorrelation Among Regression Residuals." *Geographical Analysis* 4: 267–284.

Cliff, A. D., and J. K. Ord. 1973. *Spatial Autocorrelation*. London: Pion.

Cliff, A. D., and J. K. Ord. 1981. *Spatial Processes: Models and Applications*. London: Pion.

Colaresi, Michael. 2004. "When Doves Cry: International Rivalry, Unreciprocated Cooperation, and Leadership Turnover." *American Journal of Political Science* 48(3): 555–570.

Conley, T. G. 1999. "GMM Estimation with Cross Sectional Dependence." *Journal of Econometrics* 92: 1–45.

Cooner, Freda, Sudipto Banerjee, and A. Marshall McBean. 2006. "Modelling Geographically Referenced Survival Data with a Cure Fraction." *Statistical Methods in Medical Research* 15: 307–324.

Coulton, Claudia J., Jill E. Korbin, Marilyn Su, and Julian Chow. 1995. "Community Level Factors and Child Maltreatment Rates." *Child Development* 66(5): 1262–1276.

Cressie, Noel. 1990. "The Origins of Kriging." *Mathematical Geology* 22(3): 239–252.

Cressie, Noel A. C. 1993. *Statistics for Spatial Data*, revised edition. New York: John Wiley & Sons.

Darmofal, David. 2006. "The Political Geography of Macro-Level Turnout in American Political Development." *Political Geography* 25(2): 123–150.

Darmofal, David. 2008. "The Political Geography of the New Deal Realignment." *American Politics Research* 36(6): 934–961.

Darmofal, David. 2009. "Bayesian Spatial Survival Models for Political Event Processes." *American Journal of Political Science* 53(1): 241–257.
Darmofal, David. 2012. "Modeling Spatial Heterogeneity with Geographically Weighted Regressions in R." *The Political Methodologist* 19(2): 7–12.
Darmofal, David, and Charles J. Finocchiaro. n.d. "Spatial Proximity and Roll-Call Voting Behavior in the U.S. Senate." Manuscript.
Darmofal, David, and Peter F. Nardulli. 2010. "The Dynamics of Critical Realignments: An Analysis Across Time and Space." *Political Behavior* 32(2): 255–283.
Davidson, Russell, and James G. MacKinnon. 1985. "Heteroskedasticity-Robust Tests in Regression Directions." Queen's Economics Department Working Paper No. 616. Queen's University, Kingston, Ontario, Canada.
de Graaff, Thomas, Raymond J.G.M. Florax, Peter Nijkamp, and Aura Reggiani. 2001. "A General Misspecification Test for Spatial Regression Models: Dependence, Heterogeneity, and Nonlinearity." *Journal of Regional Science* 41(2): 255–276.
Dempster, A. P., N. M. Laird, and D. Rubin. 1977. "Maximum Likelihood from Incomplete Data via the EM Algorithm." *Journal of the Royal Statistical Society B* 39: 1–38.
de Nooy, Wouter. 2011. "Networks of Action and Events Over Time: A Multilevel Discrete-Time Event History Model for Longitudinal Network Data." *Social Networks* 33: 31–40.
Dixon, Philip M. 2001. "Ripley's K Function." Manuscript. Iowa State University.
Dow, Malcolm M. 2007. "Galton's Problem as Multiple Network Autocorrelation Effects: Cultural Trait Transmission and Ecological Constraint." *Cross-Cultural Research* 41(4): 336–363.
Driscoll, John C., and Aart C. Kraay. 1998. "Consistent Covariance Matrix Estimation with Spatially Dependent Panel Data." *The Review of Economics and Statistics* 80(4): 549–560.
Drukker, David M., Hua Peng, Ingmar R. Prucha, and Rafal Raciborski. 2013. "Creating and Managing Spatial-Weighting Matrices with the Spmat Command." *The Stata Journal* 13(2): 242–286.
Drukker, David M., Ingmar R. Prucha, and Rafal Raciborski. 2013a. "A Command for Estimating Spatial-Autoregressive Models with Spatial-Autoregressive Disturbances and Additional Endogenous Variables." *The Stata Journal* 13(2): 287–301.
Drukker, David M., Ingmar R. Prucha, and Rafal Raciborski. 2013b. "Maximum Likelihood and Generalized Spatial Two-Stage Least-Squares Estimators for a Spatial-Autoregressive Model with Spatial-Autoregressive Disturbances." *The Stata Journal* 13(2): 221–241.
Durbin, J., and G. S. Watson. 1951. "Testing for Serial Correlation in Least Squares Regression. II." *Biometrika* 38(1/2): 159–177.
Durkheim, Emile. [1897] 1951. *Suicide*. London: Routledge.
Eff, E. Anthon. 2004. "Does Mr. Galton Still Have a Problem? Autocorrelation in the Standard Cross-Cultural Sample." *World Cultures* 15: 153–170.
Elhorst, J. Paul. 2003. "Specification and Estimation of Spatial Panel Data Models." *International Regional Science Review* 26(3): 244–268.
Ennis, Sharon R., Merarys Ríos-Vargas, and Nora G. Albert. 2011. "The Hispanic Population: 2010." U.S. Census Bureau, Population Division. Washington, D.C.: U.S. Government Printing Office.

Enns, Peter K., and Julianna Koch. 2013. "Public Opinion in the U.S. States: 1956–2010." *State Politics & Policy Quarterly* 13(3): 349–372.

Farley, Reynolds, and William H. Frey. 1994. "Changes in the Segregation of Whites from Blacks during the 1980s: Small Steps toward a More Integrated Society." *American Sociological Review* 59(1): 23–45.

Fleming, Mark M. 2004. "Techniques for Estimating Spatially Dependent Discrete Choice Models." In *Advances in Spatial Econometrics: Methodology, Tools and Applications*, eds. L. Anselin, R. J. G. M. Florax, and S. J. Rey, pp. 145–168. Berlin: Springer Science + Business Media.

Florax, Raymond J. G. M., and Peter Nijkamp. 2005. "Misspecification in Linear Spatial Regression Models." In *Encyclopedia of Social Measurement*, ed. K. Kempf-Leonard, pp. 695–707. San Diego: Academic Press.

Florax, Raymond J. G. M., and Serge Rey. 1995. "The Impacts of Misspecified Spatial Interaction in Linear Regression Models." In *New Directions in Spatial Econometrics*, eds. Luc Anselin and Raymond J. G. M. Florax, pp. 111–135. Berlin: Springer-Verlag.

Florax, Raymond J. G. M., and Thomas de Graaff. 2004. "The Performance of Diagnostic Tests for Spatial Dependence in Linear Regression Models: A Meta-Analysis of Simulation Studies." In *Advances in Spatial Econometrics: Methodology, Tools and Applications*, eds. L. Anselin, R. J. G. M. Florax, and S. J. Rey, pp. 29–65. Berlin: Springer Science + Business Media.

Fotheringham, A. S., M. E. Charlton, and C. Brunsdon. 1998. "Geographically Weighted Regression: A Natural Evolution of the Expansion Method for Spatial Data Analysis." *Environment and Planning A* 30: 1905–1927.

Fotheringham, A. Stewart, Chris Brunsdon, and Martin Charlton. 2002. *Geographically Weighted Regression: The Analysis of Spatially Varying Relationships*. Chichester: John Wiley & Sons.

Franzese, Robert J., Jr., and Jude C. Hays. 2007. "Spatial Econometric Models of Cross-Sectional Interdependence in Political Science Panel and Time-Series-Cross-Section Data." *Political Analysis* 15(2): 140–164.

Franzese, Robert J., Jr., and Jude C. Hays. 2008. "Interdependence in Comparative Politics: Substance, Theory, Empirics, Substance." *Comparative Political Studies* 41(4/5): 742–780.

Franzese, Robert J., Jr., Jude C. Hays, and Aya Kachi. 2012. "Modeling History Dependence in Network-Behavior Coevolution." *Political Analysis* 20(2): 175–190.

Gatrell, Anthony C., Trevor C. Bailey, Peter J. Diggle, and Barry S. Rowlingson. 1996. "Spatial Point Pattern Analysis and Its Application in Geographical Epidemiology." *Transactions of the Institute of British Geographers* 21(1): 256–274.

Gelfand, A. E., and B. K. Mallick. 1995. "Bayesian Analysis of Proportional Hazards Models Built from Monotone Functions." *Biometrics* 51: 843–852.

Gelman, Andrew. 2006. "Prior Distributions for Variance Parameters in Hierarchical Models." *Bayesian Analysis* 1(3): 515–533.

Gelman, Andrew. 2009. *Red State, Blue State, Rich State, Poor State: Why Americans Vote the Way They Do*. Princeton, NJ: Princeton University Press.

Gelman, Andrew, John B. Carlin, Hal S. Stern, and Donald B. Rubin. 2004. *Bayesian Data Analysis*, 2nd ed. Boca Raton, FL: Chapman & Hall/CRC.

Getis, Arthur. 2010. "Spatial Filtering in a Regression Framework: Examples Using Data on Urban Crime, Regional Inequality, and Government Expenditures." In *Perspectives*

on Spatial Data Analysis, eds. Luc Anselin and Sergio J. Rey, pp. 191–202. Heidelberg: Springer Science + Business Media.

Getis, Arthur, and Jared Aldstadt. 2004. "Constructing the Spatial Weights Matrix Using a Local Statistic." *Geographical Analysis* 36(2): 90–104.

Getis, Arthur, and J. K. Ord. 1992. "The Analysis of Spatial Association by Use of Distance Statistics." *Geographical Analysis* 24(3): 189–206.

Geweke, John. 1989. "Bayesian Inference in Econometric Models Using Monte Carlo Integration." *Econometrica* 57: 1317–1340.

Geweke, John. 1993. "Bayesian Treatment of the Independent Student *t* Linear Model." *Journal of Applied Econometrics* 8: s19–s40.

Gieryn, Thomas F. 2000. "A Space for Place in Sociology." *Annual Review of Sociology* 26: 463–496.

Gill, Jeff. 2002. *Bayesian Methods: A Social and Behavioral Sciences Approach*. Boca Raton, FL: Chapman & Hall/CRC.

Gimpel, James G., and Jason Shuknecht. 2003. *Patchwork Nation: Sectionalism and Political Change in American Politics*. Ann Arbor: University of Michigan Press.

Gimpel, James G., and Wendy K. Tam Cho. 2004. "The Persistence of White Ethnicity in New England Politics." *Political Geography* 23: 987–1008.

Glass, Thomas A., and Matthew J. McAtee. 2006. "Behavioral Science at the Crossroads in Public Health: Extending Horizons, Envisioning the Future." *Social Science & Medicine* 62: 1650–1671.

Gleditsch, Kristian Skrede. 2002. *All International Politics Is Local: The Diffusion of Conflict, Integration, and Democratization*. Ann Arbor: University of Michigan Press.

Gleditsch, Kristian Skrede. 2007. "Transnational Dimensions of Civil War." *Journal of Peace Research* 44(3): 293–309.

Gleditsch, Kristian Skrede, and Michael D. Ward. 2000. "War and Peace in Space and Time: The Role of Democratization." *International Studies Quarterly* 43: 1–29.

Gleditsch, Kristian Skrede, and Michael D. Ward. 2006. "Diffusion and the International Context of Democratization." *International Organization* 60(4): 911–933.

Gleditsch, Nils Petter, Peter Wallensteen, Mikael Eriksson, Margareta Sollenberg & Håvard Strand. 2002. "Armed Conflict 1946–2001: A New Dataset." *Journal of Peace Research* 39(5): 615–637.

Godfrey, L. 1988. *Misspecification Tests in Econometrics*. Cambridge: Cambridge University Press.

Gordon, Sanford C. 2002. "Stochastic Dependence in Competing Risks." *American Journal of Political Science* 46(1): 200–217.

Greene, William H. 2003. *Econometric Analysis*, 5th ed. Upper Saddle River, NJ: Prentice Hall.

Griffith, Daniel A. 1983. "The Boundary Value Problem in Spatial Statistical Analysis." *Journal of Regional Science* 23(3): 377–387.

Griffith, Daniel A. 2003. *Spatial Autocorrelation and Spatial Filtering: Gaining Understanding Through Theory and Scientific Visualization*. Berlin: Springer Science + Business Media.

Griffith, Daniel A. 2006. "Assessing Spatial Dependence in Count Data: Winsorized and Spatial Filter Specification Alternatives to the Auto-Poisson Model." *Geographical Analysis* 38: 160–179.

Guilmoto, Christophe Z., and S. Irudaya Rajan. 2001. "Spatial Patterns of Fertility Transition in Indian Districts." *Population and Development Review* 27(4): 713–738.

Hajivassiliou, V. A. 1993. "Simulation Estimation Methods for LImited Dependent Variable Models." In *Handbook of Statistics*, eds. G. Maddala, C. Rao, and H. Vinod. Amsterdam: North-Holland 519–543.

Hannon, Lance, and Peter Knapp. 2003. "Reassessing Nonlinearity in the Urban Disadvantage/Violent Crime Relationship: An Example of Methodological Bias from Log Transformation." *Criminology* 41(4): 1427–1448.

Hausman, J. A. 1978. "Specification Tests in Econometrics." *Econometrica* 46(6): 1251–1271.

Hays, Jude, Aya Kachi, and Robert J. Franzese, Jr. 2010. "A Spatial Model Incorporating Dynamic, Endogenous Network Interdependence: A Political Science Application." *Statistical Methodology* 7: 406–428.

Heijmans, Risto D. H., and Jan R. Magnus. 1986a. "On the First-Order Efficiency and Asymptotic Normality of Maximum Likelihood Estimators Obtained from Dependent Observations." *Statistica Neerlandica* 40: 169–188.

Heijmans, Risto D. H., and Jan R. Magnus. 1986b. "Consistent Maximum-Likelihood Estimation with Dependent Observations: The General (Non-Normal) Case and the Normal Case." *Journal of Econometrics* 32: 253–285.

Heijmans, Risto D. H., and Jan R. Magnus. 1986c. "Asymptotic Normality of Maximum Likelihood Estimators Obtained from Normally Distributed but Dependent Observations." *Econometric Theory* 2: 374–412.

Hill, Daniel H., William G. Axinn, and Arland Thorton. 1993. "Competing Hazards with Shared Unmeasured Risk Factors." *Sociological Methodology* 23: 245–277.

Hoechle, Daniel. 2007. "Robust Standard Errors for Panel Regressions with Cross-Sectional Dependence." *The Stata Journal* 7(3): 281–312.

Honda, Yuzo. 1985. "Testing the Error Components Model with Non-Normal Disturbances." *Review of Economic Studies* 52(4): 681–690.

Hordijk, L. 1979. "Problems in Estimating Econometric Relations in Space." *Papers of the Regional Science Association* 42: 99–115.

Hotelling, Harold. 1929. "Stability in Competition." *The Economic Journal* 39: 41–57.

Hougaard, Philip. 2000. *Analysis of Multivariate Survival Data*. New York: Springer-Verlag.

Hsiao, Cheng. 1975. "Some Estimation Methods for a Random Coefficient Model." *Econometrica* 43(2): 305–326.

Hsiao, Cheng. 1986. *Analysis of Panel Data*. Cambridge: Cambridge University Press.

Huang, J. S. 1984. "The Autoregrssive Moving Average Model for Spatial Analysis." *Australian Journal of Statistics* 26: 169–178.

Huckfeldt, Robert. 1986. *Politics in Context: Assimilation and Conflict in Urban Neighborhoods*. New York: Agathon Press.

Huckfeldt, Robert, and John Sprague. 1987. "Networks in Context: The Social Flow of Political Information." *American Political Science Review* 81(4): 1197–1216.

Huckfeldt, Robert, and John Sprague. 1988. "Choice, Social Structure, and Political Information: The Information Coercion of Minorities." *American Journal of Political Science* 32(2): 467–482.

Hunter, Lori M. 2000. "The Spatial Association between U.S. Immigrant Residential Concentration and Environmental Hazards." *International Migration Review* 34(2): 460–488.

Huntington, Samuel P. 1991. *The Third Wave: Democratization in the Late Twentieth Century*. Norman: University of Oklahoma Press.

Isard, Walter. 1956. *Location and Space-Economy: A General Theory Relating to Industrial Location, Market Areas, Land Use, Trade, and Urban Structure*. New York: John Wiley & Sons.

Jackman, Simon. 2000. "Estimation and Inference via Bayesian Simulation: An Introduction to Markov Chain Monte Carlo." *American Journal of Political Science* 44(2): 375–404.

Jenkins, Jeffery A., and Brian R. Sala. 1998. "The Spatial Theory of Voting and the Presidential Election of 1824." *American Journal of Political Science* 42(4): 1157–1179.

Johnson, Kenneth M., Paul R. Voss, Roger B. Hammer, Glenn V. Fuguitt, and Scott McNiven. 2005. "Temporal and Spatial Variation in Age-Specific Net Migration in the United States." *Demography* 42(4): 791–812.

Johnston, Ron, Carol Propper, Rebecca Sarker, Kelvyn Jones, Anne Bolster, and Simon Burgess. 2005. "Neighbourhood Social Capital and Neighbourhood Effects." *Environment and Planning A* 37: 1443–1459.

Jones, Bradford S. 1994. *A Longitudinal Perspective on Congressional Elections*. Ph.D. dissertation, State University of New York, Stony Brook.

Kaiser, Mark S., and Noel Cressie. 1997. "Modeling Poisson Variables with Positive Spatial Dependence." *Statistics & Probability Letters* 35(4): 423–432.

Kalt, Joseph P., and Mark A. Zupan. 1990. "The Apparent Ideological Behavior of Legislators: Testing for Principal-Agent Slack in Political Institutions." *Journal of Law and Economics* 33: 103–131.

Kapoor, Mudit, Harry H. Kelejian, and Ingmar R. Prucha. 2007. "Panel Data Models with Spatially Correlated Error Components." *Journal of Econometrics* 140: 97–130.

Kau, James B., and Paul H. Rubin. 1979. "Self-Interest, Ideology, and Logrolling in Congressional Voting." *Journal of Law and Economics* 22: 365–384.

Keane, M. P. 1994. "A Computationally Practical Simulator Estimator for Panel Data." *Econometrica* 62: 95–116.

Kelejian, Harry H., and Dennis P. Robinson. 1992. "Spatial Autocorrelation: A New Computationally Simple Test with an Application to Per Capita County Policy Expenditures." *Regional Science and Urban Economics* 22: 317–331.

Kelejian, Harry H., and Dennis P. Robinson. 1993. "A Suggested Method of Estimation for Spatial Interdependent Models with Autocorrelated Errors, and an Application to a County Expenditure Model." *Papers in Regional Science* 72: 297–312.

Kelejian, Harry H., and Dennis P. Robinson. 1995. "Spatial Correlation: A Suggested Alternative to the Autoregressive Model." In *New Directions in Spatial Econometrics*, eds. Luc Anselin and Raymond J. G. M. Florax, pp. 75–95. Berlin: Springer-Verlag.

Kelejian, Harry H., and Dennis P. Robinson. 1998. "A Suggested Test for Spatial Autocorrelation and/or Heteroskedasticity and Corresponding Monte Carlo Results." *Regional Science and Urban Economics* 28: 389–417.

Kelejian, Harry H., and Dennis P. Robinson. 2004. "The Influence of Spatially Correlated Heteroskedasticity on Tests for Spatial Correlation." In *Advances in Spatial Econometrics: Methodology, Tools and Applications*, eds. Luc Anselin, Raymond J. G. M. Florax, and Sergio J. Rey, pp. 79–97. Berlin: Springer Science + Business Media.

Kelejian, Harry H., and Yevgeny Yuzefovich. 2004. "Properties of Tests for Spatial Error Components: A Further Analysis." In *Spatial Econometrics and Spatial Statistics*, eds.

Arthur Getis, Jesús Mur Lacambra, and Henry G. Zoller, pp. 135–149. Basingstoke: Palgrave-Macmillan.

Kelejian, Harry H., and Ingmar R. Prucha. 1997. "Estimation of Spatial Regression Models with Autoregressive Errors by Two-Stage Least Squares Procedures: A Serious Problem." *International Regional Science Review* 20(1 & 2): 103–111.

Kelejian, Harry H., and Ingmar R. Prucha. 1998. "A Generalized Spatial Two-Stage Least Squares Procedure for Estimating a Spatial Autoregressive Model with Autoregressive Disturbances." *Journal of Real Estate Finance and Economics* 17: 99–121.

Kelejian, Harry H., and Ingmar R. Prucha. 1999. "A Generalized Moments Estimator for the Autoregressive Parameter in a Spatial Model." *International Economic Review* 40(2): 509–533.

Kelejian, Harry H., and Ingmar R. Prucha. 2001. "On the Asymptotic Distribution of the Moran *I* Test Statistic with Applications." *Journal of Econometrics* 104: 219–257.

Kelejian, Harry H., and Ingmar R. Prucha. 2002. "2SLS and OLS in a Spatial Autoregressive Model with Equal Spatial Weights." *Regional Science and Urban Economics* 32: 691–707.

Kelejian, Harry H., Ingmar R. Prucha, and Yevgeny Yuzefovich. 2004. "Instrumental Variable Estimation of a Spatial Autoregressive Model with Autoregressive Disturbances: Large and Small Sample Results." In *Spatial and Spatiotemporal Econometrics, Advances in Econometrics*, Vol. 18, eds. James P. LeSage and R. Kelley Pace, pp. 163–198. New York: Elsevier.

Key, V. O., Jr. 1949. *Southern Politics in State and Nation*. New York: Knopf.

Key, V. O., Jr. 1955. "A Theory of Critical Elections." *Journal of Politics* 17(1): 3–18.

King, Gary. 2011. "Ensuring the Data-Rich Future of the Social Sciences." *Science* 331(11): 719–721.

Klein, John P., and Melvin L. Moeschberger. 1997. *Survival Analysis: Techniques for Censored and Truncated Data*. New York: Springer-Verlag.

Klier, Thomas, and Daniel P. McMillen. 2008. "Clustering of Auto Supplier Plants in the United States: Generalized Method of Moments Spatial Logit for Large Samples." *Journal of Business & Economic Statistics* 26(4): 460–471.

Koser, K., and J. Salt. 1997. "The Geography of Highly Skilled International Migration." *International Journal of Population Geography* 3(4): 285–303.

Krieger, Nancy. 2006. "A Century of Census Tracts: Health & the Body Politic (1906–2006)." *Journal of Urban Health: Bulletin of the New York Academy of Medicine* 83(3): 355–361.

Lancaster, Jill, and Barbara J. Downes. 2004. "Spatial Point Pattern Analysis of Available and Exploited Resources." *Ecography* 27: 94–102.

Land, Kenneth C., and Glenn Deane. 1992. "On the Large-Sample Estimation of Regression Models with Spatial- or Network-Effects Terms: A Two-Stage Least Squares Approach." *Sociological Methodology* 22: 221–248.

Land, Kenneth C., Patricia L. McCall, and Lawrence E. Cohen. 1990. "Structural Covariates of Homicide Rates: Are There Any Invariances across Time and Social Space?" *American Journal of Sociology* 95(4): 922–963.

Lawson, Andrew B. 2008. *Bayesian Disease Mapping: Hierarchical Modeling in Spatial Epidemiology*. Boca Raton, FL: Chapman & Hall/CRC.

Lawson, Andrew B. 2013. Also, 2nd edition. *Bayesian Disease Mapping: Hierarchical Modeling in Spatial Epidemiology*. Boca Raton, FL: Chapman & Hall/CRC.

Lee, Barrett A., Glenn Firebaugh, Stephen A. Matthews, Sean F. Reardon, Chad R. Farrell, and David O'Sullivan. 2008. "Beyond the Census Tract: Patterns and Determinants of Racial Segregation at Multiple Geographic Scales." *American Sociological Review* 73(5): 766–791.

Lee, David S., Enrico Moretti, and Matthew J. Butler. 2004. "Do Voters Affect or Elect Policies? Evidence from the U.S. House." *The Quarterly Journal of Economics* 119: 807–859.

Lee, Hyeyoung, and Sujit K. Ghosh. 2009. "Performance of Information Criteria for Spatial Models." *Journal of Statistical Computation and Simulation* 79(1): 93–106.

Lee, Lung-fei. 2001. "Generalized Method of Moments Estimation of Spatial Autoregressive Processes." Manuscript.

Lee, Lung-fei. 2003. "Best Spatial Two-Stage Least Squares Estimators for a Spatial Autoregressive Model with Autoregressive Disturbances." *Econometric Reviews* 22(4): 307–335.

Lee, Lung-fei. 2004. "Asymptotic Distributions of Quasi-Maximum Likelihood Estimators for Spatial Autoregressive Models." *Econometrica* 72(6): 1899–1925.

Lee, Lung-fei. 2007. "GMM and 2SLS Estimation of Mixed Regressive, Spatial Autoregressive Models." *Journal of Econometrics* 137: 489–514.

Lee, Lung-fei, and Jihai Yu. 2007. "Near Unit Root in the Spatial Autoregressive Model." Manuscript. 2013. *Spatial Economic Analysis* 8(3): 314–351.

Lee, Lung-fei, and Jihai Yu. 2010. "Estimation of Spatial Autoregressive Panel Data Models with Fixed Effects." *Journal of Econometrics* 154: 165–185.

Leenders, Roger Th. A. J. 2002. "Modeling Social Influence Through Network Autocorrelation: Constructing the Weight Matrix." *Social Networks* 24: 21–47.

LeSage, James P. 1997. "Bayesian Estimation of Spatial Autoregressive Models." *International Regional Science Review* 20: 113–129.

LeSage, James P. 2000. "Bayesian Estimation of Limited Dependent Variable Spatial Autoregressive Models." *Geographical Analysis* 32(1): 19–35.

Levine, Ned. 2006. "Crime Mapping and the *Crimestat* Program. *Geographical Analysis* 38: 41–56.

Levitt, Steven D. 1996. "How Do Senators Vote? Disentangling the Role of Voter Preferences, Party Affiliation, and Senator Ideology." *American Economic Review* 86: 425–441.

Loftin, Colin, and Sally K. Ward. 1983. "A Spatial Autocorrelation Model of the Effects of Population Density on Fertility." *American Sociological Review* 48(1): 121–128.

Logan, John R., Wenquan Zhang, and Richard D. Alba. 2002. "Immigrant Enclaves and Ethnic Communities in New York and Los Angeles." *American Sociological Review* 67(2): 299–322.

Long, J. Scott. 1997. *Regression Models for Categorical and Limited Dependent Variables*. Thousand Oaks, CA: SAGE.

MacAllister, I., R. J. Johnston, C. J. Pattie, H. Tunstall, D. F. L. Dorling, and D. J. Rossiter. 2001. "Class Dealignment and the Neighbourhood Effect: Miller Revisited." *British Journal of Political Science* 31: 41–59.

Magnus, Jan R. 1978. "Maximum Likelihood Estimation of the GLS Model with Unknown Parameters in the Disturbance Covariance Matrix." *Journal of Econometrics* 7: 281–312.

Massey, Douglas S., Andrew B. Gross, and Kumiko Shibuya. "Migration, Segregation, and the Geographic Concentration of Poverty." *American Sociological Review* 59(3): 425–445.

Matheron, Georges. 1963. "Principles of Geostatistics." *Economic Geology* 58: 1246–1266.

Matthews, Donald R., and James A. Stimson. 1975. *Yeas and Nays: Normal Decision-Making in the U.S. House of Representatives*. New York: John Wiley & Sons.

McFadden, D. 1989. "A Method of Simulated Moments for Estimation of Discrete Response Models Without Numerical Integration." *Econometrica* 57: 995–1026.

McMillen, Daniel P. 1992. "Probit with Spatial Autocorrelation." *Journal of Regional Science* 32(3): 335–348.

McMillen, Daniel P. 2013. "Package 'McSpatial".' http://CRAN.R-project.org/package=McSpatial.

McNulty, Thomas L. 2001. "Assessing the Race-Violence Relationship at the Macro Level: The Assumption of Racial Invariance and the Problem of Restricted Distributions." *Criminology* 39(2): 467–490.

Mead, R. 1967. "A Mathematical Model for the Estimation of Interplant Competition." *Biometrics* 23: 189–205.

Messer, Lynne C., Jay S. Kaufman, Nancy Dole, David Savitz, and Barbara Laraia. 2006. "Neighborhood Crime, Deprivation, and Preterm Birth." *AEP* 16(6): 455–462.

Moran, P. A. P. 1948. "The Interpretation of Statistical Maps." *Journal of the Royal Statistical Scoiety B: Methodological* 10(2): 243–251.

Most, Benjamin A., and Harvey Starr. 1980. "Diffusion, Reinforcement, Geopolitics, and the Spread of War." *American Political Science Review* 74(4): 932–946.

Most, Benjamin A., and Harvey Starr. 1982. "Case Study, Conceptualizations and Basic Logic in the Study of War." *American Journal of Political Science* 26(4): 834–856.

Moulton, Brent R., and William C. Randolph. 1989. "Alternative Tests of the Error Components Model." *Econometrica* 57(3): 685–693.

Mur, J. 1999. "Testing for Spatial Autocorrelation: Moving Average versus Autoregressive Processes." *Environment and Planning A* 31: 1371–1382.

Mur, Jesus, and Ana Maria Angulo. 2007. "Clues for Discriminating between Moving Average and Autoregressive Models in Spatial Processes." *Spanish Economic Review* 9: 273–298.

Mutl, Jan, and Michael Pfaffermayr. 2011. "The Hausman Test in a Cliff and Ord Panel Model." *Econometrics Journal* 14: 48–76.

Nardulli, Peter F. 1995. "The Concept of a Critical Realignment, Electoral Behavior, and Political Change." *American Political Science Review* 89(1): 10–22.

Neumayer, Eric, and Thomas Plümper. 2010a. "Making Spatial Analysis Operational: Commands for Generating Spatial-Effect Variables in Monadic and Dyadic Data." *The Stata Journal* 10(4): 1–21.

Neumayer, Eric, and Thomas Plümper. 2010b. "Spatial Effects in Dyadic Data." *International Organization* 64: 145–166.

Neumayer, Eric, and Thomas Plümper. 2012. "Conditional Spatial Policy Dependence: Theory and Model Specification." *Comparative Political Studies* 45(7): 819–849.

Newey, W. K., and K. D. West. 1987. "A Simple, Positive Semi-Definite, Heteroskedasticity and Autocorrelation Consistent Covariance Matrix." *Econometrica* 55: 703–708.

O'Loughlin, John, Colin Flint, and Luc Anselin. 1994. "The Geography of the Nazi Vote: Context, Confession and Class in the Reichstag Election of 1930." *Annals of the Association of American Geographers* 84: 351–380.

O'Loughlin, John, and Frank Wittmer. 2005. "Taking 'Geography' Seriously: Disaggregating the Study of Civil War." Paper presented at the conference on "Disaggregating the Study of Civil War and Transnational Violence," University of California Institute of Global Conflict and Cooperation, La Jolla.

Openshaw, Stan. 1983. *The Modifiable Areal Unit Problem*. Norwich: Geo Books.

Openshaw, S., and P. J. Taylor. 1979. "A Million or So Correlation Coefficients: Three Experiments on the Modifiable Areal Unit Problem." In *Statistical Applications in the Spatial Sciences*, ed. N. Wrigley. London: Pion.

Openshaw, S., and P. J. Taylor. 1981. "The Modifiable Areal Unit Problem." In *Quantitative Geography: A British View*, eds. N. Wrigley and R. J. Bennett, pp. 60–69. London: Routledge.

Ord, Keith. 1975. "Estimation Methods for Models of Spatial Interaction." *Journal of the American Statistical Association* 70(349): 120–126.

Ord, J. K., and Arthur Getis. 1995. "Local Spatial Autocorrelation Statistics: Distributional Issues and an Application." *Geographical Analysis* 27(4): 286–306.

Øyen, Orjar, and Melvin L. De Fleur. 1953. "The Spatial Diffusion of an Airborne Leaflet Message." *The American Journal of Sociology* 59(2): 144–149.

Pace, R. Kelley. 1997. "Performing Large Spatial Regressions and Autoregressions." *Economics Letters* 283–291.

Pace, R. Kelley, and James P. LeSage. 2002. "Semiparametric Maximum Likelihood Estimates of Spatial Dependence." *Geographical Analysis* 34(1): 76–90.

Pace, R. Kelley, and Ronald Barry. 1997. "Sparse Spatial Autoregressions." *Statistics & Probability Letters* 33: 291–297.

Patterson, Samuel C. 1959. "Patterns of Interpersonal Relations in a State Legislative Group: The Wisconsin Assembly." *Public Opinion Quarterly* 23: 101–109.

Patterson, Samuel C. 1972. "Party Opposition in the Legislature: The Ecology of Legislative Institutionalization." *Polity* 4: 344–366.

Pearce, Mark S. 1998. "Geographically Weighted Regression: A Method for Exploring Spatial Nonstationarity." *Stata Technical Bulletin* 46: 20–24.

Pesaran, M. Hashem, and Richard J. Smith. 1994. "A Generalized R^2 Criterion for Regression Models Estimated by the Instrumental Variables Method." *Econometrica* 62(3): 705–710.

Pinkse, Joris, and Margaret Slade. 1998. "Contracting in Space: An Application of Spatial Statistics to Discrete-Choice Models." *Journal of Econometrics* 85: 125–154.

Pisati, Maurizio. 2001. "Tools for Spatial Data Analysis." *Stata Technical Bulletin* 60: 21–37.

Plümper, Thomas, and Eric Neumayer. 2010. "Model Specification in the Analysis of Spatial Dependence." *European Journal of Political Research* 49: 418–442.

Poole, Keith T. 1998. "Recovering an Issue Space from a Set of Issue Scales." *American Journal of Political Science* 42: 954–993.

Poole, Keith T. and Howard Rosenthal. 1997. *Congress: A Political-Economic History of Roll Call Voting*. New York: Oxford University Press.

Przeworski, Adam, and Henry Teune. 1970. *The Logic of Comparative Social Inquiry*. New York: John Wiley & Sons.

Ramsay, Timothy, Richard Burnett, and Daniel Krewski. 2003. "Exploring Bias in a Generalized Additive Model for Spatial Air Pollution Data." *Environmental Health Perspectives* 111(1): 1283–1288.

Regan, Patrick M. 2002. "Third-Party Interventions and the Duration of Intrastate Conflicts." *The Journal of Conflict Resolution* 46(1): 55–73.

Rey, Sergio J., and Luc Anselin. 2007. "PySAL: A Python Library of Spatial Analytical Methods." *The Review of Regional Studies* 37(1): 5–27.

Rey, Sergio J., and Mark V. Janikas. 2006. "STARS: Space-Time Analysis of Regional Systems." *Geographical Analysis* 38: 67–86.

Ricketts, Erol R., and Isabel V. Sawhill. 1988. "Defining and Measuring the Underclass." *Journal of Policy Analysis and Management* 7(2): 316–325.

Ripley, Brian. 1981. *Spatial Statistics*. New York: John Wiley & Sons.

Rogowski, Jon C., and Betsy Sinclair. 2012. "Estimating the Causal Effects of Social Interaction with Endogenous Networks." *Political Analysis* 20: 316–328.

Rudra, Nita. 2002. "Globalization and the Decline of the Welfare State in Less-Developed Countries." *International Organization* 56(2): 411–445.

Salehyan, Idean, and Kristian Skrede Gleditsch. 2006. "Refugees and the Spread of Civil War." *International Organization* 60(2): 335–366.

Sampson, Robert J., and Stephen W. Raudenbush. 1999. "Systematic Social Observation of Public Spaces: A New Look at Disorder in Urban Neighborhoods." *American Journal of Sociology* 105(3): 603–651.

Shaw, C. R., and McKay, H. D. 1969. *Juvenile Delinquency and Urban Areas*. Chicago: University of Chicago Press.

Shin, Michael, and John Agnew. 2002. "The Geography of Party Replacement in Italy, 1987–1996." *Political Geography* 21: 221–242.

Shin, Michael, and Michael D. Ward. 1999. "Lost in Space: Political Geography and the Defense-Growth Trade-Off." *The Journal of Conflict Resolution* 43(6): 793–817.

Smirnov, Oleg A. 2005. "Computation of the Information Matrix for Models with Spatial Interaction on a Lattice." *Journal of Computational and Graphical Statistics* 14(4): 910–927.

Smirnov, Oleg, and Luc Anselin. 2001. "Fast Maximum Likelihood Estimation of Very Large Spatial Autoregressive Models: A Characteristic Polynomial Approach." *Computational Statistics & Data Analysis* 35: 301–319.

Snow, John. 1855. *On the Mode of Communication of Cholera*. London: John Churchill.

Spiegelhalter, David J., Andrew Thomas, Nicola G. Best, and Dave Lunn. 2003. *WinBUGS User Manual Version*, Version 1.4, January 2003. Available at http:www.mrc-bsu.cam.ac.uk/bugs/

Spiegelhalter, David J., Nicola G. Best, Bradley P. Carlin, and Angelika van der Linde. 2002. "Bayesian Measures of Model Complexity and Fit (with Discussion)." *Journal of the Royal Statistical Society B* 64(4): 583–639.

Starr, Harvey. 1991. "Democratic Dominoes: Diffusion Approaches to the Spread of Democracy in the International System." *Journal of Conflict Resolution* 35(2): 356–381.

Starr, Harvey. 2002. "Opportunity, Willingness and Geographic Information Systems (GIS): Reconceptualizing Borders in International Relations." *Political Geography* 21: 243–261.

Starr, Harvey, and Benjamin A. Most. 1976. "The Substance and Study of Borders in International Relations Research." *International Studies Quarterly* 20(4): 581–620.

Starr, Harvey, and Benjamin A. Most. 1983. "Contagion and Border Effects on Contemporary African Conflict." *Comparative Political Studies* 16(February): 92–117.

Starr, Harvey, and Benjamin A. Most. 1985. "The Forms and Processes of War Diffusion: Research Update on Contagion in African Conflict." *Comparative Political Studies* 18 (July): 206–227.

Starr, Harvey, David Darmofal, and Zaryab Iqbal. n.d. "The Disease of War: Exploring Contagion and Spatiality in Domestic Conflict." Manuscript.

Stetzer, F. 1982. "Specifying Weights in Spatial Forecasting Models: The Results of Some Experiments." *Environment and Planning A* 14: 571–584.

Stimson, James A. 1985. "Regression in Space and Time: A Statistical Essay." *American Journal of Political Science* 29(4): 914–947.

Stimson, James A. 1999. *Public Opinion in America: Moods, Cycles, and Swings*, 2nd Ed. Boulder, CO: Westview Press.

Stratmann, Thomas. 2000. "Congressional Voting over Legislative Careers: Shifting Positions and Changing Constraints." *American Political Science Review* 94: 665–676.

Sundquist, James L. 1983. *Dynamics of the Party System: Alignment and Realignment of Political Parties in the United States*. Washington, DC: The Brookings Institution.

Swamy, P. A. V. B. 1970. "Efficient Inference in a Random Coefficient Regression Model." *Econometrica* 38(2): 311–323.

Testa, Mark, Nan Marie Astone, Marilyn Krogh, and Kathryn M. Neckerman. 1989. "Employment and Marriage Among Inner-City Fathers." *Annals of the American Academy of Political and Social Science*, Vol. 501: *The Ghetto Underclass: Social Science Perspectives*, pp. 79–91. Available at http://www.jstor.org/stable/1045650?seq=1#page_scan_tab_contents

Therneau, Terry M., and Patricia M. Grambsch. 2000. *Modeling Survival Data: Extending the Cox Model*. New York: Springer-Verlag.

Thomas, Andrew, Nicky Best, Dave Lunn, Richard Arnold, and David Spiegelhalter. 2004. *GeoBUGS User Manual*, Version 1.2, September 2004. Available at http:www.mrc-bsu.cam.ac.uk/bugs/

Thomas, R. W. 1981. "Point Pattern Analysis." In *Quantitative Geography: A British View*. eds. N. Wrigley and R. J. Bennett, pp. 164–176. London: Routledge.

Tiefelsdorf, M., and B. Boots. 1995. "The Exact Distribution of Moran's *I*." *Environment and Planning A* 27: 985–999.

Tobler, Waldo R. 1969. "Geographical Filters and Their Inverses." *Geographical Analysis* 1: 234–253.

Tobler, Waldo R. 1970. "A Computer Movie Simulating Urban Growth in the Detroit Region." *Economic Geography* 46: 234–240.

Tobler, Waldo R. 1975. "Linear Operators Applied to Areal Data." In *Display and Analysis of Spatial Data*, eds. J. C. Davis and M. J. McCullagh, pp. 14–37. London: John Wiley & Sons.

Tolnay, Stewart E. 1995. "The Spatial Diffusion of Fertility: A Cross-Sectional Analysis of Counties in the American South, 1940." *American Sociological Review* 60(2): 299–308.

Tolnay, Stewart E., Glenn Deane, and E. M. Beck. 1996. "Vicarious Violence: Spatial Effects on Southern Lynchings." *American Journal of Sociology* 102: 788–815.

Torrens, Paul M. 2010. "Geography and Computational Social Science." *GeoJournal* 75: 133–148.

Tylor, Edward B. 1889. "On a Method of Investigating the Development of Institutions; Applied to Laws of Marriage and Descent." *The Journal of the Anthropological Institute of Great Britain and Ireland* 18: 245–272.

Upton, G., and B. Fingleton. 1985. *Spatial Data Analysis by Example*, Vol. 1: *Point Pattern and Quantitative Data*. Chichester: John Wiley & Sons.

U.S. Department of Commerce, Economics and Statistics Administration, Bureau of the Census. 1994. *Geographic Areas Reference Manual*.

Vijverberg, Wim P. M. 1997. "Monte Carlo Evaluation of Multivariate Normal Probabilities." *Journal of Econometrics* 76: 281–307.

Visher, Christy A., Pamela K. Lattimore, and Richard L. Linster. 1991. "Predicting the Recidivism of Serious Youthful Offenders Using Survival Models." *Criminology* 29(3): 329–366.

Wang, Honglin, Emma Iglesias, and Jeffrey M. Wooldridge. 2010. "Partial Maximum Likelihood Estimation of Spatial Probit Models." Manuscript 2013. *Journal of Econometrics* 172(1): 77–89.

Ward, Michael D., and Kristian S. Gleditsch. 2002. "Location, Location, Location: An MCMC Approach to Modeling the Spatial Context of War and Peace." *Political Analysis* 10 (3): 244–260.

Ward, Michael D., and Kristian Skrede Gleditsch. 2008. *Spatial Regression Models*. Thousand Oaks, CA: SAGE.

Warwick, Paul. 1992. "Economic Trends and Government Survival in West European Parliamentary Democracies." *American Political Science Review* 86(4): 875–887.

White, Douglas R., Michael L. Burton, and Malcolm M. Dow. 1981. "Sexual Division of Labor in African Agriculture: A Network Autocorrelation Analysis." *American Anthropologist* 83(4): 824–849.

Whittle, P. 1954. "On Stationary Processes in the Plane." *Biometrika* 41(3/4): 434–449.

Wieland, Ralf, Marion Voss, Xenia Holtmann, Wilfried Mirschel, and Igbekele Ajibefun. 2006. "Spatial Analysis and Modeling Tool (SAMT): 1. Structure and Possibilities." *Ecological Informatics* 1: 67–76.

Wilson, William Julius. 1987. *The Truly Disadvantaged: The Inner City, the Underclass, and Public Policy*. Chicago: University of Chicago Press.

Witko, Christopher, and Adam J. Newmark. 2010. "The Strange Disappearance of Investment in Human and Physical Capital in the United States." *Journal of Public Administration Research & Theory* 20: 215–232.

Yang, Tse-Chuan, Carla Shoff, and Stephen A. Matthews. 2013. "Examining the Spatially Non-Stationary Associations between the Second Demographic Transition and Infant Mortality: A Poisson GWR Approach." *Spatial Demography* 1(1): 17–40.

Young, James Sterling. 1966. *The Washington Community, 1800–1828*. New York: Columbia University Press.

Zellner, Arnold. 1962. "An Efficient Method of Estimating Seemingly Unrelated Regressions and Tests of Aggregation Bias." *Journal of the American Statistical Association* 57: 348–368.

Index